DEFUND

DEFUND

BLACK LIVES, POLICING,
and SAFETY FOR ALL

SANDY HUDSON

PANTHEON BOOKS

New York

FIRST U.S. HARDCOVER EDITION
PUBLISHED BY PANTHEON BOOKS 2025

Published in the United States by Pantheon Books, a division of
Penguin Random House LLC, 1745 Broadway, New York, NY 10019.

Pantheon Books and the colophon are registered trademarks of
Penguin Random House LLC.

We acknowledge the support of the Canada Council for the Arts.

LCCN: 2024950782
ISBN: 978-0-593-70081-5 (hardcover)
ISBN: 978-0-593-70082-2 (ebook)

penguinrandomhouse.com | pantheonbooks.com

Printed in the United States of America

2 4 6 8 9 7 5 3 1

The authorized representative in the EU for product safety and compliance
is Penguin Random House Ireland, Morrison Chambers, 32 Nassau Street,
Dublin D02 YH68, Ireland, https://eu-contact.penguin.ie.

For my parents, Donovan and Juliette.
I love you dearly.

I don't think we can rely on governments, regardless of who is in power, to do the work that only mass movements can do.

—Angela Davis, *Freedom Is a Constant Struggle*

CONTENTS

DEFUND

INTRODUCTION

In August 2020, after the murder of George Floyd by Minneapolis police officer Derek Chauvin, I took a three-day trip to Portland, Oregon, to support activists who were protesting police violence. The National Guard had been called in, and several people, including journalists, had been seriously injured in the crackdown by law enforcement. It was the height of COVID-19 lockdowns, and a long road trip was my only travel option. On the day I was scheduled to leave, I checked out of my hotel early, eager to get on the road and back home to Los Angeles. I was almost out the door when I was approached by a blond woman who turned out to be the owner. She asked if I had enjoyed my time in Portland and why I had decided to visit at a time when the city was a hotbed of protest and police activity. When I told her I was there in support of activists, she beamed. She was proud of her business's support for the movement against police brutality. BLACK LIVES MATTER signs were plastered on every wall and displayed out of every window in her establishment. She was all for the movement, you see, except for one thing she just couldn't understand—a bit of messaging she thought was ruining our shot at winning, whatever that meant to her. Why, she wondered, would we be calling to defund the police?

I was exhausted, but she offered me a coffee and insisted that I sit and chat with her for a moment. She presented a thought experiment I had been posed countless times: If the police were defunded, what would she do if someone broke into her home and stole valuables? Who would she call? The question was not disingenuous, and this woman was nice enough, so I delayed my departure to work through the hypothetical with her. First, I asked who she would call today if she were a victim of theft. She said the police (of course). When I pointed out that the police would have already failed at prevention in this scenario, since she would have already been the victim of theft, she conceded that this was a good point but insisted that what would happen next was crucial: police officers would arrive, gather evidence, investigate the crime, and catch the perpetrator. Perhaps there would be an investigation, I said, but did she know the chances of the police charging someone—and not necessarily the right person—in the case of burglary in the United States? She was stunned when I told her it was less than 15 percent. There was no way, in her mind, that the rates could possibly be that low. But they *are*. Her perception of police effectiveness was wildly out of step with reality.

So, what would we do if the police were defunded? Probably the same thing we do with the police extremely funded, I told her. Call our insurance companies to recoup as much of the value of what was stolen as we could.

I understand that for many who first heard about the idea of police abolition during the 2020 uprisings, the idea can seem absurd and unfeasible. But much of that resistance is the result of pervasive propaganda that makes false assumptions about police feel like common sense, as well as narrow views of safety that position police as our best and only resource for addressing our various social ills. The consequences for this distorted view of policing are dire. Policing is currently the primary societal strategy for addressing issues related to poverty, mental health, homelessness, unemployment, disability, sexual assault, youth socialization in Black and brown communities, transportation, underfunded public schools, public revenue—the list goes on.

All the while, safety continues to be an unresolved concern. But if safety is the goal, surely there are more suitable strategies we could collectively take than spending ever-ballooning resources on a system that fails at harm prevention, perpetuates violence, and is inherently discriminatory? I hope as you continue to read this book, you allow your imagination to expand and consider the solutions so many activists and advocates have come to after decades in the fight against police brutality.

My own understanding and embrace of police abolition have developed over years of study, advocacy, as well as direct and peripheral contact with law enforcement and their methods. In August 2016, Black Lives Matter Toronto organized a prayer and picnic in remembrance of Abdirahman Abdi, a thirty-seven-year-old Somali Canadian man who less than a month before had been killed by Ottawa police—the pathologist who examined Mr. Abdi's body determined his medical cause of death to be homicide. I cofounded the Toronto chapter of Black Lives Matter (BLM) in 2014 following a string of killings of Black men by police officers in the United States and Canada. Mr. Abdi struggled with his mental health, and when police tried to arrest him near a coffee shop in his neighborhood for allegedly groping a woman, he ran for his life, desperately trying to get back to his home. The police caught up with him in front of his apartment building, mere steps from the safety of his home and family. There, the officers reportedly shoved him against the entry door and pummeled him with punches and baton blows. Some bystanders recorded the brutalization. His mother watched from the other side of the door, screaming in horror. Mr. Abdi was screaming, too, begging for help.

Help never arrived.

According to news reports, when Mr. Abdi stopped moving, neither of the officers attempted to provide CPR or medical attention. He was taken to the hospital and pronounced dead the following day. His official cause of death was hypoxic brain injury following a heart attack, meaning his brain was starved of oxygen for too long.

May he rest in peace.

Months later, Constable Daniel Montsion was charged with manslaughter, aggravated assault, and assault with a weapon. During the trial, the pathologist who examined Mr. Abdi's body said he determined that his death was a homicide, stating that Mr. Abdi would not have had a heart attack had he not been beaten and injured by police. The prosecution further argued that the injuries the officers caused by beating and using chemical irritants on Mr. Abdi—including multiple fractures to his nose and a laceration to his face—contributed to his brain injury. Nevertheless, the judge overseeing the bench trial ultimately stated that while the case was a "close call," he was left with reasonable doubt as to whether Montsion's conduct met the "criminal standard" of the charges. Montsion was found not guilty of all charges in October 2020. The other officer was never charged. On October 25, 2024, the Province of Ontario announced a coroner's inquest examining the circumstances into Mr. Abdi's death would take place starting in November 2024.

On the date of the event in remembrance of Mr. Abdi, a torrential downpour forced a last-minute change in venue. Despite this and the intimidating presence of dozens of police officers surrounding the space, hundreds attended to express our shared rage at Mr. Abdi's killing with speeches, art, and performances, including programming that honored his Muslim faith. After the closing prayer, the crowd somberly exited the venue while a handful of us stayed behind to clean up the food and child-care spaces. When we were done, we walked out into the darkness of the Toronto evening in a grave mood, quiet with one another, passing the throng of police officers that had become a fixture at BLM events in the city.

That's when we heard screaming—or maybe wailing. As we turned in the direction of the noise, we saw a Black man sprinting around the street corner. Something was clearly wrong; he seemed distressed, very upset, and desperate. The police jumped into action. Some hopped on bikes in pursuit. Others ran after him on foot. They surrounded him, barking orders, brandishing their batons.

We ran after him, too.

When we reached him, he had collapsed into a heap on the ground, crying. Two of the Black Lives Matter organizers immediately threw themselves on top of the crying man, holding him and protecting him from the police, while another organizer and I argued with the officers, who still held their batons as if to threaten us. What had he done wrong? we demanded. What were they doing to him? What did they want? They responded by threatening us with arrest for obstructing justice. Just then a woman ran towards us and introduced herself as the man's friend. Out of breath and full of concern—where had these police come from?—she explained why he was inconsolable: his mother had died in his arms only hours earlier. He ran into the night unable to contain his sorrow.

As my friends held him, the man began to regain his composure, expressing gratitude for their kindness.

The police looked somewhat dumbfounded at the entire situation, eventually slinking away when it became clear that their presence, their tools, and their approach were wholly misaligned with the situation that faced them. This is just a sampling of the irrational way policing operates in our society, and I often wonder what would have happened had we not stepped in that night.

Whom exactly were the police attempting to keep safe in this situation? How did they intend to do so by surrounding this man, crying on the pavement of a pedestrianized street in Toronto's downtown? Why did they draw their batons so soon? Why were they even there in the first place?

And why were we so much better at providing what this man needed—some humanity—than the public service assigned to the task?

Back in 2016, few were willing to question or engage in conversations about the harms of policing, let alone consider its abolition writ large. Activists working toward police abolition and confronting anti-Black police brutality were thought of as controversial. People could not even confidently say the words "Black Lives Matter" without detractors on social media or talking heads on editorial news programs countering with, Don't *all* lives matter? Even some would-be supporters felt attaching themselves to the movement beyond a superficial affirmation of the idea that racism is bad was too much of a risk to take. In 2015, for instance, my Black Lives Matter chapter was chosen as Pride Toronto's "honored group" for the year, which meant that we would lead the organization's annual parade and that our name and images would be used in its promotional materials the following year. What followed were months of meetings in which we tried get the organization to honor our values and not just our name.

This was a bittersweet moment for us. For years, Black activists had been asking Pride to make several changes to its operations, including removing police department floats from the parade. At the time, law enforcement were among the largest contingent, with a section of thirteen floats followed by squad cars and other police vehicles blaring their sirens in so-called celebration, as well as hundreds of armed officers marching in uniform. The sounds of sirens and the sight of armed police are traumatic for so many in our community, and yet Pride Toronto was asking us abolitionists to be honored at the front of a parade where this was condoned. We agreed to consider their offer contingent upon their willingness to make a few changes to the way Pride was run—changes we felt would truly honor the work of Black activists. Among those changes were the removal of police floats from the parade.

Pride Toronto organizers agreed to consider our proposals at first, but as the date of the parade approached, they were noncommittal and avoided discussing particulars. It was clear that Pride wanted proximity to an organization that could provide cover against claims of racism but did not want to make any concrete moves to support our fight for Black liberation. Somehow our plight became an opportunity for reputational gain for Pride Toronto, and not about actions the organization could take to fight anti-Black racism. What a way to be honored.

Only after we halted the parade in protest with other Black queer groups did Pride Toronto agree to remove police floats from the parade, a move that set off similar actions and changes at Pride parades around the world.

The apprehension many felt toward confidently supporting an abolitionist movement shifted in May 2020, when droves of protesters poured onto empty COVID-stricken streets to express their rage and pain following George Floyd's murder in Minneapolis. People across the United States, Canada, the U.K., and beyond started to thwart the rules keeping many of us holed up in our homes, exposing ourselves to the dangers of the novel coronavirus for the sake of racial justice. How could the police have managed to murder a man under the circumstances in which we were all living? It was enough for people the world over to throw caution to the wind, exit the safety of their homes, and mobilize to denounce the police.

Finally, it seemed that the public was open to having a true discussion about policing—a conversation that had been happening in activist circles for years. Organizers saw an opportunity to bring our message to mass media. Our rallying cry? Defund the police. We told the world: if we don't want policing to function as a force designed to uphold inequality, we have to ask ourselves some serious questions about why we continue to pour increased funding into an institution whose only consistent function is to do exactly that.

Policing ultimately does not help us meet our safety and security goals. In this book, I am going to show why police abolition is the only just and rational response one can take after examining how the police operate, how they fail us, and what their actual impacts are. I'll present other options we can employ to make us all safer. I'll give you some data and statistics that support my arguments, but mostly I am going to make this conclusion clear through story, like the ones I've told above. Stories are one of the most effective methods for understanding an issue, and injustice in policing is a many-storied issue.

The presence and scale of police are not what keeps people safe. Take the May 24, 2022, school shooting at Robb Elementary School in Uvalde, Texas. Despite nearly four hundred police officers responding to the harrowing mass shooting, eighteen-year-old Salvador Ramos was able to shoot thirty-eight people, killing twenty-one, most of whom were children, and injuring seventeen. Officers arrived at the scene within three minutes of Ramos entering the school but failed to stop the shooter for *over an hour.* How could our purveyors of safety have failed so egregiously to keep these children safe, despite the ample time they had to act?

I remember watching the horrifying reports of the unthinkable shooting while visiting my parents, a twenty-four-hour live news broadcast playing on their television screen. The questions underlying and at times explicitly posed by the anchors as they delivered updates were "What went wrong here? What caused this police failure?" Watching the coverage in her living room in Toronto, my mother kissed her teeth in the way Jamaican mothers do and proclaimed quite simply, "Isn't it obvious? They didn't want to die."

My mother's simple explanation was likely correct. They didn't want to die. No one does. It's human nature to feel fear in a situation in which there is a motivated gunman intent on murdering scores of people. Perhaps that's why, despite the massive police response from multiple law enforcement entities, including the Uvalde Consolidated Independent School District Police Department, the Uvalde Police Department, the Texas Department of Public Safety, and the U.S. Border Patrol, this tragedy was not prevented, and the lives of the affected community members in Uvalde are forever changed. Just as in the Parkland mass shooting, in which seventeen people were killed, the Santa Fe High School shooting, in which ten people were killed, and countless other incidents, police failed to prevent the loss and interruption of innocent lives. Yet stunningly, policy makers' response to the failure in Uvalde was to promise that more police will be stationed in schools.

The truth is, by the time an incident like what took place in Uvalde occurs, there has already been a failure. Could the victims have been saved if our society were more attuned to preventing tragedy rather than relying on police to respond to it? Could the shooter, who was reportedly upset that he would not be graduating, have been provided with additional support from adults with the qualifications to support youth in crisis? Perhaps the shooter required supportive, accessible mental health care his family couldn't afford. Could the funding for this sort of support in schools have been available if policy makers were not so intent on spending so much money on police officers, who have proven ineffective again and again? The shooter purchased his gun legally. Perhaps he should not have been able to; perhaps other preventative measures should have been considered, like gun control. The shooter's family reportedly had financial struggles, and he was taunted at school for wearing the same clothes over and over, as well as for a speech impediment. Perhaps his family's financial struggles contributed to his anger. There are so many unknowns about what could have prevented this tragedy. But what is certain is that police intervention *after* the shooting begins is too late.

This is the problem with our approach to safety in our societies. Rather than doing the difficult work of dealing with the root causes of many of our social issues, we throw tons of money at police. Rather than rooting out poverty, for example, we by and large make many behaviors associated with poverty criminal and subject poor people to a revolving door of surveillance, suspicion, interrogation, punishment, and banishment. And while we throw a greater proportion of public money into policing year after year, the police have largely failed by every available metric to provide a safer, more secure society. Where they have been consistent is in carrying out policing as a form of social control and punishment against particular classes, races, and sexualities in our society.

For far too long our policy makers have ignored the consistency with which policing fails to keep us safe and condoned the ways police make some of our communities—most urgently Black communities—far less safe. The stories and data I'll rely on are from the United States, Canada, and the U.K. At times, I will have the data or information from only one or two of these places, because each allows differing levels of access to information through which average people can scrutinize the police. I've chosen to focus on these three places in part because I have some experience and knowledge of the police abolition movements in each of these countries, and also because these three countries share some historical and present-day similarities. But another crucial reason is that, in each place, I've been fascinated with the ways that policy makers and skeptics in one country will use and point to the situation in another country to justify continued bad policy or inaction. For example, in Canada and the U.K., skeptics will point to the United States and its reputation for having a terrible police brutality crisis as evidence that organizers are importing a problem from elsewhere that doesn't exist in their respective countries. Or policy makers and skeptics in the United States will point to data markers in the U.K. or Canada to justify implementing unhelpful policies that are in place in those spaces. The truth is that while there may be local particularities, policing fails us in all of these countries, and it's critical to understand why so we don't make the mistake of believing there is a "better" form of policing.

Through critically exploring policing as it exists and not as we might imagine it, and by posing some simple questions, I will take a sober look at this system and show how our societies are better off and far safer without police. We will consider the following: What is policing, really? Does it function as depicted on *Law & Order* or the evening news? How do officers spend their time? What is their true societal impact? We'll then consider whom policing harms: Which communities are made to suffer from policing? Which populations do the police focus on, and how did it historically come to be that way? We'll explore why we continue to end up in a cycle of reform that never seems to resolve any of the most urgently harmed populations' concerns with policing. Then we will consider whose safety our societies value and which populations' systemic dispossession and deprivation are ignored. Finally, we'll consider what it is that we really need. Is this as simple as replacing police with another system? Or does this problem require a deeper solution?

Critically challenging the police will lead us to discover

some very difficult truths. The big spoiler is that the one thing the police do consistently well is subjugate already marginalized communities. They interrupt the lives of Black, Indigenous, Latinx, brown, poor, queer, trans, and disabled people with exacting regularity. And this has been allowed to continue because of the principles that underlie the way that we have formed our society. We're going to take a deep look at those principles and ask ourselves, Is this the society that we want? Or can we do better?

We can. And I'll make it abundantly clear that if we are to effectively root out the injustice endemic to the way we approach safety in our society today, we must release ourselves from the myth that policing has a positive effect on our safety at all.

I know what some of you are thinking. You've read the title of this book, and it has filled you with some sense of dread or anxiety about what "defund the police" really means. Shortly after George Floyd was murdered, Regis Korchinski-Paquet fell to her death from her balcony after police arrived to her high-rise apartment building in my hometown of Toronto. In news reports, Ms. Korchinski-Paquet's family members say they pleaded with police in the hallway outside her unit, telling them she was in need of mental health support. They described multiple officers following Ms. Korchinski-Paquet into her unit while blocking her mother and brother from entering. Minutes later, Ms. Korchinski-Paquet's mother says she heard her daughter cry out, "Mom, help! Mom, help! Mom, help!" Had it not been for the police, I imagine Ms. Korchinski-Paquet's night would have gone very differently. May she rest in peace.

I knew that I would not have much time to process my grief and rage before getting to the difficult work of local community support and uplifting the solution we had been raising for years. We needed to make defunding the police popular. Because of the pandemic, I was suddenly available for media interviews no matter the location. I used interviews as a tool for mass education. Over the course of the summer, I did more than one hundred interviews, wrote op-eds, taught workshops, and delivered trainings. Whether the interview was based in the U.K., the United States, or Canada, I noticed a pattern emerging. The first question was always the same: "Okay, but do you want to defund the police? Or abolish the police?" I very quickly realized that the question was a smoke screen for a very different inquiry. What these people really wanted to ask was "Are you a reasonable person worth listening to? Or are you entirely irrational?" Even after I had given a perfectly logical workshop or an even-keeled interview about the deeply upsetting subject of police murders of Black people, the first question was consistently aimed at determining whether I could be dismissed out of hand for being unreasonable and lacking sense.

It's a bizarre fixation, given the broader issue at hand, and represents a tendency toward finding fault with Black activists rather than focusing on the police or policy makers—those immediately responsible for the violence Black people experience from police. The anxiety may also be born of an attempt to ensure that the inquirer does not inadvertently attach themselves to a senseless message. Regardless, the pretextual question is a strange way of centering one's own ego at the start of a discussion about the tragedy and injustice consistently afflicting Black lives across jurisdictions, geographies, and time.

Like many, I watched Peter Hamby's famous 2020 interview with Barack Obama on *Good Luck America* in which the former president dismissed the popular call to "defund the police" as a "snappy slogan." He then went on to describe a set of policies that would be more palatable to the general public and suggested that what organizers like me *really* want are reforms like those he mentioned rather than police abolition.

I assure you that this is not the case. The talented organizers who managed to create the largest, most popular global campaign the world had ever seen during a summer when a pandemic should have made such a thing impossible could have chosen "police reform now" or "reform the police" if that is indeed what we believed would be the solution to the problem that lies before us. But reform is not what we are calling for, because for more than a century, reform has proven to be inconsequential.

In the days after President Obama's interview, trending tweets and think pieces focused on what a difficult slogan "defund the police" was to understand and how the slogan had hurt the performance of left-leaning Democratic Party candidates during the 2020 general election. But the data shows that it was not phrases like "defund the police" that hurt Democrats, but their failure to inspire people to vote. With respect to the claim that the phrase is difficult to understand, I admit to being entirely perplexed. The internet seemed saturated with people insisting that these three simple words were somehow impossible to understand. Well-meaning liberals seemed dead set on making "defund the police" mean something different from what it very clearly means.

So, let's get that out of the way, shall we? Defund the police. "Defund" is a simple concept. It means "withdraw funding from." "The" is what they call in grammar a definite article—nothing difficult there. "Police," I admit, is a more complex concept (Whom do we include in police? Only municipal forces? What about Border Patrol? Drug enforcement? Intelligence agencies?), but you and I both know that the anxieties over the phrase "defund the police" are not born of confusion over what we mean when we use the term "police."

Let's be honest. Activists, organizers, and politicians use slogans all the time to communicate complex ideas to the population quickly. "Defund the police" is no different, and it is one of the most successful campaign slogans out there. The simple phrase is supported by a well-researched road map for how it could be put into policy, as detailed in both the 2020 BREATHE Act, a bill created by the Movement for Black Lives and sponsored by Congresswomen Ayanna Pressley and Rashida Tlaib and later updated through the 2024 People's Response Act, a bill sponsored by former congresswoman Cori Bush, and members of Congress Pramila Jayapal, Summer Lee, Morgan McGarvey, Ayanna Pressley, and Jan Schakowsky. For the first time in a long time, people are having discussions on a massive scale around the globe about the function of police and the way that we approach safety and security in our society—in part because of how powerful the phrase "Defund the police" really is. It rivals the effectiveness of and is certainly more descriptive in its clear policy suggestion than President Obama's "hope and change" and "yes we can" slogans. It is certainly more descriptive in its clear policy suggestion than "Medicare for all." As activists, organizers, or political actors, we use slogans all the time to help us to effectively communicate complex ideas quickly to the population. "Defund the Police" is no different.

The simple fact is that some people don't want "defund" to mean what it means. They might be in favor of vague attempts at addressing systemic issues inherent to policing but become nervous at the prescribed action defunding the police calls for and its challenge to very deeply held beliefs, value systems, and practices that make some people feel comfortable. I get it. We are calling for a significant shift in the way society is organized and in the way we collectively provide safety and security for one another. And yes, that might change the way that you and I live. I can see how that might be daunting, but that does not mean it is irrational or an idea to be dismissed. And the reward—a more just society, wherein some of our most urgent manifestations of anti-Black racism and institutional inequality are eradicated—is undoubtedly worth it.

I have been an organizer with Black Lives Matter in various local and global capacities since 2014. Throughout my activist experience with BLM, I have been the target of countless direct acts of violence and vitriol from people who have felt similarly threatened by these three words—a simple affirmation of our inherent worth. The year 2020 was a strange year for all sorts of reasons, one of which was the palpable shift in the popularity of Black liberation movement work. In the summer of 2020, activists organized Black Lives Matter demonstrations in at least 230 cities and towns in the United States and Canada, and most of those locations had more than one protest. There were uprisings in the Caribbean, South America, Asia, Europe, Australia, Africa—all over the globe. As an organizer, I was experiencing conflicting feelings over these uprisings. There was the grief of the murders that sparked the protests. The hope that the policy changes that were being adopted as a result in some cities would spread to others. And the anger that some policy makers and police officers were using these protests as superficial photo opportunities to falsely paint themselves as anti-racist politicians ready to take action in support of Black lives.

When I saw Canadian prime minister Justin Trudeau attend a Black Lives Matter rally in Canada's capital city and "take the knee," in the style of activist and quarterback Colin Kaepernick and hundreds of athletes across the United States, I was furious. This was a man who had famously donned blackface in his adulthood—multiple times, by his own admission. This was a man who only acknowledged the United Nations–designated decade for people of African descent four years in. This is a man who ignored the increasing demonstrations and calls for policy change from Black activists, including Black Lives Matter, throughout his tenure as prime minister. Despite demonstrations in more than seventy cities and towns and growing public opinion supporting the call to defund the police, Prime Minister Trudeau has not enacted a single policy focused on ending anti-Black racism in policing. In fact, in a year when the Royal Canadian Mounted Police (RCMP), Canada's federal police force, faced scrutiny for a sexual assault scandal, police killings of Black and Indigenous people, and widely publicized video footage of RCMP officers violently interacting with multiple Black, Indigenous, and people of color, Prime Minister Trudeau's Liberal government confidently increased the budget to Canada's federal police force, never addressing the popular calls for justice occurring across Canada.

Prime Minister Trudeau and politicians like him who engage in these empty performances don't seem to realize that the protests are not aimed exclusively at the police. They are protesting *them*, powerful politicians with the responsibility to address the issue. But more important, his brand of political anti-racism—showing up at a rally, declaring oneself to be individually against racism, and doing nothing else—does not have any meaningful effect on the consequences of anti-Black racism. Anti-racism is not a simple rhetorical repudiation of the scourge of racism. Politicians the world over are happy to give lip service to the theoretical idea of anti-racism but are reluctant to use their significant power to remove the ability of police to wield violence against Black and Indigenous people. Having this power and refusing to use it are repugnant examples of how some envision the solution to racism as a simple matter of decrying vile attitudes.

But no amount of agreeing that racism is bad and self-declaring that one is not racist will stop the police killings and violence against Black, Indigenous, and other communities that experience disproportionate targeting by the police. The solution requires fundamental shifts in the way our societies are organized. The most important moments in the fight for Black liberation have not come as a result of people individually repudiating racism. The end of enslavement, the implementation of civil rights legislation, the end of segregation, and the end of South African apartheid all required significant shifts in the way we organize society. Abolition is the answer, and defunding is the mechanism through which we can achieve it.

One day we will look back at this era, at the very idea of policing, and be aghast at what we have wrought. We have to admit that if we truly want to root out the relentless interruption of life that Black people face from the police, we must be ready to make some serious changes to the way our societies are structured. As we stare down four years of Republican rule under President Trump, who is poised to give even more power and resources to police, those of us who take the issue of police violence and safety seriously are called to consider what changes must be made to bring an end to police violence and to truly address safety issues in our communities. By the time you finish this book, I hope you see it as clearly as I do: Black lives matter, and so we *must* defund the police. It won't be easy. But it is absolutely necessary.

WE'VE BEEN DISINFORMED

L ike many, I grew up watching crime investigation shows. The police procedural is the lifeblood of the television entertainment industry, consistently among the most watched television shows across the world, even more popular than sports. From dramas like *Law & Order,* comedies like *Brooklyn Nine-Nine,* and reality television like *Cops,* at any given time, policing is the one profession you can consistently watch a fictionalized account of on television. The sheer amount of available fictional material to consume about the police has created a sense of familiarity within pop culture about what police do, what they accomplish, and how. The *Law & Order* franchise, for instance, has spawned a seemingly unending plethora of spin-offs, including *Special Victims Unit, Criminal Intent, Trial by Jury, True Crime, Organized Crime, Hate Crimes, Conviction, Los Angeles, UK,* and *Toronto: Criminal Intent.* On any random date in the United States, there are nearly twenty-four hours of the *Law & Order* franchise available to watch on television and far more available on streaming platforms.

Across these shows, the police behave similarly, and sometimes the shared elements reflect things that are true. Yes, police

wear uniforms, engage in traffic stops, and respond to emergency calls. But these programs are ultimately meant to be
entertainment—to excite us, make us emotionally invested, and
keep us watching from week to week. Their purpose is not to
depict the truth. And often, the *how* and the conclusion of these
stories are largely fictionalized. Violence, harm, and threats to
safety are complicated issues that cannot be explained, let alone
resolved, in a television hour. As a lawyer, I can tell you that
televised legal serials make practicing law seem far more thrill-
ing than it actually is. The same is true for policing.

Because of how often we see the police on our screens,
whether in fiction or on the news, we all *feel* knowledgeable
about who they are and what they do—whether we have an
expert level of knowledge or not. In some ways, the ownership we collectively feel over the police is a good thing. Like
any public service, ordinary people should be able to contribute to the examination, critique, and transformation of community safety and security, much like we can with education,
health care, or other public services. What makes public safety
distinct from these other services is the level of interaction the
population has with its primary providers—police officers. To
understand what I mean, let's consider another public service:
education.

When I was a child, my parents were deeply involved in
supporting my education. My mother would order the curricula set by the provincial government before the beginning of
the school year so she was clear on the expectations for me and
my siblings. She would buttress the curriculum with additional
educational material she would find on her own, and both she
and my father would stay in constant communication with our
teachers to get updates on our progress and volunteer in our
classrooms or on field trips, even challenging instructors they
found inadequate.

While my parents might have been more intimately involved than your average parent, it's simply a fact that most of
us have had some sort of interaction with public schools: In the
United States and Canada, 91 percent of children enrolled in

elementary and secondary school attend public schools, while 93 percent do so in the U.K. As such, whether through our own experience or by way of our family members, we each have an experiential level of knowledge about how public schooling works. We have opinions about everything, from teaching strategies, curricula, and class sizes to how evaluation should work, extracurricular activities, and homework. The average person's experiential knowledge can be a valuable contribution to the expert knowledge of service providers (teachers, principals, and other education workers), those working to analyze the education system (researchers and education scholars), direct service users (students and parents), and policy makers (politicians and bureaucrats). Collaboration among these groups creates the opportunity for meaningful conversations about the future of public education systems.

In contrast, most people have no exposure to police officers, our primary recourse for public safety. Only a targeted few—primarily Black, Indigenous, disabled, and poor populations—have consistent and repeated experiences with police in their day-to-day lives. In 2018, less than 25 percent of people in the United States had any contact with police. A 2003 study of people living in London, England, found that 80 percent of Londoners primarily got their information about the police from the news media. Word of mouth was the second-largest source of information about the police at 49 percent, and a staggering 29 percent cited media *fiction* as their primary source. Only 20 percent cited direct experience with police as their primary source of information. Similar data does not exist for Canada, but we do know that there are far fewer police per capita in Canada than in the United States, which suggests there would be less opportunity for police contact with people in Canada. This is not data over the lifetime of an individual, so it isn't telling us how many of us will *ever* interact with police, and it's not telling us what the level or nature of that interaction was. But what this data does tell us is that despite how strongly we may feel about the police one way or another, for the vast majority, our understanding of police is not born of experience or firsthand knowledge. For many, our understanding of police comes from what we have been *told*.

Television shows perpetuate a powerful pervading belief about the world we live in: Police officers are heroes. Characters on police procedurals are rarely complex, and the innocent victim, evil villain, and courageous heroes are quickly identifiable. The design of the shows leads viewers to relate most strongly with the histories and principles of the law enforcement characters. This is accomplished in several ways, but one of the most crucial is simply exposure. The police characters are limited in number but recur frequently on-screen. We get to know their complexities and motivations. The villainous criminals, in contrast, are rarely recurring and do not have complex storylines. They are one-dimensional bad guys. This framing is consistently presented in television shows, in blockbuster films, and even in elementary school assemblies, where children are taught about the dangers of crimes or drugs, typically by the "hero" police officers themselves. The story is repeated so many times it's difficult to accept narratives that contradict it. That is why so many of us feel disturbed when we hear an idea like "defund" or "abolish" the police. It seems taboo; police are the "good guys," the prevailing narrative tells us. Without them, the "bad guys" will harm us.

As a result of this programming, our public safety conversations are stunted—our opinions driven by assumptions rather than reality and our discussions starting and ending with policing. Rarely are we discussing the totality of tools available to create safer, more secure communities, or to prevent harm from happening. From a young age, we are told we need to remember only three numbers, and we will be provided with immediate, personalized, professional assistance. This information is so effectively and repeatedly drilled into our heads that for many of us it has become an impenetrable truth.

The problem is that these stories of heroism are mostly fiction. They don't reflect the truth of policing. And the simple story structure of the good guy chasing the bad guy and vanquishing evil? Things are rarely that simple in real life. If

you're skeptical, I don't blame you. Popular culture has invested decades of time and money ensuring that most of us believe police can do no wrong. But as you read this book, I invite you to suspend your own notions of policing, whether you have had experience with police or not.

THE ORIGINS AND IMPACT OF COPAGANDA

LEXOW COMMITTEE REPORT: New-York's Police Described as Allies of Criminals. THE ENTIRE DEPARTMENT COR-RUPT: Evidence of a Systematic Protection of Crime, with Blackmail for Its Only Object.

—*New York Times* front-page headline, January 18, 1895

In the early days of television, policing was vilified in popular culture. Those of us who remember Saturday-morning cartoons might recall the caricature of the bumbling police officer, often depicted as eating donuts and making a fool of himself. That comedic trope has deep historical roots in Western entertainment. Modern policing as a professional organization was just concretizing at the time early police narratives began to appear in film, and the public was aware of and engaged in vigorous debate about the role of police and widespread corruption in police organizations. Early police narratives in motion picture and radio serials in the West depicted police departments as rife with corruption and hostile to average people—especially workers. The late nineteenth and early twentieth centuries, when the motion picture industry was in its infancy, were a time when workers' movements were successfully unionizing in industries across the world and police were being used to violently crack down on these movements. Many workers lost their lives. And during the 1920s Prohibition era in the United States and Canada, police enforcement of Prohibition laws was seen as overzealous and corrupt, and underground efforts to thwart these laws created plenty of opportunity for officers to profit from participating in the organized crime that flourished during this time.

One of the most famous investigations into police corruption took place between 1894 and 1895 in New York City. In a more-than-ten-thousand-page report, including testimony from hundreds of witnesses, the New York State Senate's Lexow Committee revealed evidence of rape, child abuse, electoral interference, blackmail, extortion, and corruption within the New York Police Department (NYPD), the United States' second professionally established police department. On January 18, 1895, upon completion of the hearings, the resulting front-page *New York Times* article reported that police officers were found to have engaged in "unprovoked assault," stating in particular that "many members of the force, and even superior officers, have abused the resources of physical power which have been provided for them and their use only in cases of necessity in the making of arrests and the restraints of disorder, to gratify personal spite and brutal instincts, and to reduce their victims to a condition of servility." Keep in mind that the NYPD was only founded in 1845. Organizing the widespread corruption to the scale described by the Lexow Committee likely took the better of those fifty short years between the NYPD's founding and the publishing of the report. If there was ever a time in which the police were operating to keep us safer, it certainly wasn't in its infancy.

Contemporary policing retains the character of its birth. The corruption and violence described by the Lexow Committee would be described again and again in report after report about police for decades. So, if the policing narratives of today's police television serial are not depicting some sort of changed reality, where do these narratives come from?

Almost immediately after films began depicting police unfavorably, law enforcement fought back. In 1910, the International Association of Chiefs of Police—an organization still in existence today, with more than 32,000 members across more than 170 countries—condemned popular depictions of policing in film, with its president stating: "In moving pictures the police are sometimes made to appear ridiculous, and in view of

the large number of young people, children, who attend these moving picture shows, it gives them an improper idea of the policeman." In 1916, police in the U.K. recommended to the National Council for Morals that the government establish a central mechanism through which to censor films, blaming movies for an increase in youth involvement in crime. Similar measures were proposed in the United States, and in the 1930s Congress implemented the Hays Code to enforce several rules guiding the moral content of films. The Code strictly enforced how crime was depicted on-screen, setting the stage for policing to be depicted far more positively. It stated that

> law, natural or divine, must not be belittled, ridiculed, nor must a sentiment be created against it.
>
> The *presentation of crimes* against the law, human or divine, is often necessary for the carrying out of the plot. But the presentation must not throw sympathy with the criminal as against the law, nor with the crime as against those who must punish it.

By then, the infamous Federal Bureau of Investigation director J. Edgar Hoover, who would later oversee the explicitly anti-Black policies that drove the harassment of civil rights activists, realized there was power in cooperating with Hollywood to directly influence how consumers felt about particular issues—including the police. Hollywood producers also saw benefits in shifting their approach to depicting law enforcement. Studios needed police to support required filming permits or to look the other way when their affiliated movie stars got into trouble with the law. The combination of the Hays Code and Hoover's negotiations with Hollywood resulted in a dramatic shift in how police were portrayed on-screen.

The show often credited as being the first police procedural, *Dragnet*, was the first product of the collaboration between Hollywood and law enforcement, establishing a groundbreaking partnership with the Los Angeles Police Department (LAPD). In return for help from the LAPD in the form of story ideas, financial support, and logistical assistance, as well as access to near-unlimited shooting locations, props like police vehicles and equipment, and actual police officers to serve as extras, *Dragnet*'s creator, Jack Webb, gave the LAPD authority to censor, edit, and approve every script. The LAPD was so influential it had the power to demand that entire episodes be scrapped. Webb knew his portrayal of the police did not reflect reality, and though the LAPD's edits to his scripts would at times frustrate him, the trade-off was ultimately worth it for his business interests.

Of the 37 million American households who owned a television, an average of 16.5 million were tuning in to *Dragnet* each week in 1955 and absorbing exactly what the LAPD wanted viewers to think about its operation: that police officers were responsible, kind, respectable, and worthy of being labeled heroes for keeping our communities safe. But in reality, the LAPD in this period—throughout its history, really—deservedly received the same critiques as the NYPD. The organization was known to be corrupt and open to taking bribes. City politicians would sell LAPD jobs in exchange for cash outside city hall, and the Central Vice Squad would act as an enforcer for organized crime syndicates. The force was even involved in the attempted murder of a witness in a case concerning corruption in the department. Harry Raymond survived the attack, and two LAPD officers from the Intelligence Squad were convicted of bombing his car. This legacy of corruption and gang-like activity continued right into the period when the LAPD was doing its best to portray itself differently on *Dragnet*. On Christmas Day 1951, at the height of the show's popularity, around fifty members of the department severely brutalized seven men in their custody, five of whom were Mexican American, leaving them with broken bones and severe internal injuries, including punctured organs. The incident, known as Bloody Christmas—as well as the Watts Rebellion that broke out in Black communities in 1965—was antithetical to the cop-as-hero image the LAPD was putting out about itself.

Thus was born copaganda—a word of unclear origin but

popular among abolitionists—which refers to the ways in which news media and popular culture tell stories about policing and crime to manipulate average people into believing the myth that policing creates safety. As the clever portmanteau of the words "cop" and "propaganda" suggests, the near-universal depiction of the police as heroes in popular culture is not accidental but calculated and deliberate, meant to support the goals and interests of law enforcement. Combined with the fact that most people, as stated at the beginning of this chapter, have few encounters with the police, the impact of copaganda on shaping our ideas around law enforcement is hard to understate.

Law & Order, like Dragnet before it, opens with a statement affirming that its stories are pulled from reality. The problem is that reality does not lend itself to the dramatics that make for good entertainment, nor does it neatly fit into an hour of television. Even worse, the version of policing that keeps audiences entertained is often at odds with what our rights are under the law. Viewers expect for a crime to both occur and be resolved within the span of an episode, so shows like Law & Order tend to focus on police efficiency and the relentless pursuit of revenge on behalf of innocent victims. Extrajudicial actions taken by the police within this context, such as harassment and intimidation, conducting improper interrogations, or excessive force against suspects, are nearly universally presented as justifiable means to an end. These acts, according to Normalizing Injustice, an investigative report by Color of Change, are depicted as "routine, harmless, necessary—or even noble—in the pursuit of justice, rather than as problematic, harmful, counterproductive or warranting judgment and accountability." Because these shows tend to show police infractions as useful rather than abusive, audiences are encouraged to forgive or support these police tactics, which are ultimately harmful in the real world.

After all, these abuses pale in comparison to the crimes to which fictional police officers are responding. In police procedurals, officers are constantly responding to murders, kidnappings, and instances of sexual violence—with murder being the most common crime depicted on television. In reality, the police do not deal with reports of murders, or even violent crime, nearly as frequently as *Law & Order* might have us believe. According to the Uniform Crime Reporting Program of the FBI, of the total number of violent crimes reported to police in 2019, only 1.4 percent were murders, while rape accounted for 8.2 percent. Similarly, in the United Kingdom, less than 1 percent of the total number of violent crimes are murders, as consistently reported by the Office for National Statistics from 2017 to the latest data available in 2022. An investigation by *The New York Times* found less than 5 percent of police work in the United States is spent on violent crime as a whole—a category that includes not only homicides but also robbery, rape, and assault. While the murder rates depicted on television may give the false impression that crime is on the rise everywhere, in truth much of what the police do is boring and bureaucratic and wouldn't make for good television. What's more, the rate at which fictional police are solving fictional murders gives viewers a false impression of police activity. In the U.K., for instance, statistics for England and Wales show that only 9 percent of crimes result in suspects being charged. And though the U.K. Office for National Statistics reports that the homicide rate in the U.K. has remained consistently low, with 2024 statistics showing 9.7 homicides for every million people—less than 1 percent of all violent crimes recorded by police—much like *Law & Order*, U.K.-based police procedurals like *Luther* and *Sherlock* suggest law enforcement spends most of its time solving violent crimes.

This presentation of policing as rife with danger makes it easy to dehumanize people who become suspects and therefore make light of their rights. In the *Law & Order* universe, the well-understood principle that suspects are presumed innocent until proven guilty is upended. The *charge itself*—whether the suspect is convicted or acquitted—becomes indicative of their culpability. This does significant work to color the way the general population understands people who have been charged with, much less convicted of, a crime. Few viewers have a deep

enough understanding of the criminal legal system to understand that many who have been charged and are incarcerated
today have not had their guilt proven; they are simply await-
ing trial. Or that the innocent regularly take plea deals, admitting to a crime they did not commit, because they cannot risk
the hardships and potential consequences of a trial. According
to the Innocence Project, 95 percent of felony convictions in
the United States are secured through guilty pleas and 18 percent of those exonerated in cases that have been reconsidered
after new DNA evidence was made available had pleaded guilty
despite being innocent—an unfathomable miscarriage of justice. The way fiction colors our understanding of the criminal legal system has real-world policy consequences. Because
we are generally convinced police would lay a charge only in a
situation of assured guilt, it becomes easy to garner support for
tough-on-crime political strategies encroaching on the rights
of people who have not been proven guilty of any crime, such
as the push to make it more difficult for people to be released
on bail. The consequences can be fatal.

Take the tragic case of Kalief Browder, whose story was
depicted in the documentary series *Time: The Kalief Browder
Story*, produced by Jay-Z. Mr. Browder spent three years incarcerated on Rikers Island in New York City despite never sitting
trial for a crime. He was only sixteen when he was arrested
in 2010 after being accused of stealing a backpack—an alle-
gation for which there was no evidence other than an inconsistent witness who identified him at night from a squad car
two weeks after the alleged robbery took place. Mr. Browder's
family could not afford the $3,000 cash bail, so as a minor, he
was sent to Rikers Island and imprisoned for over *one thousand
days*, more than seven hundred of which were spent in solitary confinement, to await his trial. During his time at Rikers,
Mr. Browder was beaten, starved, and tortured. He tried to kill
himself multiple times during his incarceration.

Kalief Browder should have been enjoying his teenage
years, finishing up high school, and preparing for his transition
into adult life. Instead, during these precious formative years,

this Black boy was subject to cruel punishment for a crime he always maintained he did not commit, facing a possible fifteen years in prison if he was found guilty. The prosecution in Mr. Browder's case offered him a deal: a three-and-a-half-year prison sentence in exchange for a guilty plea. But Mr. Browder refused, believing his innocence could be proven in a trial. A criminal conviction could have significant impacts on the rest of his life, limiting future opportunities and restricting his freedoms. But Mr. Browder would spend roughly the same amount of time he would have under the plea deal simply waiting for a judge to hear his case. The charges against him were not dropped until 2013, when the prosecution admitted that there was insufficient evidence to proceed with the case. Their case hinged on the alleged victim, who had by then left the country.

Mr. Browder suffered serious mental health decline because of the torment he was made to endure, and in June 2015 he died by suicide, two years after his release.

May he rest in peace.

In 2019, Mr. Browder's family and the New York City Law Department settled a civil rights and wrongful death action for $3.3 million.

————

The racial patterns of policing, too, are either weaponized or obfuscated in fictionalized police propaganda. The remarkably consistent ways policing has harmed marginalized communities, especially Black and Indigenous people, since its inception have been written out of Hollywood scripts. Racial profiling barely exists on television, despite extensive research proving its existence. Just as the racially targeted violence of the LAPD, as evidenced through incidents like the Bloody Christmas beatings and the Watts Rebellion, was kept from *Dragnet* audiences, excessive force is rarely depicted on-screen, despite consistent, repeated years of inquiries and reports that demonstrate its use and how it is linked to race. It's no wonder then that the harassment and violence understood to be fixtures in Black communities are met with skepticism and disbelief by those who experience fewer interactions with police. While some television shows have made a concerted effort to include narratives about police violence against Black people after the murder of George Floyd in 2020, these instances are still represented as the result of a few bad apples rather than a systemic issue.

In fact, unless it is a specific subject of a show, racial consequence is essentially nonexistent on television, even though race is a central determinant of our identities, our social and economic experiences, and our health. Though people of color are more likely to be victims of crime, for instance, network executives and producers reportedly instruct writers to ensure crime victims are not Black, because audiences will have a harder time empathizing with them. Color of Change reported that on police procedurals 38 percent of victims are white women, 35 percent are white men, 22 percent are men of color, 13 percent are women of color, 12 percent are Black men, and just 9 percent are Black women. As a result, according to the same Color of Change report, nearly three-quarters of white people in the United States believe people are treated the same by police, regardless of race, while some believe that people of color are treated less harshly than white people.

While racial consequence is nonexistent, race itself is still a useful propagandizing tool. Color of Change found that both race and gender were helpful toward normalizing inappropriate police behavior. In particular, it was useful for fictionalized police of color, women police officers, and even civilians of color to endorse and actively support actions and tactics police in the real world are not permitted to utilize. Despite the LAPD's well-recorded internal segregationist hiring policies, for instance, *Dragnet* was intentional about depicting Black and Latino police officers. The presence of even one Black police officer supporting wrongful behavior from fellow police officers on these television shows does significant work to normalize police behavior that is typically employed against people of color.

There are some cop shows—mostly dramas—that question and complicate the public's understanding of policing and the criminal legal system. But even these tend to suggest that the system is ineffective because police and prosecutors do not have enough power. What makes the system flawed, according to these more critical television shows, are obstacles such as legal technicalities, unscrupulous defense lawyers who represent sociopaths, and internal affairs bogeymen—a narrative that plays right into the hands of police departments angling for more resources from the public purse. In these stories, the trope is that criminals get off on a technicality.

With dozens of similar depictions of policing reinforcing a message of how policing operates, overstating its value, and erasing its consistent flaws, these shows create false ideas about policing that our culture misunderstands as commonsense. Those ideas then inform how we respond to the very real issues with policing in our communities. The message in these neatly wrapped-up stories bleeds into the ways we attempt to account for and rein in incidents of police misconduct. Despite decades of attempts to implement measures that will discourage police impropriety and thwart impunity for wrongful actions on the part of the police, the political will and public support for such measures are low. If we again consider how much the average person is learning from police procedurals, this is unsurprising. If audiences are regularly seeing exciting images of police officers bursting into homes in violation of our rights and successfully thwarting evil villains, they are more likely to forgive these actions in real life, assuming that the people harmed are villainous and deserving of these attacks. The presumption is that it must be their fault the police harmed them. If the police happened to violate someone's rights in the course of killing or harming them, at the end of the day the world is better off for it. Those trying to reform policing insist that accountability measures are necessary, but movies and television tell us that accountability measures make it harder for police to solve crimes. The paper pushers and bureaucratic disciples are obstacles to overcome, a hindrance to the hero cop whose motives are beyond reproach. Television tells us: If we care about safety, we need to limit the intrusive evaluation of police at all costs.

To be clear, I am not arguing that racial profiling and racial victimization need to be accurately portrayed in the entertainment we enjoy. But what I *am* saying is that the depictions of police in the most popular forms of entertainment we consume show a fantasyland that simply does not exist, and when people begin to believe those fantasies have a basis in real life, they have a hard time accepting reality. Research consistently demonstrates that television deeply affects the opinions of viewers, shaping public knowledge and political views. This isn't just true for policing. Citing a Kaiser Family Foundation study, Color of Change noted that viewers of *Grey's Anatomy* learned and retained useful medical information, showing how important fictional procedural dramas can be in educating audiences—or propagandizing them. With this kind of power to influence viewers, producers, writers, and network executives can significantly shape how we understand professions for which our greatest access is through a television screen.

With few exceptions, our culture rarely tells the stories or shares the perspectives of those regularly harmed by police. This absence results in the majority of people being unable to empathize with the people most likely to be charged with crimes in the real world and being reluctant to see policing as a racialized practice. For those of us who have direct experiences with police or have done work looking into the reality of how policing operates, the ease with which society turns away from what is real and true—that there is no relationship between the police heroes we see on-screen and the type of policing we are subjected to every day—is maddening. The public pressure and political support we manage to harness with each incident of horrifying police violence that does manage to become national or international news are effectively neutralized by the hundreds of millions of dollars poured into police propaganda. We are the underdogs, trying to pierce through that propaganda with our marches, research, and occasional access to news media.

COPAGANDA AS NEWS

On December 13, 2022, the topic on my podcast *Sandy & Nora Talk Politics*, in which I discuss politics with my friend, fellow social activist and journalist Nora Loreto, was about a widely reported story about retail theft. A few days earlier, on December 10, the mainstream and widely read national Canadian newspaper *The Globe and Mail* had published an opinion piece by Gus Carlson, a U.S.-based opinion columnist and communications consultant, called "Not Just Inflation: Shoplifting and Soft-on-Crime Policies in the U.S. Push Prices Up, Too." In it, Carlson argued that recent inflation was caused in part by widespread shoplifting and not enough funding for police and that movements to defund the police are partly to blame. Just before recording the episode, Nora searched for the article on her laptop so that she could have it in front of her for reference. Curiously, we came across a very similar opinion article, entitled "Top Retailers Say Theft Has Reached Historic Highs," published on December 7 in the conservative news publication *The Washington Free Beacon* attributed to Anna Allen, an assistant editor for the publication. The articles were so similar the writers seemed to have followed a formula. Both quoted the same sources, from stores like Rite Aid, Walmart, and Target, and drew the same conclusion: The solution to the massive inflationary problem caused by retail theft is more police. At the core of the writers' arguments was a claim by the National Retail Federation, an organization that represents the interests of more than seventeen thousand companies, that of the $94.5 billion in retail inventory loss in the United States in 2021, half could be attributed to organized retail crime. That astronomical number felt incredible when I read it. Aside from the publications noted above, these claims were reported in several news sources, including *The Wall Street Journal, Forbes, Business Insider,* and *Yahoo Finance*.

As it turns out, our skepticism was warranted. A year later, the trade publication *Retail Dive* found issue with these figures, and the organization was forced to walk back its claims, blaming the error on a consulting firm with which it had collaborated on the widely cited report. *The New York Times* reported that organized crime was *not* responsible for 50 percent of the $94.5 billion in lost merchandise, citing an expert that put the figure at closer to 5 percent—a massive deception by the National Retail Federation. It appears, then, that the articles were part of a public relations strategy by the federation. Alec Karakatsanis, a civil rights lawyer and cofounder of the impact litigation organization Equal Justice Under Law who publicly researches and tracks copaganda in fiction and news sources, told the *Times* that the proliferation of the Retail Federation's rhetoric and the retraction that followed demonstrate how news media is "used as a tool by certain vested interests to gin up a lot of fear about this issue when, in fact, it was pretty clear all along that the facts didn't add up."

In a Twitter thread, Karakatsanis pointed to another instance of the *exact same* phenomenon in 2021—a series of articles that quoted the same sources, appeared to be reported in a formulaic way, and argued that theft was on the rise and law enforcement needed to be beefed up to protect retailers, all opinions based on data from the National Retail Federation. In 2021, these articles were published in the *Chicago Tribune*, by the Associated Press, and in *The New York Times*. This points to a multiyear campaign to manufacture a crisis and present law enforcement as its only solution.

According to Karakatsanis, this is one of the three core functions of copaganda, which he has identified as narrowing our understanding of safety; manufacturing crises around narrow categories of crime; and manipulating our understanding of what solutions actually make us safer. The proliferation of this misleading news fed by the National Retail Federation whipped up public support for more policing to take care of a problem that is as real as the monster under the bed—when the symptoms everyone is concerned about have real solutions elsewhere. Blaming the inflationary economic impact of the pandemic on shoplifters one year after a pandemic during which supply chains were interrupted and energy costs ballooned is suspicious. It shifts the responsibility away from politicians who could have made different economic policy choices during the pandemic to regulate the marketplace in ways that would have protected average consumers and workers from businesses who chose profits over people. Blaming shoplifters gives justification for retailers to continue to increase prices (and profits) and allows politicians to avoid angering retailers. Rather than implementing economic regulations, politicians could satisfy the public that they are doing something about high prices by providing more resources to law enforcement. Crime is a great scapegoat.

With respect to narrowing our understanding of safety, the success of copaganda is palpable. As demonstrated by the articles mentioned above, discussions about public safety, especially in a political context, are often limited to heightening the perception of rising crime (whether crime is actually increasing or not), getting criminals off the streets, and increasing policing measures through heavier police presence, further militarization, and increased surveillance. This rhetoric—a remarkably narrow approach to public safety—is true across the popular political spectrum, among conservatives, centrists, and liberals alike. We could be discussing ways to keep children and youth safe and positively engaged if their caregivers are unable to be present for them in after-school hours. We could be talking about how to redesign cities so as to structurally prevent the inexcusably high number of traffic accidents that lead to injury and death each year. We could be considering ways to ensure that everyone—regardless of income—has access to stable housing, nutrition, and other basic necessities. We could be trying to figure out strategies to disincentivize and prevent burglaries like those that concerned the owner of the hotel where I stayed in Portland. The number of measures we could take to ensure we are safe go far beyond the exceptionally weak options we regularly discuss. But the impact of copaganda makes it difficult to have these commonsense conversations.

And to understand how copaganda manipulates our understanding of what makes us safe, just think about any episode of any police procedural show you may watch. The message by the end of the neatly wrapped-up story is clear. If something precious is stolen from you, the police will be there to find it. You need someone to keep you safe? Call the police. They may even personally keep watch at your door, if you need it. And police will do *anything* to set things right, make sure you are avenged, and bring evildoers to justice. To imagine how widespread this messaging is, consider this: Police procedurals and legal dramas draw the largest audiences in the U.S. for prime-time television and attract worldwide audiences in the hundreds of millions. And the ubiquity of U.S. popular culture throughout the English-speaking world means the U.K. and Canada contend with the very same consequences of U.S.-based police propaganda. But the idea that police presence is the solution to violence, or that police go to great personal lengths to protect the public, is fiction. In real life, this is not how things work. Police *do not prevent violence*. They respond to it and perpetuate it.

Police know the way that they are depicted in the media is a fantasy. It's why they spend hundreds of millions of dollars every year to ensure that they are publicly discussed in a manner that primes our societies to support ballooning police budgets and the police as our primary approach to public safety measures. In Los Angeles alone, more than $8 million of the Los Angeles County Sheriff's Department budget is earmarked for public relations, according to a 2020 report by the *Los Angeles Times*. Given the ubiquity of police communications staff across jurisdictions, we can expect similarly large expenditures are being made in police departments across the United States and Canada.

The police public relations machine has a strong copaganda partner in news media. I have often said that the police act as a stand-in for underfunded services. I was recently surprised to discover just how far this function of the police had progressed with respect to news media. At some point during 2022, I came across a tweet by Toronto-based journalist and podcast host

Jordan Heath-Rawlings. He was expressing concern about this stub of a story the *Toronto Star* published in its local crime section:

Break and Enter Reported at One East York Home (July 5) *

Police reported one residential break and enter in East York between June 28 and July 4. That's two fewer than were reported during the previous week (you can find the latest reports for the city's other neighbourhoods here). Reports across the city remained flat at 36, bringing Toronto's preliminary total break and enters for the year to 1,254—down eight per cent compared to the same period in 2021.

A fairly innocuous reporting of fact, right? Not quite. A qualifying statement at the end of the article reads,

This story was automatically generated using open data collected and maintained by Toronto Police Service. The incidents were reported by police in the past week and reportedly occurred in the past two weeks, but recent crime data is preliminary and subject to change upon further police investigation. The locations have been offset to the nearest intersection and no personal information has been included for privacy reasons.

I was completely taken aback. We rely on the media to serve as scrutinizers of public services, not mouthpieces, providing a service to readers that should include rigorous fact-checking. It's incredible that news media place such weight on the police as a trustworthy source that they are willing to cede to a degree editorial control to artificial intelligence machines populated only with police data. Law enforcement is not and should not be the only source of information for crimes. Yet in this and

---

* Torstar Open Data Team, "Break and Enter Reported at One East York Home (July 5)." *Toronto Star,* July 5, 2022.

many instances, news media treat information from the police as objective, which is striking since there is so much evidence to the contrary.

Police sources are notoriously unreliable. An analysis conducted in 2023 by *The Washington Post* concluded that in several high-profile cases in which civilians were killed by police, including those of Tyre Nichols, George Floyd, Breonna Taylor, and Elijah McClain, initial police accounts were "misleading, incomplete, or wrong." Whether in cases of police violence, or reports like the *Toronto Star* example above, the role of the journalist as an investigator is of the utmost importance when reporting on information they receive from police.

Police have a vested interest in representing themselves as faultless, because negative perceptions of policing could lead to increased scrutiny, more regulation, and decreased budgets. Their interest in appearing above reproach is at odds with the public interest in objectively understanding and evaluating the police as a public service. As such, they cannot be considered a neutral, reliable source. But the media often fail to corroborate police reports, regularly using data, sources, and information provided by law enforcement without fact-checking the accuracy of their claims. The news media are better placed than most other organizations to know that police are unreliable sources; they are the ones who later issue corrections or follow-up reports when an initial police-sourced claim proves untrue. But much like producers and executives in the entertainment industry, the media see it as in their best interest to maintain excellent relationships with police, at times to the detriment of reliable reporting.

When we watch the news, what we see is a curated report based on what producers have deemed newsworthy for an audience. There is no shortage of stories to choose from. They could prioritize coverage about the climate change crisis, rampant poverty, or corporate and political corruption—all salient issues with increasing urgency and importance in our lives. The interesting thing about all these examples is they all can be connected to action. If these topics were given more airtime, viewers would have access to more information about issues they could actually *do something* about, whether through community service or political action. But these issues generally take a back seat to crime reporting. Instead, for decades, crime has been most news programs' preferred area of coverage, receiving a disproportionate level of focus compared with other important and consequential social issues. Reported after the fact, segments on crime don't leave an audience with much but a story—the implication being that incidents of crime are relevant to viewers because they, too, could one day be victims.

––––––––

Crime accounts for 25 percent of the content in newspapers and 20 percent on television, but it is not presented in a manner that reflects how frequently it occurs. As we've learned, violent crime is uncommon, but murders are far more likely to receive coverage than, for example, property crime, which occurs far more frequently. The types of victims who receive attention are also skewed. When victims are affluent and respectable, the news is more likely to focus on their case, despite other communities being the most likely targets of crime.

Police are the number one source for information leading to crime reporting. Similar to the choice news producers have when they are deciding what is newsworthy, reporters have a choice in what sources to use. In addition to police, if journalists want to report on a crime, they could turn to victims, witnesses, paramedics, court proceedings, anonymized hospital admission records, defense attorneys, or any number of relevant sources. But the choice that is often made, especially at the outset of a crisis, is to report crime uncritically from a sole source: the police. This means that crime reporting, already taking up a giant share of mainstream news, is also disproportionately shaped by one source—one with an interest in presenting the information in a way that makes them appear faultless and necessary. This is why so much crime news amounts to copaganda.

This symbiotic relationship has been deliberately strengthened and exploited for decades, since the advent and consequent ubiquitousness of professional media departments within police forces in the late 1980s and early 1990s. Spokespeople within these departments work to disseminate information that builds and solidifies the public's trust in policing institutions and cultivate good relationships with the journalists to whom they provide crime news selectively and strategically. They essentially act as gatekeepers, deciding which crime stories to alert media about, which to keep confidential, and which to release selective information about. Their role is crucial to helping shape news coverage so that it presents the police in a manner that legitimizes their existence and emphasizes their professionalism and effectiveness. Stories are not always connected to a particular wrongdoing; often the stories highlight strategic approaches to policing activities, like drunk driving checkpoints being set up during long weekends. They also get coverage of award ceremonies and funerals, in a way that other institutions that contribute to health and safety do not, increasing public perception of their overall value to society. In this exchange, producers and reporters gain access to quick information, while police departments gain a reliable megaphone for publicity.

Yet this mutual interest is deeply uneven. When news media don't cooperate with the police, the police can use other methods to reach their intended audience, such as social media or the sophisticated government relations and lobbying apparatus developed by police fraternal organizations. On the other hand, the media are so reliant on the police that without them they would not be able to fulfill their function. Without the quick, easy access to a source audiences are willing to believe, news media would require far more resources and a complete redesign of how news is produced. As Robert Blau, a former *Chicago Tribune* reporter, put it in his book *The Cop Shop*, "The journalist is always in an inferior negotiating position—the reporter who cannot get information is out of a job, whereas the policeman who retains it is not." This can put journalists in a difficult position. Reporters and news outlets have a strong incentive to ignore or soften police behavior the public would not support.

Critical reporting on the police can make police institutions hostile to journalists, and some journalists may even feel compelled to go out of their way to "scratch the backs" of police to ensure they remain happy and willing to supply information. Police, in contrast, can be selective with the information they provide and benefit from keeping some information confidential as part of their propagandizing use of the news. Researchers in the U.K. and Canada have observed police engaging in a "freezing out technique," refusing to engage with specific journalists who write stories that question police behavior.

In part, the challenge of reporting on crime is that most coverage focuses on the discovery of the crime, which allows the police to be the first to establish an "official" version of events. Witnesses' and victims' perspectives are typically reported long after police have put their spin on a story—if ever reported at all. Consider the murder of George Floyd, for example—may he rest in peace. The initial press release published by police read, in part:

Man Dies After Medical Incident During Police Interaction

Two officers arrived and located the suspect, a male believed to be in his 40s, in his car. He was ordered to step from his car. After he got out, he physically resisted officers. Officers were able to get the suspect into handcuffs and noted he appeared to be suffering medical distress. Officers called for an ambulance. He was transported to Hennepin County Medical Center by ambulance where he died a short time later.

There is no mention of Mr. Floyd, whose murder was the inciting incident leading to the global protests in 2020, being violently removed from his car by police. There is no mention of police officer Derek Chauvin jamming his knee into Mr. Floyd's neck for more than nine minutes. There is no mention of Mr. Floyd begging for his mother or telling them he could not breathe and felt he was about to die. There is no mention of the fact that Chauvin continued to kneel on Mr. Floyd's neck even after EMTs arrived, forcing a paramedic to reach around Chauvin's knee to access Mr. Floyd's neck, only to discover there was no pulse. Once this information came to light, through witness accounts and private surveillance camera footage, Chauvin was charged and later convicted of multiple crimes, including second- and third-degree murder. The police kept this information secret to paint themselves in a positive light. While it didn't work in Mr. Floyd's case, one has to wonder how often police engage in these deceptive tactics to hide their questionable behavior.

You may be thinking that the trade-off here is worth it. Perhaps public knowledge about crime is so important that police-skewed bias is acceptable. To that I counter that crime reporting takes up the lion's share of news space *not* because reporters seek to educate the public about ongoing crimes. It is to fill content space. A crime story can fill the pages of a newspaper or the minutes of a crime report for weeks, because police will continue providing updates whether or not there is any real progress. But going to the police as a source of singular import will necessarily paint an incomplete picture of crime in any community, because *most crimes are never even reported to the police.* If crime is so important to report, news stories should not be dependent on whether a crime is reported to the police or not. If crime is among the most important news topics deserving coverage, reporters should be spending more time on developing sources besides the police. But crimes that are not reported to police rarely make it to the news, and discussions about why these news stories are missing are also conspicuously absent from the pages of our newspapers.

All this means that the public does not have ready access to information describing the ways police routinely and catastrophically fail to provide an effective safety and security service and are consistently themselves a threat to many communities. Another consequence of this preferential treatment is that the police can leverage positive news coverage to shore up political power in support of their interests. A media apparatus that is reluctant to frustrate their allies on the police force may inadvertently end up supporting the media strategy of police institutions hell bent on securing more funding to continue to carry out activities that make communities less safe, such as the proliferation of military-style resources across police departments in North America, particularly in the United States. As cities struggle to provide support for residents experiencing the brunt of defunded social services, police department funding has increased, without any effect on crime rates or the safety of residents. But together with the hero cop narrative on television and in film, the outsized way the media report on crime and police activities supports the argument that law enforcement agencies *need* the new eardrum-destroying sound cannon, eye-exploding rubber bullet, or military-grade chemical weapon. When the media fail to report on the ways these instruments and tactics seriously harm and endanger average people, they are acting as indispensable public relations partners to police.

Some of you may even notice this in your day-to-day lives. Pay close attention to news cycles prior to police budgets being approved. Several of my colleagues and I have noted the increase in reporting on police raids of supposed hotbeds of criminal activities conspicuously close to a city council vote on a budget that would see yet another increase in funding for the police, even as other services are being defunded. Reporters receive incredible access to capture police bursting through the homes of people we are told are scourges in our communities. While these trends are anecdotal when it comes to policing in my hometown, in the U.K., researchers Louise Cooke and Paul Sturges have tracked how police communications staff provide "pre-packaged news materials" for reporters and ensure they have access to activities like "dawn raids" at opportune times. This ability to manipulate reporting on police activities has become a central part of the role of police in the U.K., with all police forces in England and Wales having a corporate communications department staffed primarily by non–police officers who have a background in either journalism or marketing. The same study found that as of 1993, more than 90 percent of media interactions with police were initiated by law enforcement, and more than 90 percent of those interactions resulted in media reporting, leading researchers to conclude that there was a "high level of police control over the nature of crime reports seen by the general public."

Crime did not always dominate news reporting. In the 1980s, to ensure that the public had access to quality news media, the Federal Communications Commission (FCC) required that networks provide programming that would act as a public service. News companies in the United States used profits from entertainment programming to subsidize news programs that typically operated at a loss—they were not expected to make a profit. NBC News, for example, was losing hundreds of millions of dollars per year. But in the following decade, several important events shifted network tolerance for news media operating at a loss of millions of dollars. The FCC stopped enforcing its public service requirements; giant profit-driven media conglomerates became owners of most of what we see on television; and prime-time news programs' viewership plummeted up to 50 percent.

As news conglomerates became the norm throughout the 1990s, the news became far more focused on how to increase profit margins rather than how to provide information crucial to a functioning democracy. Networks responded by cutting back on gathering information, eliminating overseas bureaus, and increasing focus on infotainment. News media began to cover more tabloid-like news, and news with in-depth analysis fell from 70 percent to 40 percent from the late 1970s to the late 1990s. Whole books have been written on the effect of these trends on all manner of democratic participation, and it's all bad. But when it comes to the matter at hand, the bottom line is that crime and policing became easy, cheap, entertainment-like content fillers that attracted viewers and pleased advertisers.

In a paper published in the *William & Mary Law Review*, Sara Sun Beale, a professor at Duke Law School, references several studies finding profit motives can distort the way that crime is reported, with newsworthiness being determined by stories' ability to drive readers or viewers rather than by what the public needs to know. Shareholders in these news organizations, as in other sorts of businesses, demand better returns quarter after quarter, and the market is telling the owners of news media that the public has, as Beale puts it, "a taste for violence" as entertainment—which is how television networks see news. "As a result, the coverage of crime—particularly violent crime—has increased dramatically, and the nature of the coverage has shifted toward a tabloid style," Beale wrote. "Similar trends can be noted in network news, local television news, and newspapers." When reports from the first to the last third of the 1990s are compared, coverage of murder increased more than 500 percent on the three major networks in the United States. Crime stories in general increased by more than 300 percent. Research on crime reporting compared with crime rates has shown that during the period in which networks increased crime coverage during prime-time news, crime rates were *falling*. But crime stories then and now make it seem as though crime is a larger and larger problem, year after year.

The problem has worsened with the expectations of how quickly news should be reported in a post-Twitter and digital media universe. To stay relevant, news organizations now require content for a twenty-four-hour news cycle and must produce this news in the time it takes for an issue to make it to social media. In addition to the market-driven focus on entertainment-style news, news media can increase profit margins by cutting costs, and they have certainly been doing this through the decimation of their labor force. Massive layoffs at media companies and the shuttering and consolidation of media outlets are now the norm. This contributes to the media's reliance on police sources. Fewer journalists to provide analysis and investigation on the serious problems affecting our society means police public relations departments are even more alluring as cost-effective, labor-light means to obtaining content that meets a profit-focused business strategy. Reporters don't have to extend tight deadlines waiting for the police to weigh in on an issue as they might have to if they wait for witnesses or other sources, because the police are willing to deliver all the raw materials required to fill a word count without eating up crucial time in a back-and-forth discussion.

Police institutions are very aware of the status and power they hold over the media and their ability to affect public perception, and they use it, readily. In Canada, alternative media sources uncovered a strategy being used by police departments across the country to influence politics in 2021. The Vancouver Police Department, the Ottawa Police Service, and the Edmonton Police Service hired a social impact firm to justify continued increases to already bloated budgets, presumably to respond to the success of the defund-the-police message gaining popularity across the country. The firm, HelpSeeker, has published reports for these police services arguing that social safety nets are bloated and that the solution is to provide police with more funding and to ignore calls to defund the police. The police managed to get these reports published in major news media—even though analysts have shown that the numbers they rely on to make these claims are just plain wrong. Crucially, some of these reports were produced just before budget votes that would determine the amount of money going to policing. The police clearly have political motivations, and money to spend to influence political decision making. According to government records, HelpSeeker also receives funding from the Waterloo Regional Police Service, the Toronto Police Service, the Peel Regional Police, the Lethbridge Police Service, and the Winnipeg Police Service.

This kind of coordinated effort is also apparent in the coverage and responses to the Black Lives Matter movement's demands to end the very real, excessive, unprovoked police violence Black people experience every day. In response to widespread public support for activists calling for an end to police violence, headlines across the United States declared *police* were facing violence and hostility from citizens and suggested that these attacks were part of a coordinated "war on police," for which the movement for Black lives was responsible. It's stunning that this framing was able to garner as much traction as it did, given that it simply was not true. There is no evidence to suggest that violence against police has increased, and certainly nothing to suggest that the movement calling for justice for Black people has somehow created a violent situation for police, and yet reports claiming the opposite proliferated in mainstream media. This is incredibly demonstrative of the power of police propaganda: They managed to create a narrative that the problem is not the persecution of average Black people by a militarized force known for targeting their communities and using weaponry from the public purse to harm and kill them, but rather that the police, with all the money, power, resources, tools, and legitimacy of the state and having evaded accountability for its failures since its inception, are experiencing persecution. In the fall of 2015, a randomized survey of adults in the United States carried out by the polling firm Rasmussen Reports found nearly 60 percent of respondents thought there was a war on police occurring in the United States. Some police officers have even called the movement for Black lives, which is simply demonstrating against police violence, a hateful movement—equating democratic participation in critiquing the very real and measurable failures of a service we all pay for with the irrational hatred or fear of people because of immutable physical characteristics. The narrative is ludicrous, and yet they were able to get it to take hold quickly and to get that message to spread far and wide with no evidence to show its veracity. The police influence on media narratives is exceptionally powerful, indeed.

These pervasive narratives can affect the way that policy makers treat these institutions. Public institutions such as policing are under constant renewal and reshaping; new policies and regulations are introduced on a regular basis. Whether or not these policies are in the service of our tangible needs is very much dependent on what kind of public pressure average people are putting on politicians. And just like you and me, politicians can be heavily influenced by copaganda. The war-on-police narrative has affected discussions about police reform, militarization, increased access to weaponry, and gun control in the United States. In some states, the profession of policing has even become a protected class, enjoying similar protections as people who may be subject to discrimination based on immutable characteristics like race, religion, or gender. It's hard to imagine any other profession having a similar protected status—this is the power of copaganda. When average people who don't have regular interactions with police are sold a web of falsehoods and carefully curated bits of information that make police appear to be faultless, we have a perfect storm for a political apparatus that feels justified in taking such measures while ignoring its massive failure in addressing the safety and security concerns our societies desperately need.

There's a communications theory developed by late communications professor and sociologist George Gerbner that explains how our feelings about policing coincide with the way police are depicted on television. Cultivation theory argues that if you have greater mass media exposure through television or movies of a particular concept than you do in real life, your beliefs about that concept will reflect what you have consumed through the media. The thing that mass media copaganda has been most successful at delivering to mass audiences since the mid-twentieth century is legitimacy. As a society, we are far more willing to criticize and debate other service-based institutions and professions—politicians, teachers, doctors, and so on. But the power of copaganda has cultivated within us a trust in policing that prevents us from having sober conversations reflecting reality without serious backlash or confrontation.

A related concept is framing; how we frame crime and the problems in our society matters. We can talk about our social problems as crimes for which individual people bear sole responsibility, or we can talk about our social problems as related to broader issues. For example, we can understand a problem like transmission prevention during a pandemic as the sole responsibility of individuals, or we can understand that the way we live, use public transportation, and access hospitals, as well as the flexibility we may or may not have to take time off work, are not entirely under the control of individuals, and that broader social interventions might be necessary. Often, the way we discuss crime in the news places blame squarely on individuals and fails to consider that perhaps part of the problem is in the way that our society fails to provide safety—or even function—for many of us. It is critical that we have access to news coverage that tells us about the reality of policing. The public should be aware of controversial policing policies, controversial police use of force, and the reality of how effective police are at being the purveyors of safety and security in our society.

Decisions about how our news is delivered shouldn't be driven by its entertainment value. We should have an understanding of crime and its impact on our communities that is based in truth so we can make appropriate political decisions and have meaningful conversations about the services that we might want to collectively focus on as taxpayers. The consequences are real. Whether it's Republicans who support Trump's statement that "police are the most mistreated people" in the United States, or Democratic support in Biden stating that the police require more funding, the police have long-standing political support from the major parties in the United States, a trend that exists in Canada and the U.K. as well. Researchers studying cultivation theory and framing think that the way crime news is reported might have influenced public opinion in the United States, resulting in increased support for controversial punitive policies like mandatory minimum sentences and adult consequences for children who break the law. At the very least, the worldview that we cultivate from our news media should reflect reality.

As you read this book, remember that the advocates, activists, lawyers, whistleblowers, academics, and countless others who are desperately trying to get average people to understand the problems inherent in policing simply do not have access to the same communications or political apparatus that the police do. Very few politicians are willing to potentially risk their political popularity to champion our cause and go up against a massive propaganda machine. So when a case or campaign *does* manage to pierce the wall that the police and news media have created and reaches your sphere of knowledge, it has done so in spite of the very strong copaganda apparatus that makes it hard to inform the public about the horrendous realities of policing. To pierce that wall, it takes an incredible amount of effort from many, many people who do not have the same resources as the police. Those of us who are trying to break through the copaganda noise continue to engage in a monumental struggle to make this information widely available, precisely because the truth of the information, once discovered, is so verifiable, so shocking, and so unacceptable that it makes it seem absolutely implausible that this state of affairs has managed to continue for so long.

ORIGIN STORIES

The fantasy narrative that dominates what we believe about policing is that cops bring evildoers to justice. The truth is policing interacts with a complex web of legislation and institutions that consistently target and harm specific groups of people, while benefiting other groups. Rather than bringing so-called evildoers to justice, policing is focused on controlling those populations who are less valued in our society and subjecting them to surveillance. If we accept the notion that policing is actually about social control, then perhaps policing—with all its apparent failures to keep us safe and with all the ugly ways policing harms people—is working exactly as it was meant to work. It certainly does restrict the freedoms of identifiable groups of people in society. And if part of its function *is* to harm people, it is absolutely reasonable for us to consider whether or not getting rid of policing altogether is a worthy objective. The idea of defunding the police or police abolition isn't meant to do away with safety. It's meant to ensure we create systems and institutions that actually address our safety, while removing a consistent safety threat for marginalized communities. After all, why would we maintain the existence of an institution that was always meant to harm people?

In order to describe the true purposes of policing and how they persist today, I'll go back to the beginning. If we understand how policing was created, we will be able to understand how some of the consistent outcomes of policing that we find objectionable—like anti-Black brutality—were built into its design. The history of policing tells the story of how policing functions and whom it harms.

I could tell you about each of these specific groups of people, and how policing harms each of them, and how their identities are wrapped up in who we value—or rather do not value—in our society. But several other writers, academics, and public intellectuals have done that very well. There is really no denying that policing harms marginalized groups. Instead, I'll go back to the beginning and describe three of the four main purposes of policing, and how they persist today. These four main purposes are the reason why policing was created, and the reason why these aforementioned groups continue to consistently experience harm from police. In no particular order, the four purposes of policing are to create the social conditions necessary for and to enforce colonialization, enslavement, and classism, as well as to codify morals. This chapter will deal with the first three; we'll examine the fourth in chapter 6.

FOUR PURPOSES

The very origin of modern policing was a colonial endeavor that was exported around the world through European empire building. Today, the police maintain their colonial purpose in settler colonies like Canada, where they continue to attack and harm Indigenous people, and through international engagement, export their methods throughout the world.

Policing also maintains the social relationships required for a system of enslavement in which Black people *need* to be culturally understood as inhuman or lesser humans. Despite proclamations of emancipation, this purpose persists, in that police are one part of a prison-industrial complex that requires an association of Blackness with criminality and inherent deviance to supply the prison system with resources from which to make profit, and those resources are by and large Black people.

Historically, law enforcement has also been called on to suppress workers, to maintain the power relationships between the rich and the poor, and to protect the economic relationships that allow wealthy people to maintain their riches. Despite the right to unionize being hard fought and won after years of bloody attacks on workers by police, police continue to target impoverished people and do the bidding of the wealthy.

And finally, policing is meant to control morality. Whether that meant ensuring that women's hems were long enough, that people did not work on Sunday, that people did not express themselves in a manner unbecoming of their gender, or whether it means targeting drug users, sex workers, and people with disabilities, law enforcement has always been activated to police our morality.

The common theme here is that police regulate the power dynamics between different groups of people in social, political, geographic, and economic relationships. They regulate who has power in conflict. The idea of a "Karen" calling police to regulate behavior is more than just an internet meme. Think about it: Have you noticed that these popularly recorded and disseminated interactions occur in only one class direction, one race direction, one colonial direction? So, whom does policing serve? What is it for? Why do some call upon state power to regulate behavior and some don't—or can't? Why do some believe the police *belong to them* and others don't? Why are some people subject to the police as though through a paternal relationship—like the disciplining of a child—and others aren't?

COLONIALISM

To understand where policing comes from and what its original purposes were, we need to start with the activities of the British Empire in eighteenth-century Ireland. The first modern recognizable police force is the Dublin Police, and it's no coincidence that it was created in Britain's first colony. Britain's attempt to dominate Ireland was met with fierce resistance. Established in 1786, the Dublin Police was created to stamp out resistance among the colonized population, and as Britain exported its colonial strategies, the success of policing in Ireland was propagated throughout the world.

Ireland was an important landmass for Britain; it afforded the monarchy geopolitical and economic power and provided military advantages over the Spanish and French Empires. To establish control, the Brits developed strategies they would use again and again the world over: They forced the relocation of Irish people, established plantations through which English settlers would be granted land and control, and forced the local agrarian population to work the land as tenants. They implemented a system in which Irish culture and spirituality were subjugated, specifically granting privileges to Protestants and intentionally marginalizing Catholics. A system of Penal Laws meant that Irish Catholics were not permitted to own land, had limited access to education, and were punished for using their native tongue, and the traditional Irish agrarian lifestyle was subjugated in favor of an industrial lifestyle benefiting the Crown.

The British needed an authoritative body to enforce all these laws. Prior to implementing policing, an informal watch system and the British military were tasked with maintaining the rules of the colony, along with a judicial magistrate system. The informal watch was staffed with unpaid Protestants selected for the duty. They had the power to stop people whom they deemed suspicious and detain them in watchhouses, precursors to police stations. This unpaid, community-based, local system was meant to be seen as a duty of the citizenry, but these duties were generally detested and not taken very seriously. Even though there was a fine for refusing to serve, many were still resistant to the watch system, and a formal system of policing was created in part because of this unwillingness.

Prior to creating a police force, the Brits would call in the army when Irish resistance was most threatening and dangerous to their rule. But in the late eighteenth century, the army was preoccupied—especially with the rising American Revolution. So, the Brits decided to create a centrally controlled system of enforcement, with officers who would operate kind of like an army but would be stationed locally. Unlike those who participated in the watch system, these officers would be armed and paid.

This was a radical idea at the time, and local communities did not like it. England first tried to implement the idea in the city of London, and it was rejected by Parliament. Even though it also met resistance in Ireland, the Dublin Police Act was passed in 1786, establishing the world's first modern, paid, recognizable police force. The uniformed officers were employed full-time and patrolled the streets of Dublin on horseback and on foot. They had the power to search and detain people, and they created watchhouses equipped with tools for torture. Higher taxes were imposed on trades and small businesses to pay the hundreds of officers who made up the new force. Within a year, the dominion of police spread beyond Dublin into rural areas.

The Dublin Police were immediately detested—the idea of abolition is as old as policing itself.

Even privileged populations in Ireland decried the police. A petition submitted in 1786 condemned the police for being too expensive, for being ineffective, for being unnecessarily hostile, for engaging in arbitrary arrests, and for their brutality—yes, all of these common arguments against policing of the post-millennium were first raised *less than a year into policing's birth*.

Also birthed soon after policing was the idea of reform. The British government responded to the resistance to policing by ordering an investigation. Its final report concluded that "the police establishment has been attended with unnecessary patronage, waste, and dissipation." The attorney general strongly disagreed with the report, going as far as to recommend the House of Commons reject its adoption. In response to the strife, authorities *increased* day patrols, created a police watchdog body, created a bail system, and required police to identify themselves when asked by those being detained.

Some things literally never change, I guess.

Through successive advancements and revisions, the Dublin Police matured into the Royal Irish Constabulary. Their methods concretized in the nineteenth century, and their successful paramilitary tactics were dispatched throughout the British Empire. The constabulary served as the basis for policing in India, Ceylon, Sierra Leone, South Africa, northern Nigeria; its influence rocked the globe. Police officers from the constabulary were also sent to support training of police in Egypt, Jamaica, Kenya, Palestine, Northern Rhodesia, New Zealand—and of course Canada.

The North West Mounted Police of Canada

In Canada, the North West Mounted Police (NWMP) was established in 1873. Like all other colonial police, the purpose of the precursor to today's Royal Canadian Mounted Police (RCMP) was to wrest control from Indigenous people and support the colonization of the northwest territories of North America. The operating government needed a paramilitary force to do what had been done in Ireland—redistribute land and provide control of the land to settlers.

Historically, Canada has been proud to associate itself with the image of the RCMP officer, clad in a red uniform, riding a horse, and nicknamed Mountie.

But there's nothing about the RCMP to be proud of.

The RCMP and its predecessor did much of the dirty work that Canada needed to dull the impact of the fierce resistance of Indigenous First Nations, Métis, and Inuit people. They brutally attacked Indigenous communities, using several strategies. They suppressed cultural and spiritual traditions. They killed thousands of sled dogs in Inuit territory and helped to wipe out the buffalo in Canada's prairie lands, animals spiritually and culturally significant to Indigenous communities, and, in the case of the buffalo, critical for subsistence. They enforced a pass system against Indigenous communities in Canada's western territory, requiring Indigenous people to get approval from so-called Indian agents—officials representing the Canadian government—to obtain a travel document that would prove they had permission to leave their reserves. The pass detailed how long the holder was permitted to be off reserve, for what purpose, and when they would return. This system was similar to systems that would require Black people to produce papers of manumission or for permission to travel, which were used in the Caribbean and throughout North America to control and restrict the movement of people who were always presumed to be enslaved. They kidnapped Indigenous children from their families and forced them to attend mandatory boarding schools called residential schools, in which the children were not permitted to contact their families or speak their native languages and were subject to abuse. These mandatory schools were an essential prong of Canada's genocidal strategy against Indigenous people. The RCMP would arrest attempted runaways, return them to the schools, and arrest parents who tried to keep their children at home, which was against the law.

Canada's last residential school, Kivalliq Hall in Rankin Inlet, closed in 1997.

May those still impacted by the horrors of residential schools find peace. May those who had their lives stolen from them by the RCMP and its predecessors rest in peace.

In addition to their role supporting residential schools, the North West Mounted Police served as Canada's paramilitary force against Indigenous resistance, including the Red River Resistance and its culminating Battle of Duck Lake. The NWMP was not able to quash the resistance alone. The Canadian government deployed its military to support the Mounties, crushing the Métis resistance and resulting in the trial and hanging of Métis leader Louis Riel.

The RCMP's colonial legacy was so effective they assisted with the establishment of the apartheid system in South Africa and continue to export their brand of colonial policing internationally, engaging in overseas operations in Haiti, Mali, Palestine, Iraq, and Ukraine.

The Texas Rangers

Colonialism also birthed modern policing in the United States. The legacy of some of those land-based atrocities continues today through the violent policing we hear about on the United States' southern border and the subjugation of Mexican, Tejano, and other Indigenous people.

Consider the story of Jesus Bazán and Antonio Longoria.

Mr. Bazán and Mr. Longoria were well-respected members of the Tejano elite at the turn of the twentieth century. The two were related—Longoria was Bazán's son-in-law—and Longoria was a commissioner of Hidalgo County, which sits right on the U.S.-Mexico border in Texas. At the time, there was significant anti-Mexican and anti-Indigenous violence in the region. Decades earlier, the state had created the Texas Rangers to maintain control over these populations and the social conditions that made colonial expansion possible. The Rangers ensured that white Anglo settlers could thrive and claim racial supremacy over Mexicans, Comanche, Waco, and other Indigenous nations.

This is the context Mr. Bazán and Mr. Longoria were living under when their horses were stolen by raiders in 1915. In a world where the police were more concerned with justice or safety over colonialism, perhaps the Rangers would have supported the two Tejano men in recovering their property when the men reported the theft to the Rangers. But this is not what happened.

The situation presented a dilemma, given the context for Tejanos at the time. If Mr. Bazán and Mr. Longoria reported the theft, they and their families could face retaliation from raiders for engaging the police. If they refrained from reporting the theft, and the horses and assailants were later found, their *failure* to report could result in retaliation from the Texas Rangers if they were accused of helping the bandits. They could be accused of helping the bandits even if they *did* report it, because justice was not the primary concern or raison d'être for the Rangers.

Mr. Bazán and Mr. Longoria ultimately decided to report the theft. They traveled by horse to a Rangers camp and made the report to a Captain Henry Ransom. After they left, Ransom got into his car along with two other men, William Sterling and Paul West. They pursued Mr. Bazán and Mr. Longoria. When they caught up to the men, one of the passengers shot both Mr. Bazán and Mr. Longoria in the back, murdering them. Ransom, Sterling, and West left Mr. Bazán and Mr. Longoria's bodies at the side of the road. Ransom took his malevolence and desecration a step further when he commanded witnesses to let the bodies lie where they were.

May they rest in peace.

The Rangers regularly engaged in this kind of terror against Mexican, Tejano, and Indigenous communities. This period saw thousands of Mexicans indiscriminately slaughtered, with the Texas Rangers a significant part of committing the xenophobic violence.

The legacy of the Texas Rangers' colonial and ethnic violence toward Mexican, Tejano, and Black communities (the Rangers also operated as a slave patrol) in the borderlands survives today through the violence and family separation people experience from law enforcement at the border.

TODAY: STANDING ROCK AND WET'SUWET'EN

The colonial purpose of police remains in the two largest settler colonial states in North America. The United States and Canada *to this day* activate the police to carry out colonial purposes, and unlike their ineffective record in other areas, the police record on ensuring that land disputes favor colonizing forces is remarkably consistent.

Despite legal arrangements, treaties, and U.N. declarations protecting Indigenous lands in the Americas, governments in the United States and Canada continue to deploy the police as a colonial tool to combat Indigenous land defenders and water protectors. The examples of these attempts at repression and land theft are numerous and consistent. Two that remain ongoing at the time that I write this are the #NoDAPL conflict at Standing Rock and the #WetsuwetenStrong conflict on Wet'suwet'en and Gitxsan territory.

Standing Rock

Imagine learning that a foreign government had approved an infrastructure project that could endanger you and the livelihood of your entire community and then learning that it was against the law, against agreements your community had long negotiated. Imagine learning they bulldozed over sacred sites of deep importance for you and your family. Sites that carried spiritual significance, that honored your ancestors, and that were of critical importance to your culture. A thoughtless act of destruction in the service of profits. This is what happened in Standing Rock.

After the U.S. government approved the plans to build the Dakota Access Pipeline, affecting the inhabitants of the unceded Standing Rock Indian Reservation and in violation of treaties, Indigenous people mobilized to protect their land. The pipeline is a project of Energy Transfer Partners, a company worth more than $40 billion at the time of this writing. The project requires pipelines to run under Lake Oahe, a Missouri River water reservoir and a crucial water source for the Standing Rock Sioux Reservation. Standing Rock inhabitants opposed the project, certain that it would threaten the integrity of their water, making it vulnerable to oil spills. Energy Transfer Partners also demolished sacred sites in carrying out its plans, including graves and prayer sites.

The concerns of the Standing Rock inhabitants are well founded. According to Greenpeace, Energy Transfer Partners has "caused 527 incidents from 2002 to the end of 2017, spilling 87,000 barrels (or 3.6 million gallons) of hazardous liquids," including incidents that contaminate groundwater. The inhabitants of Standing Rock did what many would—and have done—the world over. They resisted the project on multiple fronts—through legal strategies, diplomatic strategies, and peaceful civil disobedience.

The police were deployed. Not to protect the residents of Standing Rock from Energy Transfer Partners, which was directly endangering their safety, but to protect the unlawful colonial land grab by Energy Transfer Partners, as approved by the U.S. government. In fact, the safety of the people being violated was not a priority for the police at all—so much so that the police used vehicles supplied by Energy Transfer Partners for their operation. Almost as though they were working *for* the company.

The resistance, popularized on social media through the hashtag #NoDAPL, set up water protector camps, where thousands of protesters from all over the world joined the Standing Rock water protectors in opposing the pipeline. The police responded by terrorizing the participants. They interrupted and dispersed people engaged in prayer. They stripped arrestees of their clothes and used military-style weaponry against protesters, including water cannons, in freezing-cold weather. They used attack dogs, tear gas, rubber bullets, concussion grenades, and pepper spray. They arrested and charged more than eight hundred peaceful protesters during the height of the resistance. More than three hundred people were injured, with protesters experiencing seizures, broken ligaments, loss of bowel control, loss of consciousness, and cardiac arrest.

Wet'suwet'en and Gitxsan

Similar issues are happening as I type in Wet'suwet'en and Gitxsan, Indigenous territory to the northwest of Standing Rock. The provincial government of British Columbia, Canada, approved the Coastal GasLink pipeline, a project of TC Energy, formerly known as the TransCanada Corporation. The land is unceded, and laws and court cases in Canada have affirmed that the land is the jurisdiction of the Wet'suwet'en First Nation.

Somehow, despite these facts, the corporate-based colonial expansion continues.

Like at Standing Rock, Indigenous land defenders at Wet'suwet'en set up the Unist'ot'en Camp to protest the project. The Royal Canadian Mounted Police were deployed. Similar to the police in the #NoDAPL protests, they collaborated with TC Energy, attending daily meetings set up by the company, as though they were working *for* it. They set up a journalist exclusion zone, to try to prevent images and accounts of what they were doing from disseminating. Dressed in military-style fatigues, they interacted with the protesters as though they were at war. They used jet boats, helicopters, and drone technology to carry out extensive surveillance. They violently raided the camp multiple times, destroying property and arresting protesters and journalists alike.

An investigation by *The Guardian* revealed documents showing that the RCMP was prepared to use lethal force on the peaceful protesters, instructing their officers before raids to "use as much violence toward the gate as you want" and be prepared to arrest minors. Apparently eager to continue RCMP's tradition of removing Indigenous children from their families as a colonial tactic, the police force went so far as to use the government's child services to separate children from their families. As Unist'ot'en land defender Anne Spice remarked, the police were there to support the invasion of Indigenous territories.

The police are not keeping anyone safe in these situations. Instead, they are protecting the collaborative economic interests of the state and corporations as they relate to land. In doing so, they are endangering countless communities and continuing long-standing legacies of violent abuse and subjugation of Indigenous people. Again, this was built into their purpose from the very beginning, and while the police are failing at keeping us safe and preventing crime in countless ways, they certainly seem to consistently succeed at one of the things they were built for: colonial expansion. These examples I have provided are just a few of many across the world, including the Fairy Creek struggle against old-growth logging in Pacheedaht First Nation, where RCMP have arrested more than eleven hundred people in the ongoing conflict; the struggle against the now-canceled TC Energy Keystone XL Pipeline, threatening several Indigenous communities, including the Smith's Landing First Nation and the Oceti Sakowin Nation, in which police in Canada and the United States arrested thousands of people over years of sustained protest; the Trans Mountain Pipeline struggle; the Enbridge Line 3 struggle; the Bayou Bridge struggle—the list is endless.

And the police are always there to protect colonial interests.

SLAVE PATROLS AND ANTI-BLACKNESS

The development of policing as a tool to control enslaved people and expand slavery in the English-speaking world also begins with the British and their colonial empire. Among the profitable colonies of Britain was the island of Barbados, where the colonizers seeking wealth determined the plentiful sugar industry required bodies to carry out the brutal, backbreaking labor necessary to cultivate the sugarcane. Of course, Britain was reliant on enslaved labor, and the Black population of the island exploded as the demand for sugar increased throughout Britain, its colonies, and its trading partners. The economic situation and the expansion of enslaved labor meant that eventually the Black population of Barbados surpassed the white population. This presented a threat to the British.

Enslaved people across the Caribbean fought for an end to their suffering. Resistances were organized and revolts were occurring against the colonizers throughout the islands with some regularity. In 1521, enslaved people outnumbered the colonizers in the Spanish colonial town of Santo Domingo, located in present-day Dominican Republic. In the first organized slave revolt recorded by historians, African enslaved people working on a plantation belonging to Diego Colón,

Christopher Columbus's son, led an uprising against their masters, determined to gain liberation and eliminate enslavement. The Spanish, with their superior weapons and military, crushed the rebellion and executed its leaders.

But the revolt was well organized, and the liberators managed to kill and wound enough Spanish settlers that the Spanish felt they needed to respond. The Spanish tried (and failed) to prevent future uprisings by implementing a set of brutal laws restricting the movement of Black people and implementing torturous consequences for enslaved people who violated these laws. For example, enslaved people who escaped and did not return within ten days were subject to having a foot severed. Execution was the punishment for people who tried to liberate themselves more than once. The 1522 "Black code" is thought to be the first of the Black codes/*codes noirs*/slave codes that delineated the restrictions and punishments that governed how African-descended people across the colonial world would live. This strategy of implementing slave codes would be disseminated throughout the empires engaged in the transatlantic slave trade.

In Barbados, the colonizers developed and implemented the first English slave code. The 1661 Act for Better Ordering and Governing of Negroes established Black people as chattel property by law and outlined the specific brutalization enslaved people would be subject to, including whippings, brandings, burnings, mutilations, and execution. The slave code also required overseers to regularly subject enslaved people to routine surveillance, requiring so-called slave houses be searched twice weekly for runaways—enslaved people who attempted to liberate themselves from their brutal masters.

This slave code was built upon in other Caribbean colonies and throughout the southern United States. The South Carolina slave code was a near-exact copy of the one implemented in Jamaica in 1684. Similar codes—*codes noirs*—were adopted in France and French colonies of the Americas, including in the Caribbean and New France, stretching from present-day Quebec to Louisiana. An important note is that these slave codes specifically included *all* Black people—meaning even free Black people were subject to the provisions in the codes.

The South Carolina slave code called upon all white men for its enforcement strategy, legally requiring the white settler population to enforce a pass system requiring enslaved people to carry permission from their masters to travel unattended and providing compensation to community members who recaptured escaped enslaved people and brought them back to their supposed owners. The law also permitted the white population to brutalize, mutilate, and kill enslaved people who resisted white authority or attempted to free themselves.

The slave code in South Carolina was a living policy that was updated and re-legislated throughout the seventeenth and eighteenth centuries. As the barbarous codes matured, they maintained and intensified their focus on the constant patrolling of enslaved people and their quarters and on doling out brutal punishments for behavior deemed retaliatory or a threat to the white settler population; much like in the Caribbean, the fear of Black people outnumbering the white settler population was of primary concern.

Similar to the initial watch patrols in Ireland, the enforcement forces of the slave codes were at first unofficial and voluntary in the southern United States. But by the early eighteenth century, South Carolina responded to uprisings among the enslaved with organized slave patrols, establishing a militia to carry out its violent purpose. By the 1730s, these patrols were compensated—a significant shift toward institutionalizing them into sustainable organizations. The slave patrols had broad powers; they didn't need warrants to search homes if they suspected they might be harboring enslaved people who had escaped and were seeking refuge. By the end of the eighteenth century, every slaveholding state had operational slave patrols, with the South Carolina patrol serving as the model for most other jurisdictions.

After the U.S. Civil War, the Thirteenth Amendment was adopted into the U.S. Constitution, reading in part,

Neither slavery nor involuntary servitude, except as a punishment for crime whereof the party shall have been duly convicted, shall exist within the United States, or any place subject to their jurisdiction.

The exception in the amendment meant that the economics of free labor the South had so desperately come to rely on could continue—so long as there were enough people considered criminals to supply that free labor. So, the former slave codes transformed to Black codes. The Black codes dictated how, when, and where free Black people could work and how much they could be paid. They restricted the rights of Black people to vote, and limited where they could travel. Importantly, the Black codes implemented new laws and harsh punishments for failure to adhere to these laws.

Among these new laws were requirements for Black people to work and apprenticeship laws forcing Black children into unpaid labor on plantations. The laws also restricted Black people from holding occupations outside farmwork or servitude. If Black people were unable to find an employer willing to pay them, which was common given social anti-Black attitudes from southern would-be employers, they could be arrested for vagrancy.

Think about this for a second. Nearly immediately after the Emancipation Proclamation, Black people were told: If you don't have gainful employment, you are breaking the law. But also—you can hold only very specific jobs. Black people, of course, did not have the power to control whether they were employed or not. But the consequence—which very well could have been due to discrimination from would-be employers— was all theirs to bear. And what if they managed to avoid being arrested for vagrancy? What could you do if you needed to survive, had no way to make wages, and had to avoid letting others know you did not have work, lest you be arrested for vagrancy? What could you do for food, water, shelter, clothing? To take care of your children? Perhaps you would be forced to try to take what you could for your survival—leaving you again open to criminalization.

During this time, states began to use chain gangs and convict leasing as sources of labor, allowing the system of enslavement of Black people to continue despite so-called emancipation. Prisoners were chained together by their ankles and forced to do difficult, backbreaking work as punishment. Chain gangs provided the labor for much of the public infrastructure in the South, including highways and roads. The system of convict leasing allowed private companies to lease prisoners to carry out free labor, and this is how some privately held plantations remained profitable after the Thirteenth Amendment.

After it passed, the prisoner population exploded.

To ensure a consistent supply of prisoners, the role of slave catchers had to change. The former slave patrols matured into police departments, and the role of these early police was to monitor the newly "liberated" Black people. Any violation of the new Black codes could mean a return to a life of enslavement. Slave patrols had fully transformed in rhetorical purpose from catching and punishing enslaved people who tried to liberate themselves, to catching and punishing emancipated people who violated impossible-to-follow, racially discriminatory laws. In both cases, police and patrols were ultimately working to maintain the social and economic conditions that maintained the subjugation of Black people.

These Black codes eventually transformed into Jim Crow laws, a system that legislated racial apartheid in the United States. For example, in Mississippi, failure to show proof of employment to police was punishable by a fine. If a Black person was unable to pay the fine, any white person who would pay the fine could lease the offender. The "employer/purchaser" could then hold the supposedly emancipated Black person in a form of debt enslavement. Chain gangs and convict leasing also remained forms of punishment allowing for the use of unpaid labor. These systems of laws and punishments continued well into the 1960s, enforced by police.

At this point, I should probably note that while I am focusing on the United States, Canada and the British Empire also had systems that criminalized the behaviors and impoverishment of Black people while simultaneously permitting racial discrimination and subjugation. The enslavement of Black people was implemented throughout the British Empire, including Canada, and the tactics to control enslaved people and ensure Black people were considered the bottom of the racial hierarchy were also implemented throughout the empire. In fact, the last segregated school in Canada closed in the 1980s. Despite the claims to innocence and benevolence of the U.K., Canada, and the northern United States, these anti-Black injustices were the norm well into the twentieth century.

After the civil rights movement of the 1960s, a number of legal challenges to anti-Black laws, and the implementation of the Civil Rights Act of 1964, Jim Crow laws as written were found unconstitutional and wiped from the books. But the well-established cycle of criminalizing behaviors and conditions of Black people continued, and importantly, the growing private, for-profit prison system became an significant driver of criminalization. Prison companies have a vested interested in maintaining a steady supply of inmates to succeed in reaching their revenue targets. Who better to focus on as a revenue-generating resource than those already considered criminal?

It's at this point that certain kinds of drug use became heavily targeted by policies and law enforcement, and they just *happened* to be the drugs most used in Black communities. The recent decriminalization of cannabis and public health approach to the opioid crisis show how these very same behaviors are treated differently depending on the community impacted. At the same time, racial profiling—driving while Black, shopping while Black, walking while Black, doing any number of activities while Black—continued to invite scrutiny and harassment by the police (more on this in chapter 6).

Discretionary anti-Black actions by police today are a continuum of activities they've been engaged in since policing was explicit about its purpose to terrorize Black people. You can draw a logical line from police in the eighteenth century stopping Black people on the street and demanding they show that they have permission from masters to travel, to the police stopping Black people in the nineteenth century and demanding manumission papers, to the police stopping Black people in the late nineteenth century demanding proof of employment, to the police stopping Black people in white neighborhoods in the 1950s and demanding their reasoning for being there, to the police stopping and frisking Black people today, demanding that we justify what we are doing.

You can draw a line between the slave patrols searching the quarters of Black people, to the police searching the homes of free Black people without warrants, to the fact that Black neighborhoods are focused on and patrolled by police today while whiter, wealthier neighborhoods are not.

You can draw that line to the actions of the Louisville police officer Joshua Jaynes, who felt so entitled that he lied when seeking a no-knock warrant to enter Breonna Taylor's home. Jaynes signed an affidavit, swearing that he had evidence that Ms. Taylor's partner was using her home to store drugs and that a postal inspector had corroborated this evidence. That affidavit served as the basis for a no-knock warrant—a warrant authorizing police to enter without first knocking or announcing their presence—that a judge approved. The warrant was later changed to a "knock and announce" warrant, meaning the officers were required to knock and identify themselves. Despite the constitutional protection given by the Fourth Amendment protecting citizens from unreasonable searches and seizures, police can get around the requirement to knock and announce themselves when executing a warrant, so long as they have reasonable suspicion that announcing themselves would be dangerous or futile or would inhibit the investigation. As a former professor of mine so aptly wrote, explaining this constitutional loophole, "The Supreme Court's legalization of racial profiling is embedded in the very structure of Fourth Amendment doctrine. . . . Fourth Amendment doctrine expressly authorizes or facilitates the very social practice it ought to prevent: racial profiling. This authorization and facilitation exposes African

Americans not only to the violence of frequent police contact but also to the violence of police killings and physical abuse."

In Ms. Taylor's case, living in a Black community and some lies told on a court document were enough to meet the requirement.

The police executed the warrant in plainclothes well after midnight on March 13, 2020. When they forced entry into her home, battering down the door, Ms. Taylor and her partner yelled out to ask who was there. While the new warrant required police to announce themselves, Ms. Taylor's partner says no one responded. Thinking they were the victims of a home invasion, Ms. Taylor's partner grabbed his legal firearm and fired a warning shot. The Louisville Metro Police Department officers Jonathan Mattingly, Brett Hankison, and Myles Cosgrove responded by firing thirty-two shots.

They shot Ms. Taylor six times, killing her.

May she rest in peace.

On November 1, 2024, a federal jury returned a guilty verdict convicting Brett Hankison of violating Ms. Taylor's civil rights. Jaynes and another former officer, Kyle Meany, are facing charges in connection with the false affidavit used to secure the warrant to enter Ms. Taylor's home. Another former officer, Kelly Goodlett, previously pleaded guilty to conspiring to falsify the affidavit with Jaynes. The city of Louisville, Kentucky, settled a wrongful death suit with Ms. Taylor's family in 2020, agreeing to pay $12 million.

CYCLICAL JUSTIFICATION

The curious thing about slave patrols is that they serve a dual purpose. Of course, subjecting Black people to the inhumane cruelty and suffering that these codes mandated was an attempt to deter uprisings. Despite being ineffective at stopping the organizing of enslaved people to liberate themselves, the patrols persisted for more than a century. So why did they endure? Because of their secondary purpose: These patrols and their corresponding codes provided a legal basis for the inhu-

man torture that Black people received. They communicated
to the slaveholding society that there was something so different between Black people and others that forms of regulation,
restriction, punishment, and torture that would be unthinkable
for other humans were *mandated* for Black people. In effect,
they transmitted the idea that Black people were not human,
thereby *justifying* the continuation of the trade and enslavement of Black people.

One of the original purposes of the police is to justify
enslavement through the association of Black people with an
inhuman monstrousness.

Today, that purpose continues, only slightly amended.

Today, one of the purposes of police is to justify the prison-
industrial complex—including the police themselves—through
the association of Black people with criminality.

Our laws continue to criminalize behaviors by Black people and to punish Black people more harshly. I could rattle off
statistics that prove it. Like the fact that Black drivers in the
United States are three times as likely to be searched during a
traffic stop. Or the fact that Black people in my hometown of
Toronto, Canada, are twenty times more likely to be shot by
police than white people. Or the fact that Black people in the
United States are more than three times as likely to be killed
during an encounter with police than a white person. Or the
fact that Greater Manchester Police in the U.K. are four times
more likely to use force against a Black person. The list of available unacceptable statistics is never ending.

I could also rattle off tales of every single time I've given a
talk or workshop to discuss these issues, when someone tries to
challenge what I am arguing by saying some version of "But we
need police *because* those neighborhoods are more violent, and
more people from those neighborhoods happen to be criminal."
The proponents of this argument avoid racial language but still
make the point: Police are needed because Black people are
more dangerous. This conclusion is circular and suffers from
confirmation bias. Of course, if the police primarily focus on
Black communities as sites for patrol and focus on Black people

as suspicious, they are going to arrest and imprison more Black people. The number of Black people being punished and criminalized cannot then be used to support an objective conclusion that Black people are inherently dangerous. And despite all the numerous academic studies proving that the overrepresentation of Black people in the criminal justice system is due to systemic anti-Black racism and not some innate propensity for being dangerous or some failure in motivation to simply *be better*, these paternalistic ideas persist.

Heavy police presence in Black communities guarantees Black people will be observed, arrested, and imprisoned at rates far beyond those of other races. And this focus serves an important purpose for the police, true to their original intent: to subjugate Black people and create the social conditions necessary to continue that subjugation, thereby justifying their existence. And it's working remarkably well.

Black communities, which do not receive the same level of resources and support from public services as wealthier communities do, desperately need programs that support safety and security. But despite their heavy presence, police fail to make these communities safer. Police are, however, remarkably consistent at continuing to deliver anti-Black racial terror. In so doing, they continue to be a crucial part of the apparatus providing a deceptive justification for the prison-industrial complex—including themselves—at the expense of countless Black lives.

CLASSISM

Prior to the police becoming the uniformed, organized force we know today, municipalities throughout Britain, Canada, and the United States typically resorted to watch systems. These so-called night watches were generally volunteer based and were meant to interrupt activities considered immoral, like sex work and gambling. By most accounts, the night watches were not orderly and were not taken very seriously. People generally wanted to avoid becoming the object of others' ire, and of course a group of people attempting to stop others from enjoying themselves was deeply unpopular. The night watch itself functioned at the mercy of the economic system; despite rules in some places requiring all landowners to contribute to the night watch, wealthy people could, and often did, pay a fine to avoid the service or paid others to do it for them. And these pre-police institutions tended to focus on controlling behaviors typically associated with poor people. In all cases, the transition from disorganized volunteer groups to formal police forces was in service of the wealthy and powerful—it's clear whom they were meant to serve.

Take the first night watch to transition to a formal police service in eighteenth-century London as an example. The first armed, paid, and centrally directed police service in London was arguably the Marine Police Office, implemented in 1798. Why would it be a marine police force? Because of the global implications of colonization.

At the time, merchants were amassing tremendous wealth by trading and selling raw materials from the Americas. As the ships carrying these goods entered the Thames, merchants became increasingly worried about protecting them. Until that time, it was an accepted custom for people who worked with material goods to take a portion of the materials they worked with as part of their payment. This was common before the imposition and proliferation of a regular wage as a form of payment. Workers would take the overages after target weights had been achieved or would take the "sweepings" from materials they had worked with—be it coal, tobacco, indigo, tea, soap, or gold. As England attempted to clamp down on this custom in favor of a standard wage, prosecutions against so-called misappropriations from workers were filed, and the defenses are revealing. The workers seemed perplexed as to why the prosecutions were taking place, freely admitted that they were taking the goods, and insisted that they had not stolen from the coffers of their employers and were simply doing what had always been done: claiming what was customary compensation for their work.

Patrick Colquhoun, one of the founders of the maritime police force created to regulate this behavior, was explicitly hostile to workers and wove that attitude into his conception and plans for the police. He thought the working class was an uncivilized lot with "evil propensities," "noxious qualities," and a penchant for pillage. His idea was that this class could be controlled and improved by the police. He believed that wealth—which was something to protect—necessitated a controlled level of poverty from the working class. They couldn't be too poor, or they would resort to crime. And they couldn't be paid too much, or they would want to work less, threatening the overall accumulation of wealth for the ownership class. And if they were working less, they may also wish to indulge in immoral activities, like entertaining themselves by enjoying alcohol. In Colquhoun's view, police could serve to ensure an orderly society where the wealthy and their property would be protected and the workers would be kept in line. Of importance was keeping workers from organizing against their employers.

The Marine Police officers, themselves paid well, were responsible for distributing wages and preventing workers from taking sweepings from ships. They were responsible for maintaining a registry of laborers, ensuring the laborers did not leave the ships during the working day, enforcing time limits for meals, enforcing a dress code to ensure items could not surreptitiously be taken from the ships, and searching the laborers for any sweepings at the end of each day. The police were essential at protecting the property of the wealthy and shifting cultural attitudes toward viewing threats to this property as a crime.

In the northern United States, policing developed similarly. The first publicly funded police force in the northern United States was, arguably, created in Boston in 1838—again to protect cargo on ships. Other cities like New York soon followed suit. Prior to the organization of these forces, businessmen hired watchmen to protect their wares; the goods were their property, they were making profit from them, and part of the cost of engaging in that sort of business was to protect their own stock. But as industrialism matured, businessmen had another growing problem on their hands. Workers were intensifying their organized disruption of the marketplace through strikes, demanding an end to the dangerous, dehumanizing exploitation of their labor for the benefit of a wealthy few. This posed significant problems for businessmen, who were spending more than they would have liked protecting their businesses and were also having their profiteering interrupted by pesky workers.

These business owners were powerful people who had plenty of influence over politics. Together, they pulled off a sleight of hand that continues to affect the way policing operates today. They made the case that the expenditure for protecting their wares should not be one that they were forced to bear; this should be the role of the public. They focused on morality, suggesting that the public play a role in ensuring the *goodness* of our society by preventing theft from businessmen—despite the exploitation they were engaged in with respect to their workers. Goodness included *order*, and that meant the public had a role to play in preventing and controlling what they might term riotous workers. Much like today, these businesspeople were reliant on immigrant labor to make profits. In making these moralizing arguments, they relied on the pervasive anti-immigrant xenophobia among the voting population, alluding to the idea that the immigrant eastern European, Italian, Irish, and Catholic workers in the city were unscrupulous and required control. In addition to making these moralizing arguments, these powerful, wealthy businessmen bankrolled politicians who would do their bidding, setting the terms for an inevitably favorable political position—a force they would not have to pay for that would ensure their continued profitability.

The accomplishment of making this a moral argument is amazing, if you think about it. At this time of changing economic relations, wealthy employers were able to persuade politicians to create policy that supported wages being the primary form of compensation, that criminalized taking subsistence from those employers in order to survive if those wages weren't enough to live off of, and that made the workers themselves pay for the police that would enforce these laws against the workers, protecting the wealth of the employers through their taxes. It really is diabolically brilliant.

Workers in England, the United States, and Canada organized unions and coordinated labor actions like strikes to fight back against their exploitation. And we're not talking about just a few strikes. From 1880 to 1900, there were more than five thousand strikes including over a million workers in New York City. In Chicago, there were more than seventeen hundred strikes involving more than half a million workers. Police responded by using brutal force to crush worker resistance, up to and including using lethal force. But for them to effectively respond, they needed more power and more tools. They created the paddy wagon system to ensure multiple workers could effectively be detained at once. They received new weaponry. They created horseback patrols to confront large crowds more effectively. They created key-access alarm boxes—a sort of prototype to 911—for which business owners received the keys. Business owners could then alert and call upon the police at a moment's notice. These strikes, rhetorically referred to as riots as a strategic way to morally criminalize the workers, were often deadly.

The use of police today to control and repress the working class and benefit the wealthy continues. One of the ways this operates is in the way that police focus their efforts on Black and poor neighborhoods, subjecting these groups to heavy surveillance and leaving the wealthy to live their lives undisturbed. But there are other, more surreptitious ways that this original purpose persists.

FEES, FINES, AND FERGUSON

In 2014, Michael Brown, a Black teenager—he was just eighteen years old—was killed by the white officer Darren Wilson in Ferguson, Missouri. I remember the moment well. The horror and anger that I and others felt led us to build the movement for Black lives with even more urgency. Michael Brown was shot six times, and his body was left on the street, bleeding, for more than four hours, in public view, in broad daylight. The infuriating incident sparked protests all over the world, with the chant "hands up, don't shoot!" our rallying cry.

May he rest in peace.

In the aftermath of the unrest, the Department of Justice launched an investigation into the Ferguson Police Department, from which the resulting report was published in 2015. The investigation revealed not only that the Ferguson Police Department targets and harasses Black people on a level I would describe as torturous but also that much of the Ferguson Police Department's law enforcement efforts were motivated by revenue generation, not keeping anyone safe.

One of the case studies the report illustrates tells the story of a Black woman whose 2007 case was still ongoing at the time of its publication in 2015. This woman was struggling to make ends meet and had experienced bouts of homelessness. So, when she received a fine of $151 for a parking violation, the fine weighed heavily and contributed to her financial burdens. She couldn't pay the fee right away, and because of her precarious living situation, she was hard to contact. She missed payment due dates. She missed court dates. Ferguson's municipal court responded by issuing an arrest warrant.

Imprisonment for the inability to pay a debt was outlawed in the nineteenth century. In the 1983 case *Bearden v. Georgia*, the Supreme Court affirmed that people cannot be jailed because they lack the resources to pay a fine. But somehow, the practice persists in poor and Black communities targeted by police. The DOJ report found that in 2013 alone the Ferguson municipal court had issued more than nine thousand arrest warrants for failure to pay fines for minor violations like parking tickets or housing code violations.

This woman was a victim of this practice. She spent six days in jail for the crime of being too poor to pay a parking ticket. And her $151 fine? They added additional charges to it as punishment for not paying the initial fee on time. She was also levied additional fines for missing court dates associated with the ticket. So, this woman, already struggling, by 2015 had paid

$550 to the court in *additional* fees stemming from the $151 parking ticket. And she was trying. She went to the court with attempts to make partial payments of what she could on the original fine. Twenty-five dollars here. Fifty dollars there. But the court returned her money, stating that she had to make her payment of the ticket in full.

At the time of the writing of the Ferguson report, she still owed $541 in fees on her parking violation. The $151 fine had turned into payments in excess of $1,000.

The report exposed the way that municipalities and police departments prey on poor communities for revenue generation—keeping impoverished people in poverty, and again maintaining social relations that keep the poor disenfranchised and marginalized. In 2015, the City of Ferguson budgeted for more than 20 percent of its revenue to come from fines and fees levied for violations, and its police officers' performance evaluations were based on the amount of revenue they produced.

A class-action lawsuit challenging the constitutionality of these actions, *Fant et al. v. City of Ferguson*, was filed in 2015. The case was settled in February 2024, with the City of Ferguson agreeing to pay $4.5 million to more than fifteen thousand plaintiffs.

The Fines & Fees Justice Center, an organization dedicated to fighting these unjust fees, reports that one in three people in the United States is affected by legal fines and fees. For the vast majority, the fees impose a debt that affects their ability to provide for their families and live their daily lives.

Asset Forfeiture

Imagine that you are a small business owner. You run a shipping company, and things are going well: You have enough money to purchase your third semitruck, if you can find it at a good price. You look around and you find the truck you want at an auction out of state. This might be it; so you prepare to travel. The institution you bank with does not have a presence in the state where the auction is happening, so to avoid banking fees, you decide to travel with the cash you'll need to make the purchase. You double-check the rules just in case, and there are no rules against traveling with the amount of cash you're willing to pay. You set off on your journey.

When you land in the state where the auction is held, you're stopped by the police. They discover the cash and become suspicious. They want to know why you are traveling with so much money. You tell them. They don't believe you and accuse you of being involved in some sort of criminal enterprise. They give you a choice: Either you can go to jail or you can sign a document that will allow you to go free. Eager to avoid jail, you sign the document. The police then say that you can go, and they won't charge you with anything, but they are taking your money.

This is what happened to Jerry Johnson in 2020.

In total, the Phoenix police took $39,500 in cash from the Black small business owner, despite never having charged him with a crime.

The police can confiscate money and assets without charges under civil asset forfeiture laws. Implemented as a law enforcement tool for the war on drugs, the laws were meant to deprive drug dealers of the money and assets acquired through or meant to effectuate drug trafficking activities. These laws only require police to be suspicious of criminal activity to confiscate the goods. And if they make an error, it's on *you* to prove that your possessions were not used or acquired through criminal activity. This isn't like criminal law, where you benefit from the presumption of innocence. When it comes to asset forfeiture, you must prove that your *possessions* are "innocent."

This means there is a much lower bar to meet in order to confiscate items from people than there is to charge them with a crime. Billions of dollars in assets have been taken by police as a result, and 80 percent of people who have their assets taken are never charged with a crime.

And it's more than just money the police take. They also take jewelry, vehicles—even homes and whole *shelters*. According to a class-action lawsuit filed by the Institute for Justice in 2017, Philadelphia police took ownership of three hundred to five hundred houses per year under asset forfeiture rules, with the revenue from seized goods amounting to an average of $5.6 million per year from 1987 to 2012.

And what happens to these possessions?

The police keep them. Or sell them for revenue.

Think about this for a second. The police can take items from you—without a warrant. Without charging you for anything at all. And then they get to keep the money. Very little is needed to prove suspicion. In forfeiture cases taking place during traffic stops, the police have cited garbage on the floor of a car, abundant energy drinks in a car, or air fresheners hanging from the rearview mirror as reasons to suspect possessions being involved in criminal activity, justifying the confiscation of the property.

This creates a perverse incentive for police to engage in what I think should be called theft.

In Philadelphia, the asset forfeiture scheme was used for funding salaries of prosecutors and the Philadelphia Police Department, according to the Institute for Justice. Its class-action suit was successful, and the resulting consent decrees prevent the police and the district attorney from funding salaries and general operations with the proceeds from asset forfeiture and limit the seizure of assets in most cases that are not criminal. A $3 million fund was awarded to victims of the brazen revenue-generating scheme.

From 2000 to 2019, at least $68.8 billion has been taken from people under federal asset forfeiture rules, according to the Institute for Justice. The problem is even worse if you consider state seizures of property. And the practice results in steady enough income that some police departments budget for it, meaning they *need* to dispossess people of their belongings to fund their operations.

An investigation by *The Washington Post* revealed some of what police are purchasing with the revenue they generate from asset forfeiture. They use the funds to purchase items police consider essential, like guns, cars, and surveillance equipment. But they also use the funds on items most people would consider superfluous at best and outrageous at worst. I'm talking poker chips, luxury vehicles, a beach party, conference food, overtime pay, and (yes, this is real) a clown named Sparkles.

To make matters worse, people who want to get their possessions back have to make their case in court. If they don't have the resources to access a lawyer or to take time off work to dedicate to the case, they are out of luck.

So not only is there an incentive to take these possessions from people, but there's also an added incentive to target people who cannot afford to fight their cases. By targeting poorer communities, the police know they are less likely to receive a challenge and more likely to benefit directly from the funds. A study by Lucy Parsons Labs, a police accountability organization based in Chicago, found that police took $150 million from Chicagoans between 2012 and 2017, focusing their asset forfeiture activities in Chicago's poorest neighborhoods. The police aren't going after the so-called drug kingpins these laws were meant to target. They're going after what little people living in poor neighborhoods have.

Asset forfeiture is essentially a transfer of wealth from the poor to the police.

The police *actually benefit* from the existence of "suspected" criminal activity and the assets used in the furtherance of that activity. Why would they want to truly stop drug crime if they stand to make billions in revenue, don't have to prove that anyone is guilty, and rarely have to face a challenge to their actions?

But you don't have to take my word for it.

John Yoder and Brad Cates, two of the architects of the federal civil asset forfeiture program in the 1980s, now advocate for its abolition. They believe the rampant corruption outweighs any benefits.

Jerry Johnson, the owner of the shipping company who had nearly $40,000 in cash seized by police, was one of the few people who was able to challenge his case. After nearly three years of fighting with legal support from the Institute for Justice, Mr. Johnson got his money back in March 2023. But even winning this case doesn't make Mr. Johnson whole. He still had to pay out of pocket for an attorney before he received support from the Institute for Justice.

Police Brutality Bonds

Police also maintain class relations between the rich and the poor by providing opportunities for investors to make money from their misconduct through what the Action Center on Race and the Economy (ACRE) calls police brutality bonds. In one of the most surreptitious—and abhorrent—ways policing benefits the wealthy, police brutality bonds provide a very safe, excellent return on investment for those who bankroll the fees jurisdictions pay to settle cases of alleged police misconduct.

Despite the rampant regularity with which misconduct allegations are made throughout the United States, jurisdictions don't budget for large payouts. Not only would that look terrible on public documents—why should taxpayers pay out in the millions for dirty cops?—but the expectation is that such payments should be made with liability insurance. Well, sometimes the payouts are so large they exceed what an insurer will pay. When that happens, if the jurisdiction cannot afford to make the payments, they may turn to bonds.

How does this work? The jurisdiction will turn to banks or other financial institutions to take out a loan. The financial institution underwrites and issues bonds for purchase to wealthy investors—either to individuals or through mutual funds. Those purchased bonds provide the liquid cash to the jurisdiction that it needs to settle cases of police misconduct. The jurisdiction then needs to pay the bondholders back over a term—with interest.

Police, financial institutions, wealthy investors, and jurisdictions that refuse to rein in terrible policing practices all benefit. The police continue with their conduct unaltered, with no effect on their budget or operations. Financial institutions benefit from the fees they make off providing the services. Wealthy investors make a profit from their initial payment in a fairly risk-free bond. And jurisdictions pay out fewer dollars than they would have paid to defend their police in court, and they can make sure settlement agreements have some other benefits—like a requirement for parties to refrain from speaking publicly about the matter.

Taxpayers, however, are still left footing the bill. And the interest for that bill can end up being nearly double the original settlement cost. ACRE studied five jurisdictions—Chicago, Cleveland, Lake County, Indiana, Los Angeles, and Milwaukee—and found that the total cost of police brutality bonds to taxpayers between 2008 and 2017 was $1.73 billion, including $891 million paid out to investors alone.

To add insult to injury, bond debt is prioritized over other necessary spending; it's not discretionary. So, while Chicago has closed schools and mental health clinics because it lacked the funds to afford these essential public services, it continues to make required bond payments on time.

Policing is quite literally eating into our jurisdictions' ability to pay for public services we all need, and misconduct cases are so recurrent they make the problem worse.

All in all, the repulsiveness of these bonds is impossible to overstate. When police wrongfully harm, and even kill, innocent people, wealthy investors reap rewards and taxpayers foot the bill. This is just another way the police stay true to one of their original purposes—maintaining the class relationships necessary to keep the poor downtrodden.

The final original purpose of policing is morality policing, which I'll discuss in chapter 6.

This might sound odd to you. You might associate morals-based police with regions of the world other than those I am discussing in this book. When viewed from the Orientalist lens in which we typically hear morality policing discussed—as a backward practice of foreign countries of the Middle East and Asia—there is fervent opposition to it. But the truth is that all police are morality police. They monitor and punish behaviors based on how society moralizes those actions. If our behaviors step outside an established moral boundary, the consequences can be severe. If you are too noisy, you might be punished after a noise complaint. If you drink alcohol in the wrong places, you might be subject to a fine or arrest. If you ingest substances considered immoral and are found out, you will be punished.

In the past, the behaviors monitored included how we dressed, which days of the week we sought entertainment, whom we loved, and how we expressed our gender.

We'll examine this more in our chapter on manufacturing crime, which contemplates whom we value, because it's not everyone's morals the police are concerned about. But consider what we've discussed: Policing is failing at keeping us safe and secure, but it is excelling at its original purposes—purposes many of us might state that we oppose today. If we oppose colonialism, the disenfranchisement of the poor, and anti-Black racism, how can we possibly argue in favor of maintaining and resourcing a societal institution that was created to ensure that those destructive functions continue? How can we possibly ignore these forms of subjugation and repression that continue through policing? So much of policing's ability to persist despite all its ugliness is due to its chicanery. At what point do we refuse to be deceived and consider policing for what it truly is?

WHAT WE'VE WROUGHT

From the perspective of a cynical politician, safety is a boondoggle. Have you noticed how often a tough-on-crime approach is promised during elections at all levels of government? It's something everyone can relate to, something we can all get behind. And when we're constantly primed by media copaganda to believe that our communities are becoming more and more unsafe, politicians can exploit our fears by promising to eradicate crime. Whether communities are actually more dangerous is irrelevant; the perception of rampant criminality creates a fear so powerful that many are willing to support even the harshest political tactics to improve safety. And without fail, whether liberal or conservative, the promises to make our communities safer generally boil down to putting more money and resources into policing. The tough-on-crime rhetoric that has become the perennial political promise of candidates seeking election is how politicians exploit the assumption that police activity leads to safer communities to retain power. But have you noticed that no politician of any political stripe seems to be able to claim victory on the safety issue? That is because the proposed solution is so monumentally ineffective, it is sure to remain an issue in the next election cycle. Wash, rinse, repeat.

Police investment is a strategy that is from conception destined to fail. The police respond only *after* a burglary has occurred, a person has been abused, or an assault has taken place. It is a reactive service. By the time law enforcement is involved, the conditions that are required for us to be safe or secure are *already broken*. Popular political responses to crime are flawed because they equate safety with retribution or vengeance for wrongdoing, rather than prevention of crime. This is a fundamentally false framing of what it means to be safe and how to achieve it.

Both safety and security are necessarily *proactive* concepts. Achieving either means creating a world in which we are liberated—free to express our truest selves and carry on with our desires without fear. Where we don't feel as though we need to constrain ourselves in order to live a life of dignity. A safe society wouldn't constrain women's freedoms by making it dangerous to be alone in a public space after sunset without alerting someone else. A safe society wouldn't make finding shelter impossible for those who do not have the means to afford housing. A safe society wouldn't make it impossible for people with certain disabilities to travel or work. But our society consistently fails to create safety in these situations and many others—in large part because law enforcement is not engaged in creating conditions that proactively support a safe society, and for the most part, neither are politicians.

It's unacceptable that we continue to be manipulated by people who are well aware that the solutions they are proposing have consistently failed. We shouldn't allow politicians to get away with handing over excessive resources to police departments without addressing what threatens our safety in the first place. Police budgets make up millions—at times billions—of dollars, representing a significant slice of public investment no matter which jurisdiction we consider. Where is that money going? What is it funding? What is it that the police are actually *doing* with all those resources?

Remember that *New York Times* study referenced in chapter 1 showing police departments across the United States spend less than 5 percent of their time on violent crime? As it turns out, most of their time isn't spent on crime at all. Writing in *The Washington Post*, Alex Vitale, an abolitionist and professor at Brooklyn College, referenced a study in the *Criminal Justice Review* concluding that patrol officers spend only "17 percent [of their time] responding to crime-related calls—the vast majority of which are misdemeanors." The lion's share of police time is spent on "random patrol," 13 percent is spent on administrative tasks, 9 percent is personal time, and 7 percent is providing nonemergency assistance and information and attending community meetings. The same study shows these numbers are borne out in the data concerning arrests as well; less than 5 percent of arrests concern serious violent crimes. Abolitionist organizer, educator, and curator Mariame Kaba said it best when she expounded on her vision for eliminating the police for *The New York Times*. "Police officers don't do what you think they do," she wrote. "They spend most of their time responding to noise complaints, issuing parking and traffic citations, and dealing with other noncriminal issues." The same is true in the U.K., where 80 percent of police officers' time is spent dealing with noncriminal matters. The British Crime Survey shows that the majority of calls to the police come from people "asking for advice or information," "social chats," "order maintenance," "alarms," "reporting accidents," "giving information," and so on.

It may be the case that we want a public service engaged in each of these tasks, but it's worth asking whether the police are the right service to call upon—and fund—to do it. Does a service providing nonemergency assistance or roaming our streets to provide helpful information to those who need it have to be equipped like the military? Knowing a bit about the police's quotidian tasks leads to another logical question: What is their actual *purpose*? A useful way to determine their purpose is to look at their historical raison d'être, much of which we have examined in the previous chapter. We might also consider what their true impact is on our society. If they aren't preventing crime, and we *aren't feeling safer* despite spending more and more money on them each year, what is it that they are accomplishing? Much of the rest of this book is going to consider the various impacts of policing, but I think I can quickly summarize their purpose in one simple concept: social control. The primary function of the police is to restrict freedoms. They do this unevenly—some people's freedoms are more restricted than others—but generally, this is what police do and have always done. Broadly, contemporary policing accomplishes this in three ways: by enforcing segregation, by targeting petty crimes through what is referred to as "broken windows" policing, and by engaging with certain communities like enemies to be controlled.

SEGREGATION

A key role of police officers is to control space. They detain and confine people who they determine are suspects. They manage crowds at crime scenes. They attempt to control access to space during protests and demonstrations. Controlling space is one of the major ways they accomplish their purpose of social control. We allow this and legitimate it by empowering police to control space even when their actions have nothing to do with crime or danger. They manage crowds at events and the flow of traffic, and in some jurisdictions they are responsible for managing the spaces vehicles use to park. There's no particular reason why police need to be the agency controlling space in these latter examples, but it makes sense to us because we have given police great latitude to determine who belongs where.

While official apartheid laws have been removed from the books in the United States, the U.K., and Canada, police play an important role in upholding de facto racial and class-based segregation, ensuring that certain groups of people have no choice but to avoid certain areas if they are to remain safe. I use the term "segregation" very deliberately, and I want to be clear that I am not invoking the term to refer to a situation in which a marginalized group *chooses* to create a space or community in which they feel safe to engage in particular activities. One of the characteristics of segregation is the removal of choice in the matter from the subjugated group.

———

When I was a student at the UCLA School of Law, I remember being utterly surprised at how much of the most crucial jurisprudence in the United States was built on case law concerning anti-Black racial discrimination. Very few cases affirmatively mention race, so the casual reader might miss it. Only by doing some digging could the underlying racial dynamics be unearthed. One case that did affirmatively discuss race particularly struck me. *United States v. Brignoni-Ponce*, argued before the Supreme Court in 1975, concerned the legality of actions by Border Patrol officers who followed, stopped, and questioned the occupants of a vehicle for no reason except for their apparent Mexican ancestry. The court decided the officers in this case were wrong to cite Mexican ancestry as the *sole* reason for the stop but determined that *it is a factor that may be considered.* Though the decision discusses only Mexican ancestry, it set a precedent that effectively allows police officers to be "free to stop people on the basis of race," as UCLA School of Law professor and critical race theorist Devon Carbado puts it.

In a Canadian example, the regulations governing "carding" in Ontario—the equivalent of "stop and frisk" in the United States and "stop and search" in the U.K.—allow for similar discrimination. The regulation was amended to explicitly forbid police officers to card solely on the basis of race after significant protest in the 2010s turned public opinion against the anti-Black practice. But while many saw the amendment as a win that eliminated racial profiling—and that is certainly how it was reported—the law maintains its support for anti-Black policing. Like the *Brignoni-Ponce* precedent, the updated carding regulation allows officers to consider race alongside additional information, which may consist of "eye colour, hair colour, or hair style," in deciding whether to stop someone.

Yes, this is what the law really says. So if someone is stopped because they are Black and have Black eyes, this does not violate the regulation. Effectively, the amendment to the regulation did not eliminate race-based carding at all.

Part of the function of the racial profiling inherent to stop and frisks is to determine whether someone appears to belong in the space they're inhabiting. Certain neighborhoods are coded white, and others non-white, or Black, or brown. And officers ask themselves, Is this person's presence out of the ordinary and open for us to scrutinize? One 2002 study completed at Oakland University by Professors Albert J. Meehan and Michael C. Ponder showed that as Black drivers drove farther into neighborhoods coded as white, they were increasingly more likely to be stopped by police. As one moves to the center of wealthier white neighborhoods, farthest away from the demarcation line where the white community begins, Black drivers were 300 percent more likely to have their plates queried. Fascinatingly, these Black drivers "were the *least likely* to have legal problems, notwithstanding the fact that they were subject to the *highest level* of query surveillance." The effect of this practice is to essentially create internal borders through which Black people are more likely to experience checkpoints if they leave their designated spaces. But a white person in a neighborhood labeled Black or brown isn't cause for police action. This kind of segregationist approach works in only one direction and restricts only the freedoms of non-white people. This results in Black people experiencing far more interactions with police based on their perceived outsider status.

Black people are often treated as suspect, which means we are always hyperaware of the image we are projecting. We have to consider the potential consequences of driving in cars in which we don't belong, sitting in parks in which we don't belong, attending events at which we do not belong, and countless other spaces while carefully strategizing about how we might avoid, reduce, or mitigate being treated as a suspect in our daily lives. While Jim Crow apartheid-like laws might have been eradicated, vague laws prohibiting vagrancy, loitering, and disorderly conduct continue to allow police the discretion to use racial profiling to determine criminality and belonging.

Spaces and neighborhoods are policed very differently depending on their residents. For example, in the recent past, when cannabis use was more widely criminalized and the target of drug war crackdowns, widespread cannabis use by students on college campuses was not met with the same scrutiny or consequence as cannabis use by people in neighborhoods racially coded as Black. While college-age young adults have regularly engaged in cannabis use without consequence, millions of Black people have been arrested and incarcerated for the same behavior.

With this in mind, consider another bit of case law making life complicated for those people who are racialized as belonging to a particular community. In *Illinois v. Wardlow*, the Supreme Court decided that fleeing from police in a "high crime area" is enough to establish reasonable suspicion to justify a stop and frisk. The Fourth Amendment, one of the most important and consequential documents regulating police conduct, reads, in part,

> The right of the people to be secure in their persons, houses, papers, and effects, against unreasonable searches and seizures, shall not be violated, and no Warrants shall issue, but upon probable cause.

While this may seem like text describing a broad protection, the phrasing leaves room for an important limitation. The Fourth Amendment gives us the right not to be subjected to *unreasonable* searches and seizures. Reasonable searches and seizures are justified. The inclusion of the word "unreasonable" in the Fourth Amendment text has as its progeny a world of justifications for police to stop and search people without a warrant.

The *Wardlow* case describes a justification for a warrantless search—a limit on this right. The case concerned the Chicago Police Department and a Black man named William Wardlow.

While patrolling a "high crime area," the Chicago police noticed Mr. Wardlow holding an opaque bag. When Mr. Wardlow saw the police, he ran. To Black people like me, this is an entirely reasonable reaction to seeing police approach. Because so many Black people have been harmed or killed by police when they have done nothing wrong, running away is a logical response. The police followed him, cornered him, and subjected him to a warrantless pat-down. Upon squeezing the opaque bag, the police felt an object they thought could have been a gun. When they opened the bag, they confirmed that the object was indeed a gun and arrested Mr. Wardlow. Mr. Wardlow's attorneys attempted to get the case thrown out due to an improper warrantless search, but in an opinion delivered by Chief Justice William Rehnquist, the Supreme Court determined that "unprovoked flight" in a "high crime area" is enough to establish reasonable suspicion of an individual to justify a warrantless search. It's worth noting that the courts that opined on the case did not all agree that the area Mr. Wardlow was arrested in was high-crime. But the Supreme Court's determination that unprovoked flight in a high-crime area is a justification for a warrantless search represents a significant narrowing of Fourth Amendment protections in Black communities that police tend to target for criminal activity.

The heavier police presence in areas racialized as Black "virtually ensures that [Black people and other people of color] will be observed, questioned, and arrested at rates that substantially overstate objective racial differences in offending," as Tufts University professor Daanika Gordon put it. In this way, not only are Black *people* criminalized through segregationist approaches to policing, so too are Black *spaces*. In making the determination that "flight" in a "high crime area" has a different meaning and potential consequence than flight in a low-crime area (presumably serving as a marker of guilt in a high-crime area and as a regular human activity in a low-crime area), the Supreme Court created an opportunity for differential treatment according to where people live.

"High-crime area" is language that is as good as meaningless. In an analysis of "2.5 million stops conducted by the NYPD between 2007 and 2012," researchers found that the designation is used indiscriminately to justify stops, and *every block* in New York City had at some point been designated as high-crime by police. This is more than just a curious quirk of a baffling Supreme Court decision. The impacts are significant. If the police are searching for and vigilant against crimes in some areas and not in others, those areas are *necessarily* going to show up more frequently in its self-reported crime data; it's an extreme form of confirmation bias. Remember the example of college kids smoking pot being ignored by police, compared with the way Black people were targeted for cannabis use throughout the war on drugs? How would crime statistics change if college students were regularly subjected to stop and frisks on campus? If running on campus was grounds for reasonable suspicion for a stop and frisk?

When considered in this way, the high-crime designation is obviously a stand-in to describe urban spaces that have high concentrations of people of color. If the area where you live is racialized as Black, that gives the police license to treat you as a suspect and use certain levels of force in pursuing you as a suspect, especially if you yourself are Black. If you are in a wealthy neighborhood coded as white, and if you yourself are white, you are free to exercise without having to fear that someone might consider you suspicious and interrupt your life with unpredictable levels of consequence to you and your safety. Not so in a neighborhood racialized as Black. You may very well make the decision to avoid *taking a walk* for fear of your safety.

And for good reason.

Larnie Thomas, Mathias Ometu, and Neli Latson are all Black men who were aggressively arrested by police officers in Edina, Minnesota; San Antonio, Texas; and Stafford County, Virginia, while simply walking, jogging, or standing on a street, respectively. Larnie Thomas and Mathias Ometu filed civil rights lawsuits in response. Neli Latson, who was eighteen at the time of his arrest in 2010, was sentenced to ten years in prison, which was later reduced to two years. He was later re-incarcerated in 2014 after a police encounter in which he threatened to kill himself. He spent 182 days in solitary confinement, only to later be pardoned and released in 2015. His family also filed a civil rights lawsuit against the police, naming his autism as a factor in his mistreatment, which was dismissed on the grounds that the defendants were entitled to qualified immunity, a doctrine that often protects police officers from facing civil liability for violating the constitutional rights of others—more on qualified immunity in chapter 5.

I know that there might be at this point some resistance to what I am saying. You've seen the crime reports on the news. I've addressed that, but it is hard to ignore. Maybe you're thinking, But there *are* spaces where more crime is happening. There *are* "higher crime" areas. I've heard this argument so many times, and I want you to remember: *Most crimes never make it to the police*, let alone the news. And since the police are the ones for the most part preparing crime data based on what comes to them, the crime data available to us is woefully incomplete.

In truth, you already know that areas racialized as Black are treated differently; what I'm pointing out isn't novel. You understand that certain spaces have a particular meaning encoded onto them that is meant to tell us something about our safety in those spaces. But these encoded meanings are neither objective nor immutable. What might be racialized as "Black" and encoded as "dangerous" and "high crime" to one community might be encoded as "home" and "family" to another. If you know that these neighborhoods are understood differently by different people across the country, it is very likely that you also know they are treated differently by police.

If so many people know that this de facto segregation exists, why is it permitted to continue? I think for some the idea of safety is as amorphous as the idea of what police actually do. So long as the police are taking care of the undefined threat happening somewhere "over there," they must be doing their job, keeping the rest of us safe. And that kind of mentality is precisely the mentality behind segregation—especially since we can disprove the discriminatory prejudices that justify these kinds of assumptions. The truth is, as Bennett Capers, a Fordham University professor of law, former prosecutor, and director of Fordham's Center on Race, Law, and Justice, puts it, "the vast majority of individuals stopped and questioned by the police are not engaged in criminal activity and are not carrying weapons or contraband. In most stops and frisks, the articulable suspicion is simply wrong."

BROKEN WINDOWS

Selling cigarettes in violation of the law is not a capital offense, punishable by public execution. Nevertheless, this was what Eric Garner was suspected of when he was killed in the streets by police officer Daniel Pantaleo. No one was in danger before the police arrived and engaged with Mr. Garner. Police were not called to the scene to support someone else's safety; the two police officers decided to stop Mr. Garner on their own. By all accounts, including his own, caught on video that day, Eric Garner was doing nothing but existing outside in public space, minding his own business.

The horror of what happened next is widely known and reported.

Daniel Pantaleo was one of five NYPD officers who surrounded Mr. Garner as he asked to be left alone and pleaded for the officers to stop harassing him. Pantaleo responded by tackling Mr. Garner to the ground as bystanders watched and recorded what was happening. Not a single police officer stopped Pantaleo from suffocating Mr. Garner to death. After Mr. Garner lost consciousness, not a single officer attempted to perform CPR.

Eric Garner was not afforded the presumption of innocence. His cries, caught on video, pleading with his killer, became a rallying cry for the Black Lives Matter movement:

I can't breathe.

May he rest in peace.

You may be thinking that the above police action could be understood as a form of prevention—police engaging an individual whom they deem suspicious and trying to prevent them from carrying out potentially harmful activity. I want to be clear that when I stress that we should be focusing on crime prevention, this is not what I am referencing. Rather than a constitutionally impermissible *Minority Report*–esque approach to safety, wherein police apprehend those they identify as likely to engage in criminal behavior, I am suggesting that we reconsider how we create safe conditions on a much more expansive level. We need to see the forest for the trees. Unfortunately, some tech companies have leaped at the chance to develop a crystal ball approach to locating crime, creating predictive policing tools that anticipate future criminal behavior—to disastrously anti-Black effect. More on this in chapter 5.

A grand jury convened to consider Mr. Garner's case decided not to indict his killer. More than *five years later*, Daniel Pantaleo's employment at the NYPD was terminated. No one was made safer in this situation, and in fact several people had their safety obliterated, including Eric Garner and perhaps even his daughter Erica, who died of a heart attack a few years after her father was killed. Daniel Pantaleo killed Eric Garner because he was allegedly breaking the law by selling untaxed cigarettes, an accusation he can be heard disputing on the recording of his horrifying homicide.

The police were engaging with Eric Garner because of a policing strategy called broken windows policing. The theory behind the strategy is that visual evidence of an unkempt community, like broken windows or vandalism, increases the likelihood that residents will feel unsafe. Because these residents *feel* unsafe, the logic goes, residents who would otherwise act as a form of social control might withdraw and spend less time engaged in the community, which will then lead to more crime. The strategy of focusing police activity on these minor issues is meant to make the public space *feel* safe so that people will reenter the community and the cycle of increased crime will end. What this looks like in practice is police roaming the streets, issuing tickets and making arrests for minor issues like loitering, disorderly behavior, and even riding a bicycle in a place where it is not permitted.

But can we honestly say that anyone in Mr. Garner's story was kept safe by the police? Or that anyone was more secure? It was Mr. Garner's safety that was shattered that day, and it was shattered by the police. In this situation, the police made a determination about Mr. Garner based on the neighborhood where he lived and used fatal force to restrict a *potential* action of one individual, who was harming no one. Selling cigarettes on the street is, at most, an economic violation of the law. Is an execution an appropriate response? Is a violent apprehension an appropriate response? What if we consider a similar legal violation at a different scale and class? Does our response change if the violation of the law and the perpetrator in question is a billionaire guilty of tax evasion or wage theft—economic violations of the law that affect millions? Is an execution appropriate then? A violent arrest? Should police roam the halls of country clubs and the streets of gated communities in search of people who have broken the law?

The huge irony in this approach is that it makes scores of communities very unsafe. The presence of soldierlike individuals roaming one's neighborhood doesn't exactly paint a picture whose thousand words are screaming, "Everything is all right here!" There's a reason we don't see the same approach in the wealthiest (and likely safest) communities in our societies. And more than just making people feel unsafe, this type of policing puts Black lives in danger, along with other identifiable communities, including people who are homeless or who have disabilities or mental health concerns.

The fear of police from these communities is for good reason. For every incident we hear about, for every incident that pierces the walls that have been set up to discourage reporting on the ways that these practices harm people, there are so many more incidents that result in death or other devastating indignities.

The very weird thing about this strategy is that the remedy doesn't seem to have anything to do with the problem. Let's say that this theory is true, and that "broken windows" and vandalism are what make people feel unsafe in their communities. Why would anyone think that the solution to those issues is increasing police presence? I cannot think of a lazier approach to addressing a set of potential problems that likely require specific and targeted solutions. If one of the windows in my home breaks, I certainly wouldn't call the police. I would contact the appropriate people who could repair it. I'm not sure what calling someone who is equipped with weapons and not much else would do for me. It's only in the linking of these minor issues to crime—an extraordinarily tenuous link to begin with—that police could even be thought of as a logical service to consider invoking.

The resources that it takes to engage in this type of policing are staggering. An analysis by the New York *Daily News* found that writing violations resulting in summonses is the most frequent activity of the NYPD, "surpassing felony and misdemeanor arrests combined." In fact, summonses for petty infractions went from about 160,000 in 1993 to more than 600,000 in 2005—the result of implementing broken windows strategies. Imagine the sheer resources—and the cost of those resources—that this sort of increase represents. What's more, over 80 percent of the people who received violations were Black and Hispanic. The analysis found that the most common offenses were the consumption of alcohol, with more than 1.6 million citations issued between 2001 and 2013; disorderly conduct, with more than 1 million citations over the same period; public urination at 334,000 citations; and cycling on the sidewalk, with more than 296,000 violations. Again, it's clear that people neither feel nor are kept safe by these tactics, and the underlying social issue remains. If public urination is a problem, for instance, perhaps funding could be spent to create infrastructure that includes public bathrooms, which cities around the world provide. If cycling on the sidewalk is an issue, perhaps a more robust cycling infrastructure could be created if roads make cyclists feel unsafe. There are obvious, logical solutions to these problems, and policing is not one of them.

WARRIOR TRAINING

There is perhaps no greater evidence of the police's function as a body for social control than the way many are trained to treat certain residents as enemy combatants. Warrior training teaches police to treat *every* potential encounter like a threat. They behave like an occupying force at war with the residents of the communities they are policing. The training takes its methodology and approach from military boot camp—and has nothing to do with the daily reality of policing. The approach encourages police to be ready to kill at all times and encourages use of militarized equipment and spy-like surveillance tools to gather information about the communities with whom they are at "war." In support of this trending militaristic approach, many police departments have adopted a new look that Radley Balko, author of *Rise of the Warrior Cop*, describes as "battle dress uniforms modeled after soldier attire." And police departments now procure weaponry and equipment directly from the military, employing helicopters, tanks, and chemical weapons. I don't think I will ever get used to the sound of police helicopters tearing through the sky several times each day in my neighborhood in Los Angeles. A paper commissioned by the Department of Justice through the Harvard Executive Session on Policing and Public Safety criticized this approach as having no evidentiary need and for training police to see constitutional rights as impediments to public safety.

There are real victims to this approach to policing. One of them is Philando Castile.

May he rest in peace.

Philando Castile, a thirty-two-year-old Black man, was killed in 2016 during a traffic stop by police officer Jeronimo Yanez. At the time, Mr. Castile's girlfriend and her four-year-old child were sitting in the car. Yanez described the reasons for stopping Castile as such: "The two occupants just look like people that were involved in a robbery. The driver looks more like one of our suspects, just 'cause of the wide-set nose." When

Yanez asked for Mr. Castile's license and registration, Mr. Castile disclosed that he had a firearm and a license to carry. Yanez responded by shooting Mr. Castile seven times. The world watched the aftermath of the incident on Facebook, where it was livestreamed by Mr. Castile's girlfriend and shared millions of times among users.

We can't know for sure what it was that ultimately made Yanez shoot Mr. Castile seven times at point-blank range in front of a child and his girlfriend, but we do know that he had warrior cop training. The course Yanez took was run by Dave Grossman, who calls the methods he teaches to police officers "killology." Grossman's reach is impressive. He has trained police at each jurisdictional level in every state.

Remember, the majority of police time is not spent on criminal matters or even violent matters. What is this training for? Why are police being taught to engage with members of the public as though they are enemies on a front line? In Mr. Castile's case, no one was kept safe. He was made unsafe by a police officer who racially profiled him and killed him, creating a violently unsafe situation for his girlfriend and her young daughter. The psychological effects could continue to impact their safety in untold ways as lifelong trauma.

STARTING EARLY: SCHOOLS

I attended public schools in Toronto during the 1990s and early 2000s. I never had cops in my schools. There was the odd fight between kids, but by and large my elementary and junior high schools felt very safe—perhaps exceptionally so. With distance, I know now what was somewhat opaque to me then. My schools felt safe because of a remarkable access to resources. For the most part, I never had more than fourteen other classmates. That meant that my teachers were able to give each of us significant amounts of attention. We had specialized programs and after-school activities to enrich our learning. The school grounds were manicured, and we had uniforms for gym class—something that wasn't common in my school district at the time. Students were encouraged to start our own clubs and initiatives with teacher supervision—I started our school's recycling program with a group of friends. We had additional teachers for non-core subjects, like drama, woodshop, computer-aided design lab, choir, and track and field. There were many adults with multiple specialties available to us. All of them had been trained in how to interact with and support the education and socialization of children. We had several school counselors, lunch supervisors, nurses, librarians, and administrators. Parents were encouraged to volunteer in the school, and many did.

What I am describing is a school in a wealthy area.

What I didn't understand until later was that the fun Spring Fling events our school would organize each year were important fundraisers. And attending school near one of Toronto's wealthiest postal codes meant that these fundraisers were critical to the elevated experience my school was able to provide.

While I happened to attend a school where most of my classmates were wealthy, I myself came from a humble upbringing. My parents are working-class immigrants from Jamaica, and I grew up very aware that I wasn't of the same class background as many of my peers. But I didn't have a sense of how that affected my experience at school until my family moved in with my grandmother in a neighborhood of Toronto called Scarborough.

Within one week, it was clear that my experience at the school in that district was going to vary significantly from my experience in the wealthier neighborhood. There were many more students in my classrooms. The school was so packed that we had portable classrooms set up outside. Our experience was so different that my mother made it her mission to figure out how we could get around the zoning rules and go back to the schools with more resources—a tactic for which Black mothers in the United States have been criminalized and incarcerated. Even though, at age thirteen, I would have to wake before dawn and take three metro buses and travel more than an hour each morning to get to school, my mother persisted, and somehow got my siblings and me back into the schools with more resources, in spite of the rules. She knew that the experience at those schools would have a significant effect on our development. At the wealthier schools, there were always supportive adults around whenever we needed them. All of them had been trained in how to interact with and support the education and socialization of children. And not a single one of them was a cop.

Increasingly, public schools in urban spaces with high populations of Black and otherwise racialized students across Canada, the United States, and the U.K. are socializing young people early to accept the differential social control they can expect throughout their lives by placing police in their schools. We are told this is a necessity to ensure schools are safe. Meanwhile, the trend across districts is to cut funding to schools, resulting in fewer school nurses, school counselors, and extracurricular offerings, as well as a higher student-to-teacher ratio and unlivable wages for educators. While these consistent cuts to education have persisted, funding for police has ballooned. And police, who are not trained in the education of children, are replacing the educational professionals disappearing from our school systems. Despite the increased police presence, fatal school shootings are more prevalent than they were a generation ago, and children themselves report feeling unsafe with police officers in their schools.

And this really isn't that surprising. If your neighborhood block was suddenly patrolled by armed police officers whom you would need to pass each day on your way to work, or if your workplace was staffed with armed officers perusing the halls, would you feel grateful for your increased safety? Or might you be concerned about what risk you were exposing yourself to that necessitated so many police officers? That is, if this isn't already your experience.

It should come as no surprise that the history of police in schools stems from the successful movement to desegregate schools in the United States in the 1950s. Newly integrated schools relied on police and military presence as part of the desegregation process. Students have been protesting police presence in their schools ever since.

In my hometown, the Toronto District School Board placed police in public schools in 2008. This was almost immediately met by protest after students at Northern Secondary School posted footage to YouTube of a classmate being handcuffed. Put up in the early days of smartphones with video capability, the post is an early marker of how important digital media from average people would become in exposing police violence generally. Reports from the time say that the Black sixteen-year-old student depicted in the video was asked for identification after a school police officer "saw [the] teen loitering in the hallway during classes." Already this sentence shows how the police view students as potentially troublemaking without reason. What does it mean to be a student "loitering" during classes at a high school? High school students in Toronto typically have spare periods and are expected to spend that time on school grounds. Why on earth is being at school as a student a problem? The student flashed his identification at the police officer, according to reports, who saw it, but "was not able to read the name on it," and so began to question the student. Recall that this student is a child. Children are not meant to be subject to questioning by police without adults present. When the student opted not to respond, the police officer decided to investigate the student for trespassing. Again, a bizarre response to a child who had done absolutely nothing wrong. The video shows the police officer putting the student in handcuffs while the student repeatedly says he did nothing wrong, asks why he was arrested, and yells out that the officer is hurting him, while what seems like hundreds of other students look on. When the police finally have the boy in cuffs, they escort him down the halls in front of his classmates.

It was later reported that the student was arrested for assaulting a police officer. It's worth noting that this charge would not be possible if there were no police at the school, and that this entire incident stemmed from a police officer criminalizing a young Black boy for acting just as students act.

The program placing police in Toronto schools was called the School Resource Officers program, and similar programs by the same name are in place across North America. Importantly, the program was not universal. The so-called school resource officers (SROs) happened to be placed in schools in neighborhoods where there is a greater population of Black students. This mirrors the safer school officers (SSOs) in the U.K., who are more likely to be stationed in schools attended by a higher number of "Black and minority ethnic students." Each of these programs places real officers who are armed and have the power to arrest in schools with minors.

In Toronto, the SRO program was widely opposed. Organizers, including myself, mobilized against it until the school board decided to discontinue the program in 2017. I remember one Toronto Police Board meeting for which police and their supporters bused in children during the school day to make statements about why they supported having police in their school. The reasons these children cited were simple enough: the police officers throw pizza lunches and help with coaching hockey, they told the room. Why would we want to take that away from children?

Of course, we didn't. But why should *police officers* be the ones throwing pizza lunches and coaching sports? These are things that existed in schools before the implementation of SRO programs—from people qualified to carry out these functions. To be a teacher in Ontario, you need at least three years of undergraduate schooling and then additional education at the graduate or undergraduate professional level. Police, in contrast, barely get any training before being placed in schools. Police received two weeks of additional training before being placed in Toronto classrooms. The same is true in the United States, where as of 2017 the majority of states—more than two-thirds—had no laws requiring SRO-specific training beyond that of a regular police officer.

At the Toronto Police Board meeting that day, one child told a horrific story that they thought was supportive of police. The look of horror on the faces of everyone in the room indicated that we all understood that this was instead a cautionary tale as to why people without proper training shouldn't be interacting with children in a public school setting. The child told attendees they had confided in an SRO about feeling unwelcome at home with their parents. According to the child, the officer's response was to invite them to live with him in his basement, an offer the student accepted, describing living with the officer as a life-changing experience. I was stunned that none of the obviously horrified authorities present said anything. Of course, children should have supportive adults to confide in, especially if they feel estranged from their parents. But a trained counselor is unlikely to have violated professional boundaries by inviting a child into their home outside required checks and balances meant to protect children. The board meeting quickly moved on, and attendees were not able to find out more about the strange story this child told.

Despite the police strategy to bus in children to the police board meeting, many more children, parents, lawyers, advocates, activists, and teachers spoke out against police in schools in Toronto, resulting in the removal of SROs from the Toronto District School Board—the largest public school board in North America—in 2018. Communities across North America are similarly fighting police in their public schools. Students cite being treated like criminals, being subject to surveillance, being forced to undergo interrogations without adults present, having their immigration status questioned, and feeling uneasy in their school environments. This, of course, has a detrimental effect on their ability to learn. #PoliceFreeSchools, a national campaign of the Advancement Project and the Alliance for Educational Justice, has tracked more than three hundred acts of violence perpetrated against students in the United States by SROs, police on school property, and security guards in what they call an #AssaultAt map. The stories contained in the map are horrendous and clearly demonstrate that police have no business on school property. In one such story, a police officer broke the wrist of an eleven-year-old child while attempting to handcuff him after he was called to the principal's office to recount an incident he had witnessed. Why was this child being arrested and handcuffed on school grounds? Why was this child's family not notified of his interrogation? And how has this incident affected this child and his classmates? What has it done to their mental health? How will it affect their education? Their development?

Between the United States, Canada, and the U.K., the United States is the jurisdiction with by far the greatest number of police officers in school, with more than 70 percent of public high schools having an SRO, a police officer, or a security guard on campus, and that awful innovation has done a lot to justify the implementation and growth of SRO and SSO programs in Canada and the U.K. In the U.K., nearly one thousand SSOs are stationed in schools as of 2023. These police officers performed more than nine thousand strip searches of children between 2017 and 2022. Yes, you read that correctly. The police in the U.K. SSO programs have for years been strip-searching children. A disproportionate number of these strip searches are carried out on Black children.

In one case that received significant media attention, a fifteen-year-old Black girl identified only as Child Q was called into the medical office when she was suspected of having marijuana on her person.

She didn't.

She was pulled out of an exam, and two police officers performed a strip search while her teachers waited outside. She was forced to strip and remove menstrual products she was using. She was instructed to spread her buttocks and cough. Her parents were not notified prior to this treatment, and there were no other adults present. When the search turned up empty, she was told to return to her exam and continue.

Child Q and her parents describe this experience as traumatic and life changing. The formerly outgoing student who was head of her class has withdrawn, "hardly speaks," is now "self-harming and requires therapy."

No amount of pizza lunches and coaching justifies this.

This is clearly not about safety. To hear police tell it, the purpose of these programs in schools is to have police serve as ambassadors. Police claim that these programs provide a positive image of police to students and help students trust them. They report that they are in these schools to counteract how students might feel about them due to what they've heard in the news or experienced in their communities. In short, they are trying to normalize their presence among poorer populations, starting from when they are young.

Because remember: These programs are not universal. Our countries' most prestigious private schools don't have police in them. No one is arguing that armed guards are needed in the wealthiest school districts to keep students safe. In fact, one of the metrics the police use to determine what schools they should be placed in in the U.K. includes the "provision of free school dinners (as an indicator of social deprivation)." If police are so excellent at keeping our youth safe, and our youth need to develop good relations with police, why wouldn't society put those efforts toward wealthy children in particular, like most resources in our society?

When we add these factors to the fact that the majority of police time is not spent on criminal matters, I think we are morally compelled to ask ourselves as a society, What in the world are we doing? We are allocating so much money to police and telling ourselves we are creating a safer world for ourselves, when really we are making life less safe for vulnerable people and continuing legacies of segregation, all while we are invoking the idea of safety as a thinly veiled euphemism for intolerance of poor and Black people. What other public service would be permitted to fail so spectacularly and still take up the lion's share of our public budgets?

What's worse is that the data also shows us that policing doesn't even do punishment well—the one tactic it seems geared toward in order to carry out its social control functions. In a study of crimes committed in sample years 1998, 2004, and 2006, the conviction rate was less than *2 percent per year.* Completed by University of Utah professor of law Shima Baradaran

Baughman, the study uses clearance rates to help in its analysis, and a case is cleared when a crime is "solved," an arrest occurs, or a suspect is identified and subsequently released. Clearance rates are an imprecise measure of police effectiveness because these can be easily manipulated, and police are known to do what they can to make clearance rates appear higher than they should be. That means that the less than 2 percent conviction rate—already staggering—could be far worse. According to the study, "97 percent of burglars, 88 percent of rapists, and over 50 percent of murderers get away with their crimes."

These are stunning numbers that truly reveal just how dissonant the public's perception of policing and its usefulness is with its actual ability to support our safety. It's a fascinatingly successful cultural lie that policing keeps us safe, and our continued refusal to do the difficult work of preventing violence and harm, and to make the policy changes that would truly make our society safe, is mind-boggling.

When I would get the question from journalists, "Do you want to abolish the police or defund the police?," I would often respond with a question I thought was far more relevant: "What do the police do well?" It's a question we should be able to answer with ease given how many public resources are spent keeping them around. As the journalist would name things they thought police did well, I would reveal statistics to show that their presumptions were not true. And there is much to reveal. Not only are police failing to prevent harm, training as warriors, enforcing segregation, harming children in schools, and failing at their stated goals, there's a whole host of things we think they do for us that they simply do not.

BETRAYAL OF TRUST

Despite the numerous ways people unlawfully harm, exploit, and threaten one another, the police tend to have a narrow purview when it comes to enforcement, focusing on only a few of the behaviors that leave people unsafe: those exhibited by people considered low- or working-class— street crimes. Behaviors wealthy people engage in threatening to the safety of others are not a priority. While social control for the behavior of wealthier people isn't absent from our society, policing, incarceration, and other forms of banishment and punishment are reserved for the poor. Social control for the behavior of wealthier people is achieved using a very different strategy, generally called regulation. While regulatory enforcement—inspection, audits, safety consultants, and the like—is deemed sufficient to keep the public safe from exploitation from corporations and other wealthy institutions, the poor are thought to require a much more punitive approach: policing.

Let's think about the implications of this.

Consider the Monsanto Company, now owned by Bayer. The company is perhaps best known for its manufacturing of herbicides, insecticides, and biochemicals such as Agent Orange and Roundup. The company has been party to numerous class-action lawsuits alleging its products cause serious harm to the environment and human health. In a release published by the U.S. Attorney's Office for the Central District of California, U.S. Attorney Tracy Wilkison said the company serially "violated laws related to highly regulated chemicals, exposing people to pesticides that can cause serious health problems." One study suggests that one of Monsanto's most popular herbicides, Roundup, increases cancer risk by 41 percent. Monsanto has been sued by thousands of plaintiffs and settled more than 100,000 cases, while tens of thousands of cases remain pending.

Despite this massive violation of human safety over decades to an unimaginable degree, no one has been arrested, and no one has gone to jail. Instead, Monsanto has paid billions of dollars in settlements, fines, and damages, but even these are incredibly lenient, given the ability of the company to pay. Take the case of Dewayne "Lee" Johnson, a school grounds-keeper in the San Francisco Bay Area. Mr. Johnson's life was forever changed when he was diagnosed with non-Hodgkin's lymphoma and told he had an estimated two years to live. Mr. Johnson filed suit against Monsanto, arguing that working with Roundup caused his cancer. Although he was initially awarded more than $200 million in punitive and compensatory damages, Bayer managed to reduce his award on appeal to $21 million. Bayer, the company that acquired Monsanto and its herbicide products, reported a net profit of $4.3 billion in 2022, in part because of higher prices for its popular herbicides. While these lawsuits have been adjudicated over the decades, countless people have been exposed to Monsanto's products.

Corporate wrongdoing such as this has significant impacts on society. Large numbers of people can be victimized with a single act, and the monetary loss to the public purse through increased cost to social services can exceed hundreds of billions per year.

Consider these unpoliced, massive threats to human safety alongside the heavy policing of other social issues. People who are homeless, for instance, are regularly harassed by police.

During the COVID-19 pandemic, as economic and public health constraints caused ballooning housing insecurity, houselessness surged. As a result, communities of houseless people set up encampments in public urban spaces across North America and the U.K. Even though public spaces are supposed to be shared with everyone, cities across jurisdictions responded brutally. Police were sent to dispossess this marginalized population of what little they had, and in some cases detained people. Not only were they subject to brutalization, detention, and forcible removal; they were also threatened by a highly contagious, dangerous coronavirus that caused a sustained worldwide emergency.

Why would people without houses be subject to such intense policing when the white-collar criminals who have injured, sickened, and caused the deaths of countless people are subject only to fines? Why are corporations subject to regulation while some of our society's most vulnerable communities, whose own safety is at risk, are subject to policing? Why isn't the safety of people who cannot afford the cost of living a priority? Who is being kept safe when we allow only certain people to access public space?

There is an element of public shaming in policing vulnerable communities in this way. The brutal tactics used by police against homeless people are witnessed by passersby and often broadcast on the news. This exhibitionism, a common feature in how poorer people are policed, attaches a stigma to the condition of being housing insecure. In contrast, the control corporations face is quieter. Regulations and fines are leveled behind closed doors, and companies like Monsanto and Bayer are given the opportunity to agree to settlements to prevent information that could be catastrophic to their business dealings from going public. In these cases, regulators might understand Monsanto products as dangerous, but it is nevertheless treated as if it has inherent value as a corporation. Human beings struggling with housing insecurity are not afforded such privilege.

Now, to be clear, I am not suggesting that large corporations should be policed and subject to raids the way houseless populations are. That would be absurd. What I am suggesting is that the way our society engages police so unevenly in the name of safety is *also* absurd. As a society, we could decide to ensure people have access to basic housing rather than spending countless resources and public money using the police to attack people who have nowhere else to go. That would address the safety issues arising from not having access to shelter. The public is harmed by what society collectively neglects to resolve because we have put so much stock into the police.

SELECTIVE SERVICE

I am a little upset right now. The reason I'm upset is because we got four young ladies that have been murdered within the last week here off of Eighty-Fifth and Prospect. We got a serial killer again. And ain't nobody saying nothing. The media's not covering it. We got three young ladies that are missing. Ain't nobody saying a word. What is the problem? Why can't we get some cooperation?

These were the words of Kansas City community leader Bishop Tony Caldwell in a video posted by *The Kansas City Defender*, an online Black publication. Bishop Caldwell was decrying the lack of attention and action missing Black women in his community were receiving. The police department called the reports of a serial killer "completely unfounded rumors."

Then one missing Black woman escaped from the home of Timothy Haslett Jr.

The twenty-two-year-old woman who survived an alleged kidnapping, beating, and sexual assault was discovered and rescued after passersby heard her crying for help. She reported being imprisoned in a basement room for a month, where she was collared, shackled, and whipped. Upon her rescue, she asserted that Haslett had killed two of her friends. She had been picked up by Haslett on Prospect Avenue—the street Bishop Caldwell was calling attention to in his video. Prosecutors have evidence of another Black woman, Jaynie Crosdale, having been at his house. Ms. Crosdale was found dead months after the surviving woman was rescued.

The police routinely fail to provide safety services to communities that need them the most, and one of the ways this disregard is evidenced is by the epidemic of missing and murdered Black and Indigenous women across North America. In the United States, Black women represent 20 percent of the more than half a million people who were reported missing in 2022—despite making up only 7 percent of the population. That's ninety-seven thousand missing Black women in one year. In Canada, Indigenous women and girls are four and a half times more likely to be murdered than other populations of women in the country. The Native Women's Association of Canada reports that while Indigenous women make up only 3 percent of the population of women in Canada, they represent about 10 percent of all femicides in Canada. And in the U.K., Black people account for more than 11 percent of missing people in England and Wales in 2016, despite making up only 3 percent of the population. Canada does not collect race-based missing persons data.

Regarding North America, note that in sharing this data with you, I don't intend to suggest that the issue of missing and murdered Black women is limited to the United States and the issue of missing and murdered Indigenous women is limited to Canada. Shamefully, Canada's data on race-based missing persons cases is nonexistent, and there is no reliable data on the prevalence of missing and murdered Indigenous women across the United States. But like so many issues faced on either side of the border, there are likely to be similar problems in both countries. In fact, given how porous the Canada-U.S. border is, these statistics should be gathered collaboratively.

Indigenous and Black women's and girls' disappearances and homicides are not taken as seriously by the media, because we are devalued by society. Ongoing impacts of settler colonialism and anti-Blackness make our communities particularly vulnerable. We are often assumed to be runaways or to be involved in crime leading to our disappearances. We are also targeted for sexual abuse and trafficking; attackers know they are less likely to be discovered if they target women from devalued communities.

These communities do not need police to continue to deny the seriousness of our safety concerns. An approach that valued Black and Indigenous women and girls would ensure that we had institutions to turn to that were interested in preventing violence and exploitation against us and would act urgently to resolve injustices committed against us.

GENDER-BASED, INTIMATE PARTNER, AND SEXUAL VIOLENCE

In a criminal law class, a professor once called on me to name my preferred theory of punishment, and to explain why I preferred it. When I answered that as an abolitionist I preferred none of them, my professor retorted, "Your answer will change when we get to the sexual assault section of the course." It didn't.

One of the most common rebuttals I have heard when discussing defunding the police is concern for women. The argument is that if the police are defunded, women will be unsafe from sexual predators. Citing sexual assault as an epidemic, a journalist once asked me, "Do you think that women would do well in a society where there were no police?" For a society that so consistently ignores the safety of people more likely to be targeted by sexual violence, it's remarkable how often sexual violence is raised as a justification for the continued support and expansion of policing. Among the most common threats to human safety—gender-based, sexual, and intimate partner violence—these violations are also our society's greatest failures where safety is concerned. And despite what we might think, the police generally do not help.

The assumption underpinning the question from the journalist and the retort from my professor is that women and people who experience gender-based violence are currently kept safe from sexual assault by police officers. Nothing could be further from the truth. A minority of sexual violence cases are even reported to police, and when they are, victims and survivors have very little support in making their case or getting any help at all. Given the dearth of support and safety measures for victims and survivors of sexual violence, continuing to rely on police is a very odd choice. Those of us who suffer from sexual violence deserve more.

In fact, one of the least discussed forms of police violence is the way that the police engage in sexualized violence against Black women. The story of convicted rapist and former police officer Daniel Holtzclaw is a sickening account of a police officer who knew that his repeated sexual violence against Black women was likely to go unpunished.

Daniel Holtzclaw is a former Oklahoma police officer and serial rapist whose victims, one of whom was a minor at the time of her assault, are Black women. Currently serving a 263-year sentence, he was convicted of several charges for his horrifying actions, including forcible oral sodomy, sexual battery, and rape. Holtzclaw specifically targeted Black women from a poor neighborhood and used his access as a police officer to find women with outstanding warrants—leverage he would use to force vulnerable women to submit to his assaults. "What am I going to do? . . . Call the cops? He was a cop," testified his minor victim.

Daniel Holtzclaw was able to harm so many Black women for nearly a year because he knew he was unlikely to face any real consequences, that he would continue to have the opportunity to harm these women, and that no one would be thinking of ways to stop him. He knew this because, in addition to the protections police officers enjoy for misdeeds, there is no broad public service addressing sexual violence or gender-based violence in our society.

Here, it may be helpful to consider some statistics. According to the U.S. Department of Justice, less than 22 percent of all rapes are reported to the police in the United States. In Canada, this figure is less than 20 percent, and less than 17 percent of rapes are reported to police in England and Wales. These are not cases that are necessarily solved, in which a conviction is secured, in which a charge is laid, or even in which there is an arrest. These are simply *reports*.

When the journalist asked how I thought women would fare in cases of sexual violence in a society without police, I responded with the truth: Women are not faring well against sexual violence *right now*. In the United States, one in five women experience a completed or attempted rape in their lifetime, and more than *80 percent* of women experience some form of sexual harassment. In Canada, nearly one in *three* women experience sexual assault at least once. Think of the absurdity of that. The majority of women—people you know, perhaps even you—experience a routinely occurring violation of their safety. And our society's response is to rely on a service that is consistent in its inability to protect us.

Most of the time when women experience sexual or physical violence, the perpetrator is someone they know. These tragic incidents of violence are an unaddressed social epidemic—and the use of the word "epidemic" is not metaphorical. One-quarter of all women in the United States will experience intimate partner violence. And the Centers for Disease Control and Prevention estimates that up to 12 percent of emergency room visits by women are due to injuries sustained from intimate partner violence. That does not account for the mental health problems that many often experience as a result. While intimate partner violence can affect people of all genders, nearly two-thirds of the more than seven million people experiencing this kind of threat to their safety are women. In addition to being a massive public health and social issue, intimate partner violence is a major economic issue, costing the United States more than $8 billion every year.

Intimate partner violence suffers the same issues with respect to reporting that sexual violence does, with some studies estimating that less than 20 percent of incidents of intimate partner violence are reported to the police. The very fact that people do not report incidents of intimate partner violence and sexual violence to the police at rates that could make police an effective purveyor of safety for these issues is argument enough to prove that police are ineffective at addressing gender-based violence. The issue of non-reporting is persistent; it has not gotten better over time. But I think understanding why people decide not to report to the police will help to underscore the point.

People refrain from reporting for all kinds of reasons, and high among them is a fear of retaliation. When a relationship becomes violent, if the victim tries to report the perpetrator while the violence is ongoing, they could increase the risk of harm. What if the violent party finds out and becomes so enraged their violence increases? Another reason is economic. If the intimate partner violence is occurring in a family unit where the violent party contributes an income essential to caring for children and making ends meet, a report could mean putting an entire family in poverty and could result in children being taken into care. Another reason is to shield the violent party. Regardless of the existence of a violent situation, the victim's care for the violent party could factor into a decision not to report. Perhaps the victim is concerned that their children will lose a parental figure. Perhaps the victim is concerned that the punishment will be a threat to the rest of the violent party's life—what if the violent party goes to jail? That could adversely affect their ability to secure a job and reduce opportunities available to them for the rest of their life. If the victim is someone who cares about this individual or relies on them, that could be a very difficult decision to make.

Women who are victims of or have survived intimate partner violence also cite reasons that are less concrete. Some women feel a sense of shame or lack of import. Society often delivers the message to women that if they find themselves in violent situations, it is their own fault. It's the "why didn't she just leave" sentiments that make many women feel a sense of embarrassment. What if others find out? Will her neighbors or other family members judge her? How will the stigma affect her life? The life of her children? Will anyone take her seriously for what they may interpret as a personal dispute? Will she be believed?

Finally, some victims simply think the police won't take them seriously. How will she prove what has happened to her? It will be her word against someone else's, especially if there are no physical signs of abuse, or if the physical signs are in a location that she may not be able to show. How will she persuade the police to believe her story? What if she is unable to be calm or clearly express herself due to the trauma of the violence? What then?

The belief that police will not help women is well founded. Police officers often disbelieve and mistreat women when they turn to them for help. When that happens, think about what will happen to those women if police respond to a domestic violence call, are unconvinced by the claims they make, and leave. How might the person who harmed them respond?

All these factors point to the conclusion that police are not only ineffective at responding to gender-based violence; they may be entirely inappropriate. At worst, the dangers that women and other people who are victims of this kind of violence face are often exacerbated when they call for the only form of support our societies have chosen to invest real resources in, and victims know it. So why do we continue to not only rely on policing for this epidemic but constantly use it as such a justification for policing?

Though my professor was certain that my opinion would change when we studied sexual violence, he was wrong. In each of the cases we studied, the victims were not protected; they had already been harmed. And if we were as committed to prevention as we are to punishment, perhaps things could be different.

Let's talk about how punishment has worked out for us.

Several states have implemented rules requiring police officers to make an arrest in cases of intimate partner violence. Called mandatory arrest laws, these rules force police officers to detain someone whenever they determine they have probable cause that abuse between intimate partners has occurred. Since the widespread adoption of these rules, studies have shown that these arrests have had the opposite of the intended effect. These arrests have not deterred intimate partner violence and can in fact increase the likelihood of gender-based violence. Nearly two-thirds of protective orders that result from police involvement in intimate partner violence cases are violated. And while these cases are being prosecuted, upward of 30 percent of those apprehended *continue to abuse their victims*. In some cases, the abuse is worsened as the violent party seeks vengeance against their victim for reporting their behavior to authorities. These impacts are exacerbated by mandatory reporting laws, which require social service agencies and health-care institutions to report suspicions of intimate partner violence—typically to police.

Since the adoption of mandatory arrests, arrests of men in intimate partner violence cases have increased by 60 percent. And the arrests of women have increased *by more than 400 percent*. How is this possible? In these situations, police have cited having probable cause that an incident of intimate partner violence has occurred but being unsure which party is the aggressor. Perhaps both parties have physical signs of abuse, because one party injured the other while defending themselves. Because an arrest is mandatory, they sometimes end up arresting both adults and letting the system figure it out. In cases of dual arrest, charges against women are more likely to be dropped. In New York, a study showed that a whopping 94 percent of charges against women in these cases were dropped. That means that, often, the victim is needlessly further victimized rather than protected by the system.

Even though these cases may be dropped, think about the effect of this approach on people having experienced a violent trauma. Not only have they been physically and emotionally harmed; they have now been detained. Taken away from their home. Forced to go through the traumatic experience of detention processing. If they are unable to be released quickly, perhaps their ability to take care of family and go to work is affected. These situations can lead to serious economic hardship and even the loss of one's children to the child welfare system.

Now imagine that this happened to you once. Are you going to call the police the next time you experience violence?

One study showed that the primary effect of implementing mandatory arrest laws—forcing police to engage when a victim reaches out to what is largely the only safety support available to them—was to *deter women from calling for help*.

So let's recap.

In cases of sexual violence and intimate partner violence, victims are by and large not reporting to the police. When victims *do* end up reporting to police, their risk of being abused can be markedly increased. And the system's focus on ensuring that police act when faced with cases of intimate partner violence has led to victims being arrested and has deterred women from calling police when they face violent situations.

Who is being kept safe in these situations?

Violence is not being prevented. And yet the majority of the funds allocated to addressing these problems from the Violence Against Women Act, meant to address these kinds of gender-based violence against women, is going to policing and punishment.

This situation is nothing short of absurd.

If we truly care about gender-based violence and keeping women safe, we must be willing to have a conversation about *preventative* measures and strategies that don't *increase* violence against women. And that means letting go of the police as a solution. They have been worsening the problem for decades.

Think about what people need to leave a violent situation with an intimate partner. They need a place to go. They need financial security. What have we done as a society to make sure that these resources are in place? Our shelter systems are weak, under-resourced, and inadequate. What if some of the money we put into policing was put into the shelter system? What if a woman facing a violent situation wasn't in danger of losing access to necessary health care or pharmaceutical coverage for her children, because we put money into a free and accessible universal health-care system instead of subjecting the systems we have to never-ending cuts or, in the case of the United States, refusing to implement a universal system at all? What if a person who cared deeply for their abuser was able to get their partner the help they needed for the issues that they face? What if we took some of the money we were putting toward an ineffective policing and punishment approach, and instead put it toward a preventative approach? It's worth mentioning that the police tend to get involved with intimate partner violence only when the issue is concerning poorer, working-class communities. And that the resources and backstops I suggest above are already available in wealthier communities through networks and services they can rely on for the support they need.

Knowing how many people at risk we are failing, why would we continue to rely on police as the solution to gender-based violence?

Unless policing is accomplishing something else that our society does want to maintain. We have already established that the police's main function is social control. But whom are the police controlling, and why? Who benefits? And who is harmed? We'll discuss this more in chapter 6, but for now suffice it to say that in any collective attempt to build something new, we cannot replicate our tendency to value certain communities over others, lest we end up re-creating an institution as harmful and as ineffective as police.

We have to consider what kind of work we have ahead of us if we are serious about ending the harm policing brings to our societies. Why is it that these inclinations to discard and judge people persist? Unfortunately, the answer is that they are popular. Our societies are addicted to punishment. We want people whom we consider deviant or sinful to be punished. We'd prefer not to be confronted with those our society deems worthless. We don't want to be reminded of the existence of people who have less than we do.

These are deeply ingrained cultural beliefs, and as much

as they are embedded in the institution of policing, they are also embedded in other institutions that reinforce the ways we devalue people. Getting rid of policing will solve a lot of our problems, but if we are honest with ourselves, that will be just one piece of the puzzle. We must be ready to remake our institutions and start thinking about how to proactively create safety, rather than reactively punish and discard people.

HOW WE'VE FAILED

I f policing's original purpose is so reprehensible, why don't we just change it? Take out the ugly pieces and work with what's left? This is the question that inevitably follows the recognition and acceptance that yes, indeed, police are harmful and hurt people in ways that reinforce social stratifications most of us do not want to be associated with. It's the natural question for those of us who see the ugly but still cannot imagine a world without 911 or 999 at our fingertips—a comfort for the ever-present possibility of chaos that could befall us. I admit to being here once, too.

With the benefit of having contemplated these issues in depth for more than half of my life, my perfunctory answer is that there is nothing redeeming to grasp from the steel-enforced encasement of the policing institution. And why should we want to? I can't imagine a more unserious conversation than one that asks us to find the "good" parts of enslavement, of anti-Blackness, of colonialism, of poverty, and of classism to work with and discard the remainder. Anything *beneficial*—not even an approximation of "good"—could be so only for the select few who benefit from such isms anyway. But we give a primary tool of those isms a new nomenclature—policing—and somehow the conversation is considered worthy. Policing cannot be purified. No amount of confession and public reckoning will save it. Its purposes have been so effectively protected, so walled off from public reach, they are impossible to shift; that's part of the reason they have persisted so effectively for so long.

The *how* of policing is similarly immovable.

The impulse to excise the bad parts of policing piece by piece in the hopes of finding some sanitary form of policing we can hold up and be proud of is what comprises the entirety of the conversation on police reform. The ideas we have for reform never fundamentally alter the stuff policing is made of, which is why reform efforts always leave us dissatisfied.

Throughout its existence, several attempts at policing reforms have been tried. Invariably, these fail to solve the multitude of problems that policing unleashes on our societies. There is a cyclical nature to reform attempts: a widely reported incident of abusive police behavior sparks a flurry of political activity; activists and community members make demands as to what should be done, ranging from middling reforms to radical overhauls; politicians commit to a study or inconsequential reform of some kind that will placate the public and keep police fraternal organizations happy; and then the cycle repeats.

It's exhausting and disrespectful to all those who perish and whose lives are irreparably harmed waiting for something real to be done.

Recognizing the unending nature of these cycles reveals the primary purpose of reform: placating populations concerned with police violence, enriching the corporations offering up solutions, and preventing any deep, comprehensive, resource-heavy reckoning with public safety and inequality.

Still, examining the logic popular reforms are built on is a useful exercise. I remember engaging in thought experiments and research myself when I was younger and still convinced that policing was an inevitability in our lives. Giving reform suggestions serious consideration was in part what ultimately convinced me that police abolition is the only way forward. The process of considering oft-suggested modern reforms of policing to their natural conclusions is a discussion worthy of engagement, and one too few have seriously entertained.

POLICING IS PROTECTED

Like no other public service, policing is protected from attempts to shift it and officers from having to face consequences for their actions. The legal system is set up to protect police, even if they violate your rights. So whether we're talking about a reform that is implemented to shift police behavior—like ensuring all police wear body cameras—or laws that are already in existence that are meant to protect you—like the Fourth Amendment protection against unreasonable searches and seizures—the likelihood is that whether or not police violate the reform or your rights, they will not suffer any consequences, and you will have little recourse, despite violations on your rights that should be sacrosanct.

I'll give you a couple of examples.

You might have heard about the concept of qualified immunity; against all odds, activists, academics, journalists, and unlikely social media stars have made this muddy legal concept somewhat well known. Qualified immunity protects police officers from civil liability in cases where they violate someone's constitutional rights if the violation has not been clearly established by *constitutional precedent*. That means that there must have been another case considering the same constitutional violation under very similar circumstances where the officer in question was found liable. The constitutional violation could be clearly written in law; hell, it could be clearly written in the Constitution! But qualified immunity still protects police officers from prosecution if the violation hasn't been "clearly established" in *precedent*—in previous legal decisions. Those two words, "constitutional precedent," do a ton of work.

The level of protection for police under the doctrine of qualified immunity is astounding and pales in comparison to the level of responsibility the law requires from average citizens. Think about it: If you break the law, you cannot claim ignorance as a defense. But police—whom one might expect to be held to a higher standard, given that they are ostensibly meant to uphold the law and are the only body sanctioned to use weaponry and state violence against citizens—are able to be protected from civil liability through a doctrine that essentially says that they should be given a break if the constitutional violation wasn't clear enough to them.

Even when a police officer is proven to have acted *with knowledge* that they have violated an individual's constitutional rights, qualified immunity will still protect that officer. The doctrine of qualified immunity doesn't care about intent. It cares only about whether or not the violation was clearly established in legal precedent.

I admit to learning all sorts of doctrines I thought were unjust as a law student. But qualified immunity was among the most absurd.

The fatal case of Alabama's Khari Illidge, may he rest in peace, exposes the absurdity of this doctrine. As I recount Mr. Illidge's story to you, keep in mind that there is already law prohibiting police from using unreasonable force during an arrest. Keep in mind that the first officers on the scene had dashboard cameras that recorded some of the interactions between Mr. Illidge and the officers but did not capture the events directly surrounding and including his killing. Keep in mind that the police used a Taser, often referred to as a "less lethal" weapon. Keep in mind that the police submitted a statement from a bystander in their defense that was later stricken from the record after the bystander complained that it contained false information. Keep these facts in mind as I recount for you how the police escaped civil liability for their fatal killing of Khari Illidge.

In May 2013, Mr. Illidge, a twenty-five-year-old unarmed man, was walking down the street in Lee County, Alabama. The deputy sheriffs Steven Mills and Ray Smith were dispatched to respond to a report that a Black man—Mr. Illidge—was running down the street. When they came upon him, the officers knew he was unarmed; he was naked. The police understood that Mr. Illidge, who was clearly in distress, might have been experiencing a mental health crisis.

When Deputy Mills called out to Mr. Illidge to stop, he turned to walk in Deputy Mills's direction and said, "Excuse me, out of the way." Deputy Mills said he felt threatened, and tased Mr. Illidge twice, after which he fell to the ground. Deputy Mills then claimed that the five-foot, two-inch, 201-pound Khari Illidge overpowered the five-foot, nine-inch, 230-pound deputy, and that the tased man somehow "slung him at least 10 feet." As Mr. Illidge walked away, Deputy Smith deployed his Taser. Mr. Illidge again fell to the ground, this time face-first, with his arms under his body.

Imagine how terrifying this situation must have been for Mr. Illidge, already experiencing some mental distress and persistently attempting to walk away from the situation. He hadn't hurt anybody. He hadn't threatened anybody. He wasn't armed. Perhaps he needed help. Perhaps he didn't. But he was not an apparent threat to anyone. And yet his presence and behavior—walking naked—were enough for police to tase him multiple times.

The police then got on top of him to handcuff him, and while doing so, Deputy Ray Smith tased Mr. Illidge thirteen more times using the highest voltage available. The police later testified that this Taser deployment was inconsistent with their training, in which they are told not to repeatedly tase individuals having a mental health crisis. Police *admitted* in this case that the excessive use of the Taser was to inflict pain and "shut down" Mr. Illidge's nervous system. After torturing Mr. Illidge with the Taser, the officers hog-tied him, shackling his ankles. Officer Joey Williams, who had arrived to provide backup, knelt his 385-pound frame, using both of his knees, onto Mr. Illidge's back.

Khari Illidge went limp, and blood and white froth seeped from his mouth as he lay facedown, handcuffed and shackled. When the paramedics arrived, they found Mr. Illidge still hog-tied. They took Mr. Illidge to the hospital, where he was pronounced dead from a fatal arrhythmia, a known potential effect of being repeatedly tased.

Overall, Mr. Illidge was tased nineteen times.

Gladis Callwood, Mr. Illidge's mother, filed a civil lawsuit against the officers. The U.S. Court of Appeals for the Eleventh Circuit granted summary judgment for the police under the doctrine of qualified immunity, finding the officers did not violate clearly established law. Despite naming other cases in which police were found to have used excessive force when Tasers were deployed fewer than nineteen times, the court decided these cases had facts dissimilar enough from Mr. Illidge's case that they did not establish precedent proving excessive force was used against Mr. Illidge in *this* case. For example, the court discussed a case in which police were found to have used excessive force when a victim was tased seven times while lying on hot asphalt. The court said that Illidge's case is different because Illidge "acted erratically" and "ignored commands to stop." These differentiating facts were enough for the court to determine that police did not have a clear precedent to draw from to understand that they were using excessive force against Mr. Illidge. Whether or not the police violated Mr. Illidge's constitutional rights by using excessive force is beside the point in a qualified immunity analysis. As the court states in a footnote, "Because we conclude that neither Mills nor Smith violated clearly established law, we do not decide whether they violated Illidge's constitutional right"—and they don't have to.

In the matter of the hog tie, the court cited a case in which it had previously decided that officers were entitled to qualified immunity because "they did not violate clearly established law when they physically restrained and hogtied a suspect because he repeatedly ignored their requests to calm down and continued to resist even after being placed in handcuffs and leg restraints." Since the precedent was not clearly established in that previous similar case (because the officers were granted qualified immunity), the precedent remained unestablished in Mr. Illidge's case. Make sense?

The NAACP Legal Defense Fund and Ms. Callwood peti-
tioned the Supreme Court to hear the case in 2018. They were
denied.

―――――

In Mr. Illidge's case, and countless others, the camera that
recorded a portion of his interaction with police did not save
him. The fact that there is a law against excessive use of force
in an arrest did not save him. The use of a "less lethal weapon"
proved to be in fact lethal, and did not save him. The fact that
the police conduct was inconsistent with their training did not
save him. The fact that the *Constitution* contains the Fourth
Amendment protection against unreasonable seizures did not
save him. The fact that the police knowingly submitted an affidavit on behalf of a bystander witness with false information on
it did not open the police up to liability after the fatal incident.
Ultimately, neither the facts nor the officers' potential violation
resulted in consequences.

What reform can be an effective deterrent to bad behavior
in a context where police are so absurdly protected?

Even in civil cases where police are *not* shielded by qualified
immunity, they are still protected. Very rarely are individual
police officers ever required to personally contribute to settlement payments or financial damages awarded to plaintiffs. We
talked about police brutality bonds in chapter 2. The munici-
pality, state, or other jurisdictional bodies are often covering
these payments—even the cost of legal counsel. And criminal
cases? Most police misconduct doesn't even get to the point
of being investigated criminally, even when the circumstances
warrant it.

Take the case of Kurt Reinhold, may he rest in peace.

Mr. Reinhold was a forty-two-year-old unhoused Black man
residing in San Clemente when he was shot and killed by the
Orange County sheriff's deputy Eduardo Duran during the
noon hour on September 23, 2020. Deputy Duran was working as a homeless liaison officer at the time.

According to the Orange County Sheriff-Coroner Department, a homeless liaison officer is meant to use "outreach and

enforcement to assist the homeless population and provide them with access to available resources and services, while protecting the quality of life for the citizens of Orange County." They receive additional training to take up this role, including a forty-hour crisis intervention training and an hour-long session on "dealing with the homeless population." This stated purpose and additional training did not help Mr. Reinhold, however, who was treated like a criminal by these so-called liaison officers. (As an aside, we should question why this duty is allocated to police. Keep that question in mind for the next chapter.)

The night before Deputy Duran killed Mr. Reinhold, he watched Mr. Reinhold on video surveillance from San Clemente City Hall at the outdoor pool center of the private Ole Hanson Beach Club. The City of San Clemente operates the outdoor pool during off-hours. Deputy Duran decided to go to the Beach Club to confront him for trespassing. According to the district attorney's investigation of the situation, Deputy Duran and two other deputies arrived at the Beach Club at about 10:00 p.m. and tried to talk to Mr. Reinhold, who refused to answer them, except to say that God had given him permission to be there. The deputies determined that they could not take action against Mr. Reinhold for trespassing since they did not have an active "no trespassing letter" from the Beach Club.

The following day, Deputy Duran and his partner Deputy Jonathan Israel were driving on patrol when they saw Mr. Reinhold walking. The two decided to observe him, parking in a 7-Eleven lot where they could watch him. According to the district attorney's report, Deputy Israel saw Mr. Reinhold jaywalk and decided to approach him. In the dashcam video of the encounter, the two deputies seem to disagree about whether Mr. Reinhold actually jaywalked, but they decided to engage him anyway.

The deputies drove past Mr. Reinhold, who was standing on the sidewalk, parked, exited their vehicle, and Mr. Reinhold walked away. The deputies ordered Mr. Reinhold to stop, but he ignored them. The vehicle dashcam captures some of the audio of what follows, but the three men are outside the range of the camera. The officers tell Mr. Reinhold to stop a few times, and he does not respond. According to the district attorney's investigation, Mr. Reinhold ignored them and walked away. The district attorney's account states that Deputy Israel then told Mr. Reinhold he was detained (this discussion is not captured by the dashcam). On the dashcam video, you can hear Mr. Reinhold ask why he needs to stop, and one of the deputies says, "Because I asked you to," and later tells him he was being stopped for jaywalking. Reinhold denies that he ever jaywalked—saying he had been on one side of the street the whole time. On a bystander video taken on a mobile phone, you can see Mr. Reinhold walk into the street as he attempts to get away from the two officers, who have blocked his way forward on the sidewalk. One of the officers extends his hands to stop Mr. Reinhold from walking forward, and Mr. Reinhold responds by demanding that they stop touching him. The officers begin to push him.

Mr. Reinhold, clearly frustrated, continues to try to walk away, telling the officers that he is just trying to eat. "What is your problem? Stop touching me!" he exclaims. But every which way he turns, the officers block his path, escalating the situation. They tell him to sit on the sidewalk and that he is now going to be arrested for resisting arrest, as he continues to plead with them to leave him alone. On the fourth minute of the video interaction, the deputies yell at Mr. Reinhold to get down on the ground as he continues to try to walk away. He is unarmed, not threatening them, and insisting that he is just trying to eat.

As seen from the bystander video, the officers then tackle Mr. Reinhold onto the sidewalk, slamming him facedown. Almost immediately after, Deputy Israel yells, "He's got my gun! He's got my gun! He's got my gun! He's got my gun! He's got my gun! Shoot him!" Deputy Duran complies immediately, shooting Mr. Reinhold in his upper torso. Deputy Israel then yells again, "Shoot him!" and Deputy Duran fires another shot.

The district attorney's account, written in a letter to the Sheriff's Department, claims that Mr. Reinhold said, "I'm gonna get it," after Deputy Israel yells. It's the only thing Mr. Reinhold allegedly said that is not captured on the recorded accounts. Apparently, within the moment of time between Deputy Israel screaming and Deputy Duran killing Mr. Reinhold, Deputy Duran said to Mr. Reinhold, "Drop it or I'll shoot." Again, this is not on any of the footage that captured the homicide.

The district attorney found that Deputy Duran was "justified in believing Mr. Reinhold posed a significant threat of death or serious physical injury to his partner, himself and the surrounding civilians." Even though the district attorney's account concedes that Mr. Reinhold was correct in asserting that he *was not jaywalking*, it still determines that another vehicle code violation (crossing the street against a red light, apparently) allowed the deputies to approach Mr. Reinhold.

Assistant District Attorney Stephen J. McGreevy wrote,

> In order for Deputy Duran to be justly and lawfully charged and convicted with a crime, it is the [Orange County district attorney's] burden to prove beyond a reasonable doubt that Deputy Duran did not act in reasonable and justifiable self-defense or defense of another when he shot Reinhold. . . . A jury analyzing these facts would justly conclude that it was reasonable for Deputy Duran to believe his life and the lives of others were in danger. It is clear from the evidence in this case that Deputy Duran did not commit a crime, and that he was justified when he shot Reinhold and carried out his duties as a peace officer in a reasonable and justifiable manner. . . . [I]t is our legal opinion that there is no evidence of criminal culpability on the part of Deputy Eduardo Duran.

I'm just going to pause here to make a remark: Mr. Reinhold would be alive if not for the police. Mr. Reinhold was not hurting anyone. Who were these officers keeping safe? It was the officers who initiated contact with Mr. Reinhold. It was the officers who badgered him and blocked his path such that he had little choice but to enter the street. It was the officers who tackled him—on an initial *incorrect* assessment that he was *jaywalking*. It was the officers who brought guns to the vicinity of a man simply trying to eat. And it was the officers who shot and killed him.

I disagree with Deputy District Attorney McGreevy. I don't think it's so clear that a jury would side with the officers claiming self-defense in a manslaughter trial. And I believe that Mr. Reinhold's estate and the broader public should have had the opportunity to witness a trial that proved that such a crime did not take place.

Unfortunately, Mr. Reinhold's family and countless others did not get this chance, and that is a function of how the system is set up. The only advocate available in these circumstances in Orange County and many jurisdictions across the United States is the district attorney. The same district attorney who needs a good working relationship with the police to carry out much of their roles. The police are one of the primary bodies through which they gather evidence they then use in cases and investigations. In places like Orange County, where district attorneys are elected, there is often another reason to suspect the objectivity of district attorneys in matters of police criminality.

The district attorney in Mr. Reinhold's case and as of the writing of this book is Todd Spitzer, a Republican first elected in June 2018. For his 2022 reelection, Mr. Spitzer received campaign contributions and endorsements from the Association of Orange County Deputy Sheriffs ($4,100), the Santa Ana Police Officers Association ($4,100), the Huntington Beach Police Officers' Association ($4,100), the Westminster Police Officers' Association ($2,100), the Pasadena Police Officers' Association ($1,000), the Anaheim Police Officer's PAC ($2,100), the City of Orange Police Association PAC ($2,100), the California Statewide Law Enforcement Association ($2,100), the Orange County Coalition of Police and Sheriffs PAC ($2,100), the PAC of the Irvine Police Association ($2,100), the Tustin Police Officers Association PAC ($2,100), and the Garden Grove Police Association ($2,200). Mr. Spitzer has a personal financial interest in ensuring that the police fraternal organizations continue to support him—significant campaign financing dollars. These organizations represent police when they are accused of improper behavior. How might they respond if Mr. Spitzer were to act against police officers?

I am not making the argument that Mr. Spitzer decided not to pursue a criminal case against Mr. Reinhold's killers to protect the significant campaign finances he receives from police organizations. But there is a serious conflict of interest. How can the people of Orange County be assured that Mr. Spitzer's decision is in the interest of the community he serves if he has a personal stake in the outcome? Worsening the problem is the fact that there is no way for the public to examine the process through which Mr. Spitzer came to his conclusion. This is not an open and transparent process. We don't get to see what method the district attorney used to collect his evidence. We don't get to examine whether anything was ignored. There was no process by which an adversary could poke holes in the district attorney's determination that he could not make the case that Deputy Duran's actions were criminal.

In December 2020, Mr. Reinhold's family filed a wrongful death civil suit against the county. The case never made it to court; Orange County made the extraordinary and rare decision to settle the lawsuit with a $7.5 million payment to Mr. Reinhold's family. Perhaps I am not the only one who is skeptical that all the available evidence supports Deputy Duran's "self-defense" justification for killing Mr. Reinhold.

Prosecutors across the United States rely on police testimony to secure convictions and on evidence gathered by officers to secure plea bargains. But when the wrongdoer in question is a police officer, the prosecutor is required to stop thinking about the police officer in question—with whom they may have a personal relationship—as an ally, and start being skeptical of their claims, as they would any other defendant.

This isn't a book about prosecutors or the entirety of what's known in academic and activist circles as the prison-industrial complex—the ways the entire structure of the criminal legal system and its institutions works to enrich corporations and harm the poor. But it's useful to understand how prosecutors work to see why police are so protected when they engage in harmful actions that many average people may consider worthy of a criminal investigation or trial.

By and large, prosecutors make their decisions to take a case to court in virtual secret. There are rarely processes that provide any amount of transparency or accountability to the people they serve. Even in jurisdictions where a prosecutor must make use of a grand jury process to pursue charges, the process is obscured from the public—by law. The Federal Rules of Criminal Procedure contain a secrecy clause, preventing participants from disclosing what happens at a grand jury. In a grand jury, the process is overseen by the prosecutor; there is no judge. The prosecutor may call witnesses to support their case, but there is no cross-examination. The prosecutor can provide evidence, but they do not have to show the jury any evidence that is favorable to the defendant. The defendant does not have the right to counsel, and media cannot record the proceedings. This results in a system significantly skewed to favor the prosecutor and whatever outcome they would like.

In a world where securing convictions could mean career success and promotions for prosecutors, and prosecutors are reliant on the work, testimony, and cooperation of police officers to prepare for convictions, it's not hard to see why these same prosecutors might choose to sway a grand jury *against* voting for an indictment when the defendant is a police officer. Add to this our cultural inclination to believe the police are the good guys, and in most cases the prosecutor has a jury primed to support the police officer and all the tools they need to secure a no-indictment decision against a police defendant.

Some jurisdictions use a special prosecutor, who is not working with police every day to secure convictions against civilians, to try to avoid these conflicts. Even in these cases, special prosecutors may be reliant on evidence from police to charge one of their colleagues—how cooperative do we imagine police will be in those situations? Special prosecutors are also still bound by other laws and policies that strongly favor police impunity, from collective agreements secured by police fraternal organizations that limit the ways police can be questioned, to laws and precedent that make the burden of proof on a prosecutor incredibly difficult to surmount. Finally, a special prosecutor answers to an elected representative somewhere down the line, whether it's the district attorney or another elected body. If that body can be politically influenced by police advocacy organizations, that special prosecutor can be compromised through the pressure they experience from their supervisors.

So, to recap, we have a system where the people charged with keeping police accountable are allied with police in the way they carry out their day-to-day jobs, are potentially influenced by police advocacy organizations in elections, need police cooperation to be professionally successful, and are able to operate in secrecy and with near-total power to decide whether to criminally indict officers.

The data tracking the type of accountability police face in these situations is stark. According to Mapping Police Violence, a nonprofit organization dedicated to collecting data revealing the quantitative impact of police violence in the United States, 1,364 people were killed by police in 2024—more than were killed in any other year in the past decade. Of those cases, only nine charges were filed. In most of these incidents of police killings, law enforcement was responding to nonviolent offenses or cases where no crime was reported.

The Police Integrity Research Group at Bowling Green State University found that between 2005 and 2019 only 104 nonfederal law enforcement officers have been arrested for murder or manslaughter. Of those, only 35 have been convicted.

The truth is that the outcomes like that achieved in the George Floyd case—in which former police officer Derek Chauvin underwent a trial, was convicted, and is now serving a sentence for murdering Mr. Floyd—are exceedingly rare. The structure of our criminal system is set up to strongly discourage prosecutors from holding police accountable, because they are so reliant on them. Even when the stakes are criminal misconduct, police are protected and can act with impunity.

No matter what reforms are implemented—body cameras, less lethal weapons, policies against particular types of physical restraints police can employ—there are virtually no consequences faced by individual police officers when the rules governing their use are ignored.

What good is a reform if police aren't compelled to follow it? What policing reform can crack through such an armor of impunity? I don't know which reforms are going to make a lick of difference to how police operate given those circumstances. If it doesn't matter whether police follow the rules, when we allocate even more money to police through attempted reforms, we are effectively incinerating public dollars that would be put to better use by focusing on prevention of violence within our communities as a primary approach to safety.

That said, I know some of these reforms can sound so promising that it's hard to immediately see that not only are they largely useless because of the protections police enjoy, but they also tend to operate in practice much differently than we expect.

CIVILIAN OVERSIGHT

A popular reform that has the support of the American Civil Liberties Union (ACLU) is the implementation of a police oversight body made up of civilians that operates outside the existing criminal legal apparatus. The idea is that these organizations could hold police accountable and perhaps provide a level of transparency to the public more effectively than existing institutions that have conflicts of interest, as is the case with prosecutors.

In Canada's province of Ontario, where I am from, a police oversight board exists, and it is called the Special Investigations Unit (SIU). It was implemented after significant demonstrations protesting police violence against Black people in the late 1980s and early 1990s. Since then, many of the Black activists who campaigned for this body have expressed to me what a disappointment the civilian oversight board has been. Rather than being an effective body independent of police, it has been captured by police interests. In Ontario, when police kill, seriously injure, or are accused of sexually assaulting civilians, the Special Investigations Unit determines whether charges will be laid. Another body, the Office of the Independent Police Review Director, investigates public complaints against police that fall below the SIU threshold of severity. The director of the SIU is appointed by the province's attorney general, who is an elected member of the provincial government—subject to similar political influences from police advocacy bodies as district attorneys. Over the years, its directors have primarily been former crown prosecutors, the Canadian equivalent of deputy district attorneys—people who would have worked closely with the police for the majority of their careers as allies and would have developed good working relationships with the police.

And thus a familiar set of issues emerge.

———

Andrew Loku, may he rest in peace, was a forty-five-year-old Black man who came to live in Toronto as a refugee from South Sudan. He was shot and killed by Toronto Police Service constable Andrew Doyle on July 5, 2015. Andrew Loku was a former child soldier. In a coroner's inquest held after his homicide, the public learned that Mr. Loku was a husband and father of five children, whom he had left behind in South Sudan. He suffered from post-traumatic stress disorder from his horrendous experiences in war, including two months of brutal torture after being kidnapped by rebel forces. Mr. Loku lived in an apartment building unit designated for people with mental health challenges by the Canadian Mental Health Association. He had recently graduated from a construction program at a Toronto college and was hoping to reunite with his family in his new home.

According to the SIU report, on the night he was killed, a neighbor of his called police, saying he was armed with a hammer and threatening to kill her. At the coroner's inquest, the public heard that Mr. Loku and this neighbor had been at odds for some time over noise issues, and that Mr. Loku was frustrated that the noise was making it impossible for him to sleep. The officers arrived at the scene within minutes. I recall sitting at the coroner's inquest and listening to the audio of the 911 call, which recorded the mere seconds that pass between the time that the police arrive on the scene and the time that they open fire, killing Mr. Loku. Days after the shooting, a witness told the *Toronto Star* that she had personally calmed Mr. Loku before the police arrived on the scene, and that Mr. Loku "posed no danger to anyone, including the officers." In one officer's account, Mr. Loku is alleged to have said, "What you gonna do? Come on, shoot me," words not captured in the 911 audio. According to another officer, Mr. Loku did not say anything. A strange inconsistency. Witnesses say Mr. Loku used his hammer to bang on the door of his noisy neighbor to make a point about how loud they were being—not to threaten them. They also said the calm Mr. Loku did not ask the police to shoot him, but instead said, "What, you gonna shoot me now?" seemingly in disbelief. Despite the 911 tape not recording this exchange, the SIU report made a decision about which of the conflicting accounts was true. You can probably guess that the report went with the account most favorable to the police, determining that Mr. Loku apparently demanded police shoot him—as if this were justification for them doing so.

The vast majority of the cases sent to the SIU—about 95 percent—result in the body deciding not to lay charges against police. In Mr. Loku's case, the SIU again decided not to charge the police officers. Mr. Loku's case is exceptional, because it was the first case in which the Special Investigations Unit made a portion of its report public. After widespread public protest—including a two-week occupation of Toronto Police Headquarters I helped organize—the SIU released a heavily redacted version of its investigation into Mr. Loku's homicide. In the previous sixteen years of its existence, every other report had been kept secret.

Even though the report was heavily redacted, it *did* concede that an officer had acted improperly sometime after the shooting. There is video surveillance in the apartment hallway where Mr. Loku was killed. The report reveals that a police officer accessed the video surveillance in an "attempt to review and download the video." The SIU's report says that there was no "adequate explanation for the officer's conduct" and states that the officer's action appears to be in violation of provincial regulations. The surveillance footage contains a convenient gap: It records the moments leading up to Mr. Loku's killing, and the moments following, but it does not include the killing itself. The SIU report remarks, "Based on a forensic examination of the recording, it would not appear that there was anything nefarious about the so-called 'gap' in question and that the camera had simply not recorded the shooting." There is no way for the public to verify this forensic account.

There are other examples of the SIU deciding to clear police officers, even when police have clearly acted improperly. Consider the case of Jermaine Carby, may he rest in peace, whose killing by Peel Police constable Ryan Reid in 2014 sparked the Black Lives Matter movement in Canada. Officers claimed Mr. Carby had a knife, and that this is the reason they killed him. But when SIU investigators arrived on the scene, there *was* no knife. Constable Justin Chittenden revealed at a coroner's inquest that he removed the knife in order to "preserve evidence." The kitchen knife, which did not match any of the knives in Mr. Carby's home according to his family, was presented to the SIU by police hours after SIU investigators arrived on the scene of Mr. Carby's homicide. The SIU report in Mr. Carby's case remains a secret, but the director of the SIU at the time, former crown attorney Tony Loparco, expressed his frustration at the police tampering with evidence, stating in a press release, "This conduct is hard to fathom. . . . [A]s a result of the officer's actions, the SIU, and in a broader sense the public, is asked to accept that the knife it retrieved from police was in Mr. Carby's possession when he was shot, when that same inference could have more readily and safely been made had the scene not been tampered with."

Mr. Carby's family remains suspicious that police planted the knife.

Mr. Loparco raised another critical issue in his revealing release, stating, "The subject officer chose not to provide the SIU with any first-hand evidence regarding his conduct and state of mind at the time of the shooting. While the officer was within his legal rights to choose to remain silent, the SIU is without any direct evidence regarding . . . whether the subject officer believed he was acting to defend himself or his colleagues when he shot Mr. Carby." Despite this admission describing a massive deficiency in the information the SIU had access to, the SIU *still* refused to charge the police officer in Mr. Carby's case.

Far from a panacea on the issue of police oversight, civilian oversight bodies like the SIU come with their own set of problems that exist regardless of what jurisdiction or country we consider—because of the way the institution of policing is set up. The SIU, like many other civilian oversight bodies across the United States and Canada, has no power to compel police cooperation into its investigations. Police can refuse to participate in interviews and can refuse to provide notes to investigators. Similarly, in the United States, several jurisdictions have what are called Law Enforcement Officer Bill of Rights (LEOBORs). These rights typically protect police from having to undergo the same level of scrutiny as a civilian in an investigation into their misconduct. According to the Cato Institute, LEOBORs typically protect police officers from undergoing investigations carried out by "non-government agents," rendering civilian oversight boards useless if they are in place. Similar protections are often contained within collective bargaining agreements negotiated by police fraternal organizations, which are protected by labor laws.

The idea of a civilian review board sounds good, but if the system is set up so that they lack any bite in their attempts to hold police accountable, what is the point of allocating millions of dollars to establish and maintain these institutions?

The former Ontario ombudsman André Marin released two scathing reports criticizing the SIU in 2008 and 2011. In them, he detailed an internal culture influenced by the large number of ex–police officers that make up its staff, a consistent issue with delays in notifying the SIU of cases (at times lasting days) or a failure to notify them at all, and a persistent issue with police refusal to cooperate with investigations.

In the United States, more than 160 jurisdictions have implemented some form of civilian oversight, representing a small fraction of the more than eighteen thousand policing bodies across the United States. While the existence of these bodies has increased throughout the decades, the number of police killings has remained consistent.

The truth is that these bodies have failed to provide the type of oversight and transparency hoped for by those who advocate for them. Instead, they become a way to placate the public into thinking that a fix to police impunity is being implemented. Only later does the public realize that the oversight body cannot surmount the level of protections police have, and calls to reform the reform begin. More funding will fix the problem, we are told. More resources, more staff, new laws. But none of these approaches can defeat the infinitely thick shield of protection police enjoy from policies, laws, collective agreements, institutional systems, and even culture.

In the case of the SIU, every major review of its effectiveness except one has recommended increased funding and resources. And while these measures are approved, for the SIU and other civilian oversight boards nothing about their lack of effectiveness seems to change.

TECHNOLOGY

A popular set of reforms are those based on the idea that technology can provide accountability and safety where human measures have failed. Most popular are calls to outfit police officers with body cameras and calls to increase police access to weaponry thought to be less lethal than guns. In the case of body cameras, the idea is that the cameras will show us when police act improperly, allow us to appropriately hold them accountable, and potentially act as a deterrent against excessive use of force. But we cannot forget about the countless incidents of police violence caught on camera that result in no accountability. The body camera suggestion is a convenient distraction—and one that has been tried. Studies suggest they have no effect on use of force, and at least one study shows that they may *encourage* it.

The promise of body cameras is tantalizing. They seem to offer a way to objectively see and evaluate the actions of police with your own eyes. What's more, the police and their advocates generally *agree* with the implementation of body cameras. When the majority of reform measures spark disagreement between police, politicians, and police reform advocates, body cameras can feel like an easy win. But the truth is, while most major police departments in the United States, Canada, and the U.K. use body cameras, the devices haven't lived up to their promise and come with a whole host of other problems.

Proponents of body cameras argue the visibility they provide is a way to hold police accountable and provides a deterrent to bad behavior. This is an incredibly naive position. Given what we know about how intensely police are protected, how could a recording overcome the litany of policy, law, and agreements that protect police from prosecution or civil liability?

Even if a recording itself persuades a prosecutor to contravene the overwhelming structural discouragement to initiate a charge, a body camera recording can show only so much and is not the objective witness we may want it to be. The cameras are affixed to the body of police, they point outward, and they make use of wide-angle lenses. This creates a view from the perspective of police, mostly showing us what is in front of police; we may not be able to see the totality of what police are doing, and the angle of the lens creates distortion that can make the resulting footage hard to interpret accurately. In a world where footage from mobile phone cameras, which can record more information than a body camera, consistently makes little to no difference in whether police officers face criminal or civil liability, what would this limited angle add?

The scientific research on body cameras in one of the largest randomized trials ever completed has found that they have no detectable, meaningful effect on documented use of force. In studies suggesting body cameras may encourage use of force, researchers have hypothesized that part of the reason is that police don't believe they are doing anything wrong and believe that the body camera footage may exonerate them. Police have so much latitude permitting them to use force at their discretion—it's not just the fact that they *use* force that's the problem; it's the entire apparatus that permits and encourages it that requires dismantling.

Even though body cameras demonstrably represent little more than another money pit that allows us to feel as though we are addressing a problem, they remain popular among police and politicians alike; more than eight thousand police departments across the United States outfitted their police with body cameras since 2014. In fact, the global market size of body cameras was valued at $1.2 billion in 2020 and is projected to multiply significantly over the next decade, with some market research firms estimating a growth within the hundreds of billions of dollars. If it's not their effectiveness, what is it that is driving the significant expansion of this market? Perhaps some of that will become clear when we consider some of the problems body cameras create.

An agreement within a jurisdiction to implement body cameras can be an important placating strategy. Politicians and police looking to quell protest and public concern over police brutality can easily point to body cameras as a demonstrable reform without ruffling many feathers. What is far less popular than the body cameras themselves is any accompanying legislation or policy providing access to the resulting footage—to the public or to individuals filing complaints.

When the public doesn't have the right to the footage, whom does the footage benefit?

The police.

Police see body cameras as a surveillance tool for monitoring communities they deem dangerous. Subjects being recorded are not required to consent to their image being captured. What's worse is that these cameras can be outfitted with facial recognition software that has been widely reported to be remarkably ineffective at distinguishing the facial features of Black people. When used as identification tools, facial recognition software in body-worn cameras that can be activated when a police officer is walking down the street further criminalizes Black people in neighborhoods frequently patrolled by police. These tools can be used to create databases identifying people living in particular neighborhoods. We know police patrol poor and Black communities more than others. Body cameras can become just another tool in the arsenal of ways these communities are already marginalized.

Another unintended issue is the security of these cameras. In 2018, *Wired* reported on research completed by Josh Mitchell of the security firm Nuix, who found that the cameras were vulnerable to hacking. Mitchell said he could "connect to the cameras, log in, view media, modify media, [and] make changes to the file structures." So not only do body cameras cost millions to implement and maintain, they don't even protect the integrity of the recorded footage—a problem that would likely be a significant expense to correct.

Rather than solving any problems, body cameras and their related issues have created more distractions in the struggle against police brutality. Now advocates have whole new areas of advocacy they are engaging in to try to address some of these problems. Instead of focusing our efforts on real solutions grounded in solving the root of our safety concerns, some of us are now dedicating our efforts to shifting policy so body camera footage can be accessed or limiting the ways body cameras can be used as surveillance; all the while, the cameras remain an ineffective accountability tool.

The rush to outfit police officers with body cameras has transferred billions of dollars to police departments and additional tools that harm marginalized communities, and they have not lived up to their promise of being a deterrent for police considering using force. For most people who still believe in the utility of body cameras and are concerned about police violence, I think there is hope that the visibility of police violence caught on camera will open the eyes of people who refuse to acknowledge policing is a problem.

I understand the allure. In Black communities, having footage that makes the horrors of policing visible to people who don't regularly encounter police can feel validating. But more than thirty years after the brutal beating of Rodney King was caught on camera, I think the visibility goal has been accomplished. Footage showing the violence and terror police inflict on individuals and communities alike is ubiquitous. At this point, if you haven't seen it, you are willfully avoiding the truth.

I haven't watched it, but the knowledge that there is a nearly half-hour video depicting Memphis police officers beating Tyre Nichols, may he rest in peace, to death after a traffic stop only makes me horrified. At the very best, all a body camera can do is record behavior. Given the choice of how to spend the hundreds of millions that go toward police body cameras every year, wouldn't we prefer for those efforts to be spent on *preventing* police brutality, rather than just recording it?

Stun Guns and Weaponry Diversification

Another popular technology-based reform is to outfit police with more choice in the weaponry they use against civilians. Of course, it is never framed that way, but reforms calling for increased use of "less lethal" weapons are just that—a call to increase harmful weaponry as tools for police officers. This does not reduce the prevalence of police brutality; it just changes the nature of how that brutality takes place. And let me be very clear: "less lethal" is an extremely low bar to aspire to—and is a misnomer. The so-called less lethal weaponry that police use can still kill, maim, and seriously injure. Rubber bullets, water cannons, sound cannons, chemical weapons, and, perhaps most popularly, stun guns—like the popular Taser manufactured by Axon Enterprise.

Take the case of Zodoq Obatolah, may he rest in peace, a fifty-two-year-old South London Black man who was killed when a Met Police officer shot him with a Taser on his balcony on April 12, 2023. Mr. Obatolah was in distress that day. Neighbors saw the typically quiet man crying out on his balcony for hours, threatening to jump. According to reports, the police arrived at Mr. Obatolah's apartment and left after he did not respond to them. They returned hours later, this time forcibly entering. In footage taken by a bystander and shared to Facebook by Black Lives Matter London, you can hear Mr. Obatolah responding to the officers demanding they leave his home. Police shot the unarmed Mr. Obatolah with a Taser, and he fell from his fifth-story balcony. The names of the police officers have not been released, but the Independent Office for Police Conduct is investigating two officers for gross negligence manslaughter.

Perhaps Mr. Obatolah needed help. But what he received instead was an attack from armed strangers who entered his home and sent a shock through his body with a weapon that has the power to temporarily eliminate muscle control. If he was experiencing distress, fear, and confusion before that moment, I don't imagine the police showing up and assaulting him helped his situation. If only there had been an alternative option for him. A service that could have attended to his needs without the use of weapons.

Proponents of stun guns and other such tools tout the fact that this increase in weaponry provides the police with options besides guns that they hope will lead to fewer fatalities. But let's be perfectly clear: these are brutal, torturous weapons that can lead to sudden cardiac arrest and death, especially if they are repeatedly deployed or deployed for long periods, as happened to Alabama's Khari Illidge; recall that he was tased nineteen times before his death. These tools can temporarily paralyze and cause excruciating pain. They pose increased dangers to people who experience seizures, have heart conditions, or use drugs or alcohol, as well as to the elderly, pregnant people, and children. A Reuters investigation found that the list of people for whom the use of stun guns poses a higher risk is nearly *one-third* of the population of the United States. And yet most patrol officers in the United States carry them. And remember—patrol officers are focusing on already marginalized, low-resource communities with higher proportions of Black people, people with disabilities, and impoverished people. Being from one of these communities means you are more likely to have health problems associated with poverty—in part because of the reduced likelihood of having access to preventative care and health insurance. Lower incomes are associated with a higher prevalence of heart disease, so the target population most likely to experience stun gun use by police is far more likely to include people from that one-third of the U.S. population who are at higher risk of experiencing complications.

Even though children are at higher risk, nearly half of school resource officers at secondary schools and nearly 30 percent at primary schools are armed with stun guns, and at least 143 kids have been tased by school officers in the United States since 2011. Children. The Taser is designed to incapacitate a fully grown adult. But somehow, they have been used in the United States and in cases in the U.K. against children as young as seven years old.

Even when the stun gun does not cause physical harm, its use can lead to an escalation rather than de-escalation of violence. An American Public Media Reports investigation found that more than 250 fatal police shootings between 2015 and 2017 occurred after a stun gun failed. In over one-third of those cases, the subject the police were trying to subdue became more agitated after the failure of the stun gun, which could have led to the escalation involving a gun. By police officers' own admission, Tasers are only effective at incapacitating a subject "as little as 55 percent of the time, or just a little better than a coin flip," according to the APM Reports' investigation.

Imagine a situation in which police are called because of a

person who is in medical distress. The police are not health-care providers, so they respond with the tools available to them. They use a Taser in an attempt to incapacitate this person, who is already confused and simply needs care. The stun gun deploys, and it delivers the overdose of pain promised, but this is just one of those 45 percent of cases where police report the Taser failing to incapacitate. The person in distress is now even more confused, perhaps angry, and has just experienced level 10 pain. How might that person respond? What might their reflexes do to try to protect them? And how might the police, realizing the stun gun was ineffective, respond to the subject's agitation?

It's not hard to see how these cases escalate. Crucially, the escalating violence is directly caused by the presence of police and the violent strategies they employ. If another approach was taken in Mr. Obatolah's case and countless others, fatalities could have been avoided.

Tasers are just one of the weapons often described as less lethal and cited as reforms that can help curb police brutality. There are also alternative projectiles, like rubber bullets, which can cause injuries from exploding eyes to fatalities. In the 2016 case of Montreal's forty-six-year-old Bony Jean-Pierre, may he rest in peace, a plastic bullet to the head fired by Service de Police de la Ville de Montréal police officer Christian Gilbert resulted in fatal brain damage. Officer Gilbert was acquitted after a rare trial on charges of manslaughter and aggravated assault in 2021.

Then there are chemical weapons, like tear gas. During the 2020 uprisings, I joined a peaceful gathering in Portland led by mothers whose children had experienced brutality at the hands of police. We were singing and chanting, gathered in one spot in the city's downtown. With no warning, police arrived and started shooting tear gas canisters into the crowd. I was prepared for this; I had seen the increasing crackdowns from police against protesters, passersby, and journalists during the 2020 uprisings. I put a helmet and mask on and ran, along with the hundreds of others who were at this demonstration. It had been peaceful until police escalated the situation. They seemed to be shooting the tear gas canisters indiscriminately, which themselves are dangerous weapons—hence the helmet. We were not given any instructions from police, just attacked. As we ran, I couldn't help but wonder what the point of the police attack was. It almost appeared as though it were for sport. We gathered at another part of the city after running from the police to continue our vigil. They once again came and launched tear gas canisters at the previously calm crowd. I am not sure what happened to our First Amendment rights during the 2020 uprisings, but those nights felt like a dystopic fever dream. Police officers were the only ones making our gatherings unsafe.

In addition to stun guns, chemical weapons, and projectiles, police are now using sound cannons, which can rupture eardrums, and water cannons, which can be deployed with chemical irritants that can lead to serious injury from the blunt force of the water, including blindness.

As I sit here describing all the tools with which we continue to outfit police in the name of reducing police brutality, I just can't help but marvel at the nightmarish scenario we find ourselves in. Are we so out of ideas that the only thing we can think of to make interactions with police safer is to give them more *stuff* in the hopes that maybe, just maybe, they will choose a weapon that will probably harm us but perhaps won't kill us?

It's absurd.

The truth is that police officers have harmed and killed with their bare hands and any other tool at their disposal. No increased diversity of weaponry will stop the oppositional position they take when they are interacting with people. They are trained to respond to everything from perceived noncompliance to atypical behavior to resistance to arrest with the tools that they have, none of which are de-escalating. And yet companies are developing even more weapons with which to arm law enforcement, like the recently released BolaWrap, a device that fires a Kevlar cord that wraps around the subject to restrain them, like something out of Looney Tunes.

All these weapons come with their own set of problems, and

again pull police reform advocates into distracting piecemeal campaigns to implement policies or standards to govern the use of this weaponry—which will likely never matter, given the level of protection from accountability police enjoy. All the while, the reforms that aim to give police more choice of weaponry take money from the public purse and enrich the manufacturers of these tools. The primary beneficiaries of expanding weaponry reforms are profitable corporations and their wealthy investors.

And throughout the time all this new tech has proliferated, the rate of police killings in the United States has not changed.

Automation

The final form of technological reform I'll discuss are the efforts to use predictive and artificial intelligence tools to automate policing. Proponents of this strategy often believe the pervasive myth that anti-Black racist policing is the fault of a few bad apples—individual police officers who harbor racist thoughts targeting Black people and give the entire system of policing a bad name. By this point I've roundly refuted that logic; while these racist individual officers certainly exist, it's policing's various institutions that operate through anti-Black racism and various other forms of discrimination. But this persistent desire to believe that the problems with policing all boil down to individuals leads to the automation strategy—the belief that if policing is assisted by robots, unplagued by the discriminatory intentions of rogue humans, it will be impossible for individual acts of discrimination from police to affect civilians.

The problem is that robots are racist, too.

A plethora of companies have emerged promising to offer unbiased policing tools that will solve the problems of discrimination. There are predictive policing tools that use algorithms based on available crime data to predict where crimes will happen next. There are facial recognition tools, which try to match the faces of average people to suspects. These tools are their creators' attempt at figuring out what crimes will happen before they occur, who the perpetrators will be, and who the victims will be. A way to forecast crime. Like the weather.

Very *Minority Report*.

But the thing about technology is that it does what *we* tell it to do. And while the technology may be devoid of discriminatory intent, the ways discrimination is baked into our institutions are reflected in the technological tools we make.

For example, most dark-skinned people—including myself—will be able to describe interacting with automated tools that simply don't work for us. From hands-free dispensers and dryers in public restrooms to smartphone cameras that just won't focus on a Black person's face, technological tools often cannot recognize us. These technologies were trained on people with pale skin, and at times cannot detect a person with dark skin. The designers might not have had a discriminatory intent, but the way their products were made resulted in a massive flaw with a discriminatory outcome.

These problems are present in policing tools, too, and their resulting consequences are far more dire than the awkward dances some of us perform hoping the soap dispenser will notice us.

Take the case of Porcha Woodruff, a thirty-two-year-old resident of Detroit. Facial recognition tools led police to send six officers to her home on February 16, 2023, with an arrest warrant for robbery and carjacking. At the time, she was helping her two young children get ready for school. She was incredulous. "Are you kidding, carjacking?" she asked. "Do you see that I am eight months pregnant?"

That's right, Ms. Woodruff was eight months pregnant. The victim of the robbery and carjacking had his items, including his mobile phone, stolen on January 29, 2023, at gunpoint by a man. The victim suspected this man was associated with a woman he had met and had intimate relations with earlier in the day. The victim later informed police that his mobile phone's location tracker indicated it had been returned to a gas station. A detective obtained surveillance video of the woman who returned the phone from the gas station (who was not, to be clear, eight months pregnant) and ran it through facial recognition software, which identified the person who returned the mobile phone as Porcha Woodruff—using a source photo from nearly a decade prior. The victim was presented with a lineup of potential suspects including Porcha Woodruff and identified her as the woman he had interacted with on the day he was robbed.

On the day of her arrest, Ms. Woodruff was forced to send her young children upstairs to wake her fiancé and tell him that "Mommy is going to jail." Ms. Woodruff was searched and arrested in front of her children, fiancé, and neighbors, and their pleas for the police to double-check whether the suspect they were looking for was pregnant were ignored.

Ms. Woodruff's charges were later dismissed due to insufficient evidence. In August 2023, she filed suit in federal court against the City of Detroit and one of the detectives who arrested her for civil rights violations including false arrest and imprisonment and malicious prosecution.

Ms. Woodruff's is just one case in which reliance on facial recognition technology has resulted in actions being taken against innocent civilians because the software has difficulty distinguishing between Black people. In fact, a study on the accuracy of facial recognition algorithms completed by the National Institute of Standards and Technology found higher false positive rates among Black, Indigenous, Pacific Islander, and Asian faces when compared with white faces. As mentioned earlier, this faulty technology can be paired with body camera technology to further criminalize and subject to surveillance innocent civilians going about their daily lives.

Not only are the systems themselves faulty, they also bolster existing issues with anti-Black policing.

Consider the way predictive policing changed Robert McDaniel's life. As reported by *The Verge*, predictive policing algorithms used by Chicago police might have led to Robert McDaniel being targeted for violence in his community. Chicago uses the data it has collected about gun crime to create a heat map, and in 2012 it also created a "Strategic Subject List," through which it allocated a "threat score" ranging from 1 to 500 to anyone the police arrested. Yes, arrested—not everyone charged, not everyone convicted—everyone arrested. The Chicago police considered those with higher threat scores more likely to commit crimes in the future, using the scoring mechanism as a predictive policing tool.

Police visited Mr. McDaniel, a Black man, at his home in 2013 and told him that an algorithmic policing tool predicted that he would be a party to violence. They told him that he was "more likely than 99.9 percent of Chicago's population" to be either a victim or a perpetrator of gun violence. Mr. McDaniel was surprised. He had no violent criminal history. But still, the police warned him that because of what the predictive tool told them, they would make sure to be watching him going forward.

And watch him they did. The Chicago police started following him around the city, including harassing him at his place of work and asking people connected to him about his activities. According to reporting by *The Verge*, McDaniel's friends and neighbors became suspicious. Why were the cops around so often? Some stopped associating with him. And some people thought he might be working with the police against other community members—a snitch.

Mr. McDaniel was later lured out of a friend's home and shot in the knee, with people connected to the perpetrators suggesting to him he had been targeted because they were suspicious of him given how often the police were around.

Had the police never used a predictive policing algorithm and begun targeting him, he would not have raised such suspicions. Also, the police tool predicted that Mr. McDaniel could possibly be a victim of violence—which, yes, he did become. But it was police activity arising from that prediction that made him a target, and even though the police started observing him, they seem to have been entirely focused on Mr. McDaniel potentially being a perpetrator of police violence. Their increased activity did nothing to protect him from the violence he experienced.

Chicago stopped using the Strategic Subject List in November 2019, acknowledging that the program "hadn't reduced violence" and referencing studies calling it ineffective.

What happened to Mr. McDaniel is problematic not only because it resulted in him being a target for violence but also because of why the predictive policing system focused on him. Predictive policing systems are trained on past incidents *that the police know about.* We already discussed that most crimes are never reported to police. Police focus only on crimes in particular areas and target only certain communities for surveillance. If you feed a machine information that is already skewed based on the selective, racist, anti-Black, class-based approach to crime police already employ and ask it to predict where the next crime is going to happen, all it is going to do is spit out predictions that justify police continuing to engage in these skewed policing practices. Except now the police can say, "The machine made me do it." The technology becomes a futuristic tool to justify treating certain communities like second-class citizens. An Orwellian version of the presumption of innocence: Everyone is innocent until proven guilty, but perhaps some of us are more innocent than others.

But let's take a step back and look at the broader picture of what we are really doing when we rely on these tools. In jurisdictions around the world, we would rather give millions of dollars to police and enrich private companies to provide ineffective snake-oil chicanery to *magic* our way into finding crime that has not happened and therefore cannot be prosecuted— instead of spending that money on services that we *know* have an impact on making communities safer.

Part of the call to defund the police is to stop these farcical efforts and admit that, rather than try to crystal ball our way into safer communities, we should maybe—just maybe—put our resources into strategies and solutions that actually work.

On October 3, 2009, seventeen-year-old Victor Demarius Steen, may he rest in peace, was killed by the Pensacola Police Department officer Jerald Ard. The Black boy was riding a bicycle at night. Officer Ard was on routine patrol in his squad car and saw Mr. Steen riding down the street. Officer Ard asked the teenager to stop his bike. Mr. Steen continued to ride his bike. Officer Ard followed Mr. Steen, even riding in the wrong lane of traffic to follow him. Officer Ard did this because he was suspicious of Mr. Steen for "operating a bicycle at night without proper lighting."

The one-minute chase ended when Officer Ard shot his Taser outside his patrol car window at the cycling teenager. Mr. Steen lost control of his bicycle and crashed.

Officer Ard then made a sharp turn and ran Mr. Steen over with his vehicle, killing him.

The dashcam video footage did not save Mr. Steen. The Taser did not save him either. Laws preventing excessive force did not save him. There was no case precedent finding the use of a Taser on someone fleeing on a bicycle was excessive force, so Officer Ard was granted qualified immunity and therefore found not liable for Mr. Steen's homicide in a civil case brought by his mother.

None of the reforms discussed above saved Mr. Steen. And other reforms I haven't discussed—like new training or making police forces more diverse—would not have saved him either.

How do I know?

Because we have been trying those types of reforms for nearly a century and have not seen any shift in police behavior.

In the 1960s, civil uprisings occurred in Detroit, Chicago, Newark, and Los Angeles following incidents of police brutality against primarily Black victims. As a result, officials undertook a study resulting in the report of the Kerner Commission, also known as the National Advisory Commission on Civil Disorders. When I first read excerpts of the commission's report, I was stunned. It could have been written yesterday. The commission identified the forces' own practices as the root causes of anti-Black violence by police, but also poverty, inadequate housing, inadequate education, white supremacist attitudes, discrimination in the legal system, and inadequate social services. Unfortunately, in the decades that followed, policy makers failed to address any of the underlying issues and instead focused on reforming police practices. The result has been abject failure.

Various investigations and commissions into policing over the years recommended shifts in oversight, more training, diversity, and so on—from the 1895 Lexow Committee, to the Curran Committee, to the Hofstadter Committee, to the Stephen Lewis Report on Race Relations, to the Mollen Commission. We've had more than a century of reports and commissions recommending surface-level shifts and changes that *never work*.

As the Knapp Commission of 1972, convened to report on corruption in the New York Police Department, asked, "Will history repeat itself? Or does society finally realize that police corruption is a problem that must be dealt with and not just talked about every 20 years?"

What could have saved Victor Steen as he was riding his bicycle is there not having been an officer there to harm him in the first place.

At this point, the only reform efforts we should entertain are those that take power away from the police to harm us. We should not be fooled again by recommendations that increase their power. If Officer Ard did not have the option to tase Mr. Steen, perhaps that could have saved him. Perhaps taking Tasers away from Met Police could prevent future tragedies like that of Zodoq Obatolah, the South London man who fell to his death after police shot him with a Taser as he stood on his balcony. If Deputy Duran was not armed with a gun and if homeless liaison outreach in Orange County were assigned to people other than the police, perhaps that could have saved Kurt Reinhold. If it was accepted that police are an absurd response to mental distress calls, and instead another unarmed emergency response service was the norm, perhaps Mr. Illidge would be alive today. The elimination of faulty tech tools could have saved Mr. McDaniel and Ms. Woodruff the harm and distress they experienced.

So many reforms have been tried for more than a century, and none have had an effect on any of the problems endemic to policing. To continue to believe we can reform our way out of this mess is naive and lazy and represents the carelessness with which people in power treat the communities for whom policing is an urgent and persistent encroachment on their safety. Policing's problems are embedded in the institution, and the only way to reduce their impact is to reduce the power of policing altogether.

At what point over this several-hundred-year attempt at police reform do we admit to ourselves that the cancer lies at the root?

MANUFACTURING CRIME

Policing is a scourge. Its purposes are antithetical to the kind of society most of us want—a democratically run place where people have equal opportunities and can live in dignity, free from oppression. And it cannot be reformed into being an institution that supports that kind of society.

But this is not a pessimistic take. I am eternally optimistic about the capacity of human creativity to solve the problems that face us. We can come up with a way to build safe, secure communities with one another that don't include an institution that operates as an enemy combatant with the most vulnerable groups of people among us.

We must build something different.

I don't think it's useful to think of a simple new institution that we can replace policing with. That, I think, would be tantamount to a useless reform. Keeping society exactly as it is and replacing the institution would not change much.

Instead, if we truly want to solve the myriad ways policing is destructive, demeaning, and oppressive to so many of us, we need to start with how we want our society to function, how we want to feel within it, and what we want it to be.

The origins of policing are so intimately tied to power and maintaining that power in the grasp of the people society values the most and ensuring power remains out of reach for those valued the least. At the time of policing's origins, our individual inherent value was tied to race, ethnicity, gender, sexuality, wealth, ancestry, faith, physical ability, perceived normality, and educational status. Though we may think of our societies differently, not much has changed.

In order to rethink our approach to safety in our society, the most useful place to start is to reassess whom among us society values. If we genuinely want to create a world in which none are devalued based on immutable characteristics, we need to examine how we are failing at this right now.

If you've read this far, it should already be clear that certain groups among us face barriers not because they are deserving of them; the barriers are a reflection of how our society is set up. The ways our communities are constructed can tell you about what we value. Communities that lack bike infrastructure and public transportation but have many highways value people who drive over people who don't—or can't. Restrooms with very small stalls value people who do not use assistive devices over those who do. Colleges that provide an advantage to applicants whose parents or other family members attended the same school value certain ancestral relationships over others.

One of the most consequential ways we express whom we value and whom we do not is through what we designate as a crime. The behaviors we criminalize may be designated as crimes because they are harmful to the broader community, or they may be designated as such because we don't value the groups who tend to engage in them. When we criminalize behaviors based on the perceived value of the people who engage in them, we add discriminatory fire to the structure of policing, resulting in disparate treatment by police for different communities.

For example, consider the different approaches to substance

use our societies employ. Alcohol dependency is dealt with as a medical problem, a public health problem, and a social problem. We engage multiple institutions in our attempt to address those problems, but we do not criminalize alcohol use. Cannabis was once primarily associated with Black communities, and for much of my life, its use was primarily dealt with as a crime. While cannabis and alcohol may be used recreationally in similar ways, our societies decided to engage with their use very differently. Even though marijuana has been popularly used among college students in the United States, Canada, and the U.K., the policing of the drug was never focused on students; we value education and students. The criminalization of cannabis created criminals out of the devalued communities police targeted for cannabis criminalization—Black communities. As cannabis use becomes more popular among more valued communities and is no longer primarily associated with Black people, there is a widespread trend toward legalization. Just like that, we eliminate crime and the need for policing by legalizing cannabis and regulating its associated market.

Compare the way political leaders of the past engaged the crack cocaine epidemic with the opioid crisis. Associated with Black communities, crack cocaine and its dependency was ruthlessly criminalized and led to widespread targeting and incarceration of Black people through the "war on drugs." The people affected by its use were not considered valuable enough to treat or even understand. Addiction to crack cocaine was considered a personal fault and deficiency. The opioid crisis is certainly being processed through the criminal system, but it is also being engaged as a serious medical and public health crisis. We have engaged multiple institutions to support and treat people who struggle with opioid use. What makes our approach to crack cocaine and opioid dependency so different? The primary communities affected and how we attach value to them.

One way to eliminate some of the power police possess to harm us is to make different decisions about whom we criminalize. What if we simply labeled fewer behaviors as criminal?

WHAT IS A CRIME?

On New Year's Eve in 2019, SaTae'zja Devereaux, a Black twenty-two-year-old resident of Oakland, was traveling home from work during the daytime on the public Bay Area Rapid Transit (BART) system. She did not pay the $3.60 fare; she thought the transit ride was free for the holiday. She took the train to her stop, and as she was exiting, BART police officers Karl Carpio, Casey Tyler, and Brian Lucas approached her, accused her of fare evasion, and told her she was being detained. Ms. Devereaux asked if she could simply pay the fare. On body camera footage of the encounter, a police officer can be heard insisting that she hand over her ID to another officer or she would be placed in handcuffs. Ms. Devereaux pleads with the officers and asks why she cannot simply pay the fare. "This is not a debate. This is not a discussion . . . that's not the way this works," the officer replies. They ask her to turn around, face a wall, and start advancing toward her. "Please don't touch me," she says, before the body camera footage becomes impossible to make out; the officer is now presumably on top of her as Ms. Devereaux releases bloodcurdling screams.

According to a suit Ms. Devereaux filed against the police officers, all three officers jumped on top of the 135-pound young woman. They slammed her onto the ground, pinning her for seven minutes. "I can't breathe! Stop! I can't breathe! You're hurting me!" she cries. She was punched in the face, twice. "You just punched me in my face!" The police officers shout back, "Stop moving!" She cries back, "I can't, you're hurting me!" On the footage, bystanders can be heard saying, "She can't breathe!" and "She's bleeding!" as well as berating the officers.

As Ms. Devereaux is being beaten, she vomits and urinates on herself.

She was taken to jail and charged with resisting arrest and fare evasion and was forced to post a $15,000 bail.

For a $3.60 fare.

Ms. Devereaux's case against the officers was settled in 2023.

Think for a moment about the absurdity of this situation. Extensive resources in the form of three transit cops, equipped with deadly force, were deployed against a single Black woman who did not pay a fare of $3.60. They could have issued a citation. They could have simply *let her pay*. But instead, they physically assaulted her. They spent resources on the response to the resulting lawsuit, and even more resources on the resulting settlement. That we would spend these resources on attacking a person who fails to pay a $3.60 fare tells us something about how we value people who take public transportation, those who try to avoid paying, and those who cannot pay.

In a world where most are living paycheck to paycheck, trying to avoid paying $3.60 is not unreasonable.

Whether a person makes a simple mistake, cannot afford the fare, or intentionally tries to save themselves from spending the $3.60 because they need to spend it elsewhere—all these people are lumped into the same category and criminalized.

We could make other choices about how to spend the extensive resources currently being used to criminalize people on public transportation systems across North America and the U.K. We could, for example, use the funds currently allocated toward policing people taking transit toward making public transportation free of charge. If we did that, we would completely eliminate the so-called crime of fare evasion.

But instead, we choose criminalization. This represents a significant contempt for the poor and those living in poverty. If we valued the poor, we would not criminalize them for what they cannot control. Broadly, we have an expectation that people contribute to society by getting a job. While we have this expectation, we haven't guaranteed a way to ensure people can *get* to that job. We haven't even mandated a minimum wage that guarantees everyone can pay for all the things they need to live. And instead of spending our public resources on ensuring that all people can take transit to the various places we require them to be, we have deployed officers to criminalize them.

DETERRENCE

Some may argue that these seemingly arbitrary roadblocks are deterrence strategies—ways to discourage others from breaking rules for fear of impending punishment. A paternalistic apologism clearly rooted in social control. But these roadblocks are not arbitrary; they are targeted at specific types of people, primarily people who cannot afford the consequences of those roadblocks. But more important, deterrence is a losing game.

For behaviors designated as crimes that really represent our society's contempt for the poor, people may have little choice but to try to thwart the system. If you are living paycheck to paycheck to make ends meet, like most people in the United States, and nearly half of people in the U.K. and Canada, all it takes to upend your life is one unexpected issue that results in unforeseen financial expenditures. A car crash, a child's illness, a death in the family—these already difficult situations can be compounded by existing economic insecurity. It's unreasonable to label behaviors in which people are trying to stretch their dollars a crime when so many are living in economic precarity.

We cannot deter people from being poor. No one *wants* to live in poverty. No one wants to live paycheck to paycheck. But inequality is a central feature of the economic system in which we live. Low-wage workers are the engine that makes our societies run. For some, there are potential consequences whether you pay the $3.60 fare or not. If you don't pay, maybe you get a citation and a fine costing far more than $3.60. If you do, maybe you cannot afford the next round of prescription medicine you need for your child. It may be unbelievable for those who want for nothing, but many calculate their costs down to the dollar, and even the smallest hitch can affect their ability to afford basic expenditures. For people who live paycheck to paycheck, or a paycheck behind, money is not an intangible floating in the stock market; it is counted in bills and coins doled out with exactitude. For those who struggle to make difficult choices about how to allocate their limited resources every day, witnessing a woman being beaten to the point of soiling herself on a subway platform—or, God forbid, experiencing it yourself—does nothing to change the crushing consequence of either choice.

The studies on the deterrent effect of the criminal legal system are somewhat inconclusive. Some say there is a minor effect when the threat of punishment is certain; some say there is no effect or that the effect is impossible to determine. What we know for sure, however, is that for those who *do* get punished through incarceration, recidivism rates—the rate at which someone who has been convicted of a crime will reoffend— are high. In fact, research in both the United States and the U.K. shows that incarceration can *increase* the likelihood that someone will engage in criminal activity in the future. This is in part because the punishment from incarceration goes far beyond the period of captivity. Once released, someone who has been incarcerated faces significant obstacles to reintegrating into society. A criminal record can negatively affect one's chance of employment and make certain careers and jobs completely unavailable. It can make it difficult to obtain housing and admission to college. These ongoing punishments push people who have a criminal record into very difficult economic situations. When survival is on the line, the options are to risk reincarceration by breaking the law to make ends meet or to suffer, become homeless or ill, fail one's family, or worse—it's an impossible choice.

This is not a book about incarceration; plenty have written about the failure of prisons as a strategy for anything other than discrimination and the provision of a cheap labor force, and I won't recount those arguments here.

But suffice to say the deterrence criminalization strategy is a failure in part because it can make the likelihood that someone will engage in criminal activity higher.

CRIMINALIZING POVERTY

Targeting people who attempt to take public transportation without paying the user fee is not the only way we criminalize the poor. There are countless examples ranging from cruel to absurd. Each of these laws is a choice that reflects whom we value.

> Good Morning All, I just wanted to let you know that the scheduled cleanup with sanitation will take place on Thursday June 29th. Everyone will be arrested and all their belongings will be taken away by sanitation. . . . As always, do not approach these individuals experiencing homelessness. I want to make sure all are there at the encampment on the 29th so I can arrest them. This is a hush hush task force.

This is a portion of the text of a real email sent by Los Angeles Police Department senior lead officer, Brittney Gutierrez, in June 2023 to residents of Los Angeles's wealthy West Hills neighborhood. It's a crushing admission of the fact that police do not serve all of us and part of their work is the punitive targeting of poor people. In this example, the police are so committed to positioning themselves as an offensive opponent to homeless people, they recruit the wealthy community members in one of the United States' most expensive cities to be their ally in launching an attack against them by preserving the element of surprise.

How can we view this as anything other than outsized loathing for people who find themselves in circumstances in which they have very little?

The sentiments expressed in the email by Officer Gutierrez are not unique. They represent the way police are engaged to harass homeless people throughout our societies. This awful public policy strategy to address homelessness became much more visible in the post-pandemic era. There were several unexpected economic crises caused by the COVID-19 epidemic. I experienced some hardship, and the likelihood is that you did as well. But some of us had it far worse than others. For those who were laid off or made the difficult decision to leave work to preserve their health, the inability to afford expenses

month after month had dire consequences, and government aid
packages might have been helpful but were not able to stem
the tide of disaster. As economic insecurity grew, the ability
to make rent or mortgage payments became increasingly difficult. Evictions skyrocketed. Supply chains and corporate greed
made food unaffordable for some. While some people might
have had resources they could rely on in such circumstances—
emergency funds, family members, and community members—
others were not so lucky.

If one's circumstances were so dire during the pandemic,
there might have been very few options available. Traditional
shelters might have been full—which is always a problem,
pandemic or not—or shuttered for safety. Some people might
have turned to a personal vehicle, if they had access to one, to
serve as a shelter. Those with the fewest resources among us
might have had little choice but to seek shelter in the spaces
we collectively share—public space. Parks, alleyways, boule-
vard medians—spaces one could try to be as safe as possible.
Being in a community with other people where mutual support and sharing of resources is possible could help provide a
measure of safety to one another. It's no wonder that during the
pandemic, tent cities were erected in urban spaces across the
United States, Canada, and the U.K.

Imagine what a difficult circumstance it would be if you
were pushed into homelessness by a system that does not have
supports for all of us. Imagine the upending of everything representing stability in your life. Your immediate circumstance
will require unending strategizing. You will need to deal with
the lack of certainty as to where and what your next meal will
be. How you will plan for weather you cannot survive without
shelter. What you will do if you are sick. Where your backup
locations will be if the one you are currently staying at becomes
unsafe or is raided by police. In addition to your present circumstance, you may also try to strategize as to how to overcome the
situation you find yourself in. How will you make money? Can
you find a place to use as an address so you can apply for jobs? If
you are able to get an interview, will you be able to attend with-

out risking your possessions or the certainty of your next meal? Perhaps you find an organization or government program that may help you. Do you qualify? Do they have space for you? Do you have the proper documentation they require in order to support you? On top of all of that, imagine the emotional toll. Every day, the weight of your circumstance rests heavy on your soul. There is little time for leisure or respite. Average people walk by you every day and avoid your eyes. You have become invisible, somehow. The trauma is crushing.

This is one of the most unsafe, most insecure daily conditions you could find yourself in. And whom are you to call in this nightmare situation? The police are certainly not your ally in safety here.

In fact, the police may come and raid your tent city, taking all your possessions, thwarting all your strategies, physically roughing you up, and forcing you to leave. Because of their actions, your already unsafe situation has become markedly more perilous. Who could argue that the police are acting in the interests of safety when they target and attack homeless people?

Let's break this situation down and examine what's really happening. When a person becomes homeless, it is not simply an individual circumstance. It represents a societal failure. People who have experienced housing precarity have had to contend with regular financial pressures, a system that allows rents and the costs of other necessities to rise faster than wages, compounded by an unexpected life situation, like an underinsured family member needing caretaking. In this scenario, we have the failure of our employment policies to ensure people can earn a living wage interacting with the failure of housing policies to ensure rents do not become a burden interacting with our societal choice to have our needs provided through corporations who care little about their affordability interacting with a failure of our meager or nonexistent employment insurance, medical insurance, pharmaceutical insurance, and pension provisions to do what they are meant to—provide a safety net in these very scenarios.

For someone who has no private space options—whether a purchase, a rental, a motel, or a family member or friend's home—the only thing available is *public* space. And there simply is not a lot of public space available for the purpose of sheltering people. When all other options are exhausted, the only remaining choice is to take up residence in accessible public space not intended for living.

And in all fairness, whether intended for living or not, it *is* public space. It is meant for general use, and we all contribute to its upkeep.

When we then pass laws, ordinances, and bylaws prohibiting people from using public space to survive, ask police to enforce them, and fail to provide alternatives, we are essentially asking unhoused people to *disappear*. We do not want to face the visible reminder of our failure to these members of our community. We would rather try to make them and their struggles invisible.

But whether or not we want to face the consequences of our neglect, we *do* pay for it. When we deploy the police to raid and arrest homeless people, we are taking public funds that could be put toward providing shelter and other services that can support people and instead using those funds to resource attacking them and taking what little they have. We are saying that we value them so little, we would rather spend money making their lives more difficult than making up for the ways our institutions have failed them.

There are so many ways we have decided to criminalize poverty rather than work to eliminate it. Not only do we make it a crime to use public space in a way that results in tent cities and encampments, but we have decided to criminalize asking for support through panhandling or busking, and we've made initiatives to build tiny homes to support people experiencing homelessness unlawful. Take the story of Khaleel Seivwright of Toronto. Mr. Seivwright is a carpenter, and he watched as homelessness ballooned in Toronto during the height of the COVID-19 pandemic. As colder temperatures made outside encampments more dangerous, Mr. Seivwright decided to do what he could. He began an initiative to build tiny homes as shelter for people who needed it. His initiative was widely popular, hitting six-figure support on crowdfunding services in no time.

And then the City of Toronto took him to court to stop him.

He didn't have the right permits, said the city. Mr. Seivwright had been careful with his tiny homes, which he saw as a temporary solution to a problem worsened by the pandemic. His homes were insulated, water-resistant, fire-resistant, fire tested, and fitted with fire and carbon monoxide detectors. The city *could* have spent its resources trying to work with Mr. Seivwright to make sure the tiny homes addressed any concerns and met permit requirements. It could have expanded his quick, temporary solution as it worked on a long-term plan to combat housing insecurity. Instead, consistent with the cruelty of encampment raids police had engaged in with increased frequency since the pandemic began, it took those resources and spent them in court.

Our system is set up so that it pushes those who are the most vulnerable into homelessness at the most difficult times in their lives. Being homeless is itself dangerous and very difficult to overcome, and we have spent resources making nearly impossible any ad hoc initiatives to lessen the burden that individuals experiencing homelessness and their communities attempt. To make matters worse, we have criminalized homelessness, regularly sending in the police to attack encampment communities, confiscate their belongings, and arrest them, making the condition of being homeless even less safe and even less secure.

But do we need police to be involved in homelessness at all? What would it look like if we valued the lives of homeless people? Perhaps rather than deciding to create crimes with the sole purpose of rendering the plight of homeless people invisible, we might try making it impossible to be without shelter. Some reports suggest that it costs three times as much to police homelessness as it would cost to provide homeless people housing. What if we collectively decide to spend the resources we are currently spending on creating further strife for these people on caring for them instead? These questions are exactly the kind we need to ask ourselves in order to strategically increase safety and security conditions for people in our community in a preventative way; we do not need to rely on the reactive response of the police.

I don't want to live in a society where we punish people simply because they have fewer resources than they need. I want to live in a society where we collectively provide one another with what we need to survive. And isn't this one of the clearest ways we can provide safety for one another?

MORALITY POLICING

In chapter 2, we discussed the purposes of policing. Here, I'll expand on how the police forcefully impose cultural morals, whether these are mutually agreed upon or not.

I recall the fervor with which Western media rightfully condemned the actions of the repressive Iranian morality police in their fatal beating of Mahsa Amini in the fall of 2022, may she rest in peace. Ms. Amini was arrested for failing to adhere to rules governing appropriate dress for women, namely wearing a hijab. In discussing the atrocity, Western media spent a lot of time criticizing the morality police as an unconscionable institution in its punishment of women who do not live up to the morality standards of those in power. I agree: The idea of an all-seeing eye policing one's morality is repugnant.

But all police are morality police. It is a central feature of policing.

When police in the United States, Canada, or the U.K. are doling out punishment for drug use, sex work, or even a hungry person's theft of bread, they are engaging in morality policing. The labeling of these activities as crimes does not keep people safe, nor does it stop the behavior. It merely justifies the punishment of these activities based on arbitrary moral standards that reflect the beliefs of people in power. This often includes targeting actions taken by groups historically devalued by society, typically those with marginalized identities.

This has always been the case. It's why we occasionally discover laws on the books that seem appropriate for the cultural morals of another age but out of step with the morals of contemporary society—like the 1931 Michigan law banning "any man or woman, not being married to each other, who lewdly and lasciviously associates and cohabits together." Living together before marriage was considered so morally unacceptable that it was punishable by up to one year in prison. That law was repealed in 2023.

If we are to create a world without police, a world where all of us can live in dignity, without behaviors associated with our identities repressed by police, we must reexamine the ways we currently devalue these communities through our laws and consider whether the associated crimes could simply be eliminated.

Morality Policing: Identity

In July 2015, twenty-two-year-old Meagan Taylor, a Black trans woman, was on her way to a funeral with a friend. On the way, she stopped at an inn in Des Moines, Iowa, for the night. The concierge and manager at the inn treated Ms. Taylor and her friend, another Black trans woman, with hostility and disrespect. Ms. Taylor's official identification listed her gender incorrectly, and this seemed to have set off the inn staff. They told her the prepaid credit card she provided did not work. The staff gave her and her friend dirty looks and asked to photocopy their IDs. Their check-in process took more than half an hour. The two women watched other guests check in for an overnight stay in no more than five minutes. They considered leaving, concerned that the inn staff were prejudiced and could put them in danger. But ultimately, against her gut feeling, Ms. Taylor and her friend decided to stay the night at the hotel. The following day, they were accosted by plainclothes police officers banging at their door.

The manager of the inn had called 911. In an audio recording of the 911 call released by the American Civil Liberties Union, the inn manager describes Ms. Taylor as "someone unusual" and asked if there was a way to discreetly "run their name," since Ms. Taylor and her friend were dressed as women but "had a man's driver's license." She admitted to taking pictures of the women, stating they were "dressed over the top," and she wanted to make sure they "weren't hookers."

Everything about this call suggests that the issue was not that the hotel manager felt unsafe but that she was prejudiced and felt the two Black women themselves were morally objectionable.

Feeling anything but safe, Ms. Taylor and her friend were brought to tears when the police arrived. The police searched Ms. Taylor's belongings, finding hormones she takes. They asked her to produce a prescription for the hormones. Ms. Taylor did not have her prescription with her.

The police arrested Ms. Taylor, leaving her friend to make the rest of her way to the funeral alone. Her bail was set at more than $2,000 and was paid with the help of an online crowdfunding campaign.

A complaint filed against the inn by Ms. Taylor and the ACLU was settled in 2016.

The dehumanization Ms. Taylor experienced at the will of the hotel staff person was aided by the police. Public resources should not be used to support discriminatory action, but if you've read this far, you know that the police have historically and consistently been accomplices to bigotry against women, Black people, queer people, trans people, and people with disabilities who failed to live up to arbitrary anfd often discriminatory moral standards.

In the early twentieth century, police were part of the apparatus implementing harsh punishments to women who did not adhere to expectations of chastity and modesty. Women's desires and personal agency were devalued, and those who did not meet these standards risked losing (more of) their freedom. One of the ways this was operationalized was in the targeting and arrest of women who were suspected of having a sexually transmitted infection (STI). Empowered to enforce women's morality, police would reportedly arrest women who were with men, walking "suspiciously," or just sitting in a restaurant alone.

One day in 1919, "using suspicion as their only guide," a "moral squad" appointed by the chief of police arrested twenty-two women suspected of having sexually transmitted infections in Sacramento, according to an article detailing the incident in *The Sacramento Bee*. The previous year, President Woodrow Wilson signed the Chamberlain-Kahn Act into law, which, among other things, provided funding to states to "[care] for civilian persons whose detention, isolation, quarantine, or commitment to institutions may be found necessary for the protection of the military and naval forces of the United States against venereal diseases." The government believed the spread of sexually transmitted infections among the troops was the fault of sex workers, who were believed to often carry STIs. After being arrested, the women were subjected to humiliating and invasive examinations to test for STIs. Those who tested positive could be incarcerated without due process, tortured, put into solitary confinement, or even sterilized. Sometimes incarceration was mandated even without a positive test. While only one of the women tested positive, *The Sacramento Bee* reported that six of the twenty-two women were "detained over night" and "were not allowed communication with any one."

The targeting of women's morals by police made them less safe and more vulnerable to sexual assault by authorities under the guise of public health. All women were at risk, but women of color and immigrant women were disproportionately targeted. Margaret Hennessey, a white woman, was one of the twenty-two women targeted by police in 1919. As she walked to the meat market in the morning, she and her sister were arrested by police and told that they were "suspicious characters." Ms. Hennessey pleaded with the police. She told them she had a son in school that needed looking after. She offered to give her identification. But the police would not listen to her; she had already been pegged as potentially amoral. She would have to be taken and examined. In an interview, Ms. Hennessey said, "At the hospital, I was forced to submit to an examination just as if I was one of the most degraded women in the world. I want to say I have never been so humiliated in my life. . . . I dare not venture on the streets for fear I will be arrested again." Public health officials claimed that each arrest was valid, because the circumstances in which the women were observed were deemed suspicious.

While society's expectations might have shifted, women are still policed for their morality, in ways that make them less safe. One example of this practice is the treatment of women who use social assistance.

———

Enacted in 1974, the U.S. federal government's Housing Choice Voucher program, sometimes referred to as Section 8, provides financial assistance to low-income people to aid them in securing housing. The government created the program in response to criticisms of public housing projects, which were said to concentrate poverty. Proponents of Housing Choice, through which families whose income was below a certain threshold could obtain vouchers to use on privately owned homes, envisioned a system that allowed recipients choice in where they lived and would result in mixed-income communities. Recipients pay up to 30 percent of the rent of their unit, while a local public housing agency pays the rest. The program is strictly regulated; certain kinds of criminal records could make someone ineligible, and recipients who fail to report their income or violate other terms—like having unauthorized residents— can lose the housing support they so desperately need. The program depends on private landlords being willing to accept Housing Choice recipients as residents.

Housing Choice recipients face discrimination from landlords and community members alike. Landlords often refuse to accept vouchers, with a 2018 study sponsored by the U.S. Department of Housing and Urban Development and conducted by the Urban Institute finding the rate of denial for landlords in Fort Worth, Los Angeles, and Philadelphia to be 78 percent, 76 percent, and 67 percent, respectively. Writing for the American Bar Association, Deputy City Attorney for Santa Monica Gary Rhoades suggests three reasons landlords discriminate against tenants using the Housing Choice Vouchers: (1) a false belief that they may need to reduce their rents; (2) a false belief that they may have untenable administrative burdens; and (3) bigoted concerns about the racial background, economic class, disability status, or other immutable characteristic of the potential tenant, which they use to refuse tenants despite these being protected from discrimination in the Constitution. This latter reason is also the reason community members may fight affordable housing efforts and the use of programs like the Housing Choice Voucher in their communities—the NIMBY (not in my backyard) approach to community development.

The foreclosure crisis, the Great Recession, and the resulting pressure on homeowners made landlords in the 2000s more willing to accept Section 8 recipients as tenants in order to guarantee themselves steady income that could cover their housing costs. Cities like Antioch, California, whose residents were overwhelmingly white, began to change demographically because of this shift. The city's Black population increased from 3 percent in 1990 to 20 percent in 2005.

Mary Scott was a Housing Choice Voucher recipient when she moved to Antioch with her three daughters in 2003. The Black mother and cancer patient had lived in Antioch as a child and thought the quiet community with high-ranking schools would benefit her family. Instead, she found herself harassed by police.

Ms. Scott had a difficult relationship with her partner at the time and had called the police to her home on a few occasions because of domestic disputes. Instead of valuing her life and trying to support her, the police took action against Ms. Scott in an attempt to have her evicted.

In January 2007, police arrived at her door and entered without consent—Ms. Scott had not called them. "This is a nice house. How can you afford a house like this?" one of the officers asked her, suggesting that she did not belong there. She asked if they had a warrant, and the police incorrectly claimed they did not need one because they had an arrest warrant for her partner, who was visiting at the time. They threatened to handcuff her in front of her children and make her lie on the ground if she did not consent to a search. The police continued to search her house after they arrested her partner, who was the father of her children. "You people are always causing something in this neighborhood," they grumbled to her during their search. Though Ms. Scott explained to the police that her partner was not living there, in an apparent attempt to have her Housing Choice eligibility revoked, the police sent word to the local housing authority of his presence as an unauthorized tenant. The officers did not stop there. They also sent a letter to Ms. Scott's landlord, saying that he could be held responsible for criminal activity on his property and letting him know about Ms. Scott's visitor. They then called Ms. Scott's landlord *nearly weekly* from January 2007 to October 2007 to check if he had evicted Ms. Scott.

The local housing authority terminated Ms. Scott's housing voucher following another visit by the police in spring 2007. The decision was reversed and her voucher reinstated after she sought a judicial review of the decision.

In this case, Ms. Scott was a target of the police because she was poor and receiving social assistance. But because she is a woman, she was also morally scrutinized for the man she was spending time with, which opened her up to police harassment and endangered her housing security.

As it turns out, the police actions were part of a coordinated campaign between police officers and Antioch's white residents to push out recipients of the Housing Choice Voucher program. A report issued by the city in 2006 claimed that Antioch's Section 8 residents were problematic, bringing "crime, drugs and disorder to the neighborhood." The city's residents began to systematically target the Black women who were Housing Choice Voucher recipients, collaborating with police to submit complaints against them. Police would place door hangers on homes where they suspected Housing Choice tenants resided, which served as a signal to neighbors to submit complaints against the residents. They focused on the romantic partners of these women, as they did with Ms. Scott, making complaints if they suspected them of having unauthorized tenants. They would engage in surveillance, sitting outside voucher recipients' homes in squad cars. Some complaints submitted by residents focused on the children in the households, perceived as troublemakers for playing basketball in the street and listening to loud music—normal leisure activities for any youth.

These targeted actions were accepted in a community and culture that devalued the Black women who were simply trying to live their lives and needed support to do so. Instead of just providing the support these women needed, the community treated them as though they were undeserving and did everything possible to ensure their eventual eviction. Mary Scott was a named plaintiff in a class-action suit filed in 2008 against the City of Antioch, the Antioch Police Department, and individual officers for discrimination against Black Housing Choice Voucher recipients. Her case was settled in 2012. Though Mary Scott was ultimately able to stay in her home, other women were not so lucky, and the actions of Antioch police officers represent a broader trend of harassment toward women who rely on the welfare system.

The stereotypes of Black women as fraudulent recipients of social assistance, as sexually deviant, and as unsuitable mothers are the cultural myths that bolster activities like those taken by the Antioch police. Women, especially poor women of color and Indigenous women, are deeply scrutinized for the ways they raise their children, and child welfare systems are often destructively and improperly deployed against these women to remove their children from their care. In the aftermath of the overturning of *Roe v. Wade* by the Supreme Court, women in the United States seeking reproductive health resources are also subject to higher scrutiny, with potentially criminal consequences now in place for women who access abortions against the law—with moral arguments as the basis for these anti-abortion laws.

Why do we need police to engage in these ugly enforcements against women? What would a society that valued women's agency and safety look like? What might be the impact of redirecting the resources that were used toward antagonizing Ms. Scott and the other Section 8 recipients who joined in the class-action suit against the City of Antioch? Could we have instead given these women and their families the resources they need to live full, safe lives instead of deploying public resources to prove they are immoral and undeserving of support?

───────

Police have also quite famously been deployed to target gay men, their sexuality considered immoral. In the past, policing that targeted queer people included raids of popular bathhouses and gay bars. This kind of targeting does still continue today, but in ways that focus on gay people who are particularly vulnerable, so as not to upend the sensibilities of a society that might believe institutional discrimination against queer people ended with the legalization of same-sex marriage in Canada in 2005, in the U.K. in 2014, and finally in the United States in 2015.

Consider the Toronto Police Service's Project Marie operation. In 2016, after an undercover operation, the police raided a park in the city's West End, arresting and laying eighty-nine charges against seventy-two people, mostly men. Because it is relatively hidden, Marie Curtis Park was known in the queer community as a safe place to cruise for consensual sexual partners. For six weeks, Toronto Police Service constable Kevin Ward cruised undercover in the bushes, citing men for sexual activity when his cruising was successful. Police also ticketed motorists who were cruising in their cars. "I want anyone engaging in these illegitimate activities to know that this is no longer a safe place for this to happen," said Constable Kevin Ward at the time. "We are going to be at the park every day and we will not be tolerating it."

Constable Ward later pleaded guilty at a disciplinary tribunal to carrying on an inappropriate sexual relationship with a youth group member associated with the Toronto police.

According to reports, youth group member participants are between eighteen and twenty-six years of age.

While the police actions were clearly aimed at behaviors associated with queer people, most of the charges they laid in connection with Project Marie were for trespassing, since the park is closed after midnight—a pretext for targeting an identifiable and marginalized community. Remember, the punitive measure is not just in the charge itself; it is in how the charge and resulting case could affect the rest of one's life, including job prospects, housing, and opportunities for higher education.

For some of these men, cruising in a public park after dark may be the only way they are able to express their sexuality. Our society is not completely welcoming of queer communities, despite progress in certain areas. Some people remain steadfastly homophobic, and queer people are still at higher risk of homelessness and other forms of reprisal due to homophobia. Men who are seeking sexual satisfaction with other men in clandestine ways may be at risk in the communities and institutions they frequent if they express their sexuality openly. Police targeting these men makes them far less safe.

In a society that valued queer identities, would we spend public resources on attempting to trick consenting men into agreeing to have sex with an undercover police officer so that we could then charge them for trespassing? It's absurd that this would be a priority and something the Toronto police proudly announced in a press conference to the city. If we valued the safety of queer people, and if cruising at night is a safety concern for any community, wouldn't a better approach be to make sure there are places where men who have sex with men, and need to do so covertly, would have a place to meet others searching for the same thing safely? Why should we criminalize these behaviors?

Morality Policing: Behaviors

In addition to morality policing focused on identities, police engage in morality policing against specific behaviors. Because of the ways we devalue the people who engage in them, these behaviors have been made criminal. The most urgent criminalized behaviors are those relating to drug use and sex work. We are often told that the laws surrounding sex work are in place to protect the sex worker; the crimes related to drug use are to protect the potential drug user. But the evidence shows that this couldn't be further from the truth. Heavy policing of drug users and sex workers punishes some of the most vulnerable people in our society, and policy makers have known this for years. Society largely accepts this because our culture considers drug use and sex work to be behaviors that land somewhere between indecent and a personal failure on a moral spectrum.

If you approach these issues with concern for the drug user and sex worker and their safety, the plain truth is that policing makes these activities less safe. Criminalizing drug users and sex workers means they will need to hide their activities to continue engaging in them while avoiding criminal sanctions. The more hidden and underground these activities are, the less access the people engaging in them have to spaces and health care that can make these activities safer. If you approach these issues with a moral goal of eliminating these activities from our society altogether, decades of experience tell us that criminalizing and policing these activities will ultimately fail.

The war on drugs has not eliminated drug use. More than a century of criminalizing sex work has not eliminated sex work. Abolitionists take a different view: decriminalize drugs and decriminalize sex work.

Drugs

One of my many jobs as a young adult was as a don (also known as resident adviser) in my undergraduate residence at the University of Toronto. My job was to support fellow students, most of whom were younger than me, in their personal and academic transition from high school to on-campus life. Many of these students were living away from home and being treated as adults for the first time. As a don, I was there nearly around the clock to listen to student concerns and help in a crisis, whether it was an on-campus fight or a harrowing experience with drugs or alcohol.

It's no secret that there is a lot of experimentation on college campuses. From sex to alcohol use to drugs, young people experiencing independence for the first time can be eager to try things that might have been considered vices at home. In Ontario, where the University of Toronto is located, the legal drinking and smoking age is nineteen. Many of the people engaging in substance use on campus, who were freshmen as young as seventeen, were doing so against the law. Dons had different approaches to the way they would deal with these situations. Some saw their role as akin to a community disciplinarian. The approach I took mirrored the one my own don took when I was living in residence for the first time. My don promised students that she would never call the police to report us and that we could come to her for anything without fear of being penalized. If someone was unconscious because they were engaging in illicit activity, she stressed, we were to call her. She would be there for us and do everything she could to keep us safe without getting us in trouble.

I saw firsthand the effect this approach had on students. Students were bound to experiment despite potential consequences, but students whose dons promised confidential support did not try to hide the repercussions of their activities. An attempt to hide when someone is unconscious or is having a physical reaction that requires immediate care could have disastrous and potentially fatal consequences. Dons were trained in first aid, crisis management, and conflict resolution, and were therefore well equipped to help students through the panic of a dangerous situation. Without this support, students would have been on their own—equipped only with the broad knowledge we provided about supporting someone who was intoxicated by drugs or alcohol. I'm glad I was there to support students who needed it, and I'm glad they felt comfortable contacting me.

A similar approach should be used for drug use in broader society.

Whether you agree with drug use or not, what is very clear after decades of prohibition and a disastrously ineffective war on drugs is that a zero-tolerance societal approach does not work and is counterproductive to its purported goal of eliminating drug use. There is no refuting it. Currently, more people in the United States and the U.K. are dying of overdoses than ever before. The war on drugs has failed to protect users from overdose deaths. The number of people arrested and incarcerated for drug-related crimes has ballooned. About a decade into the war on drugs, in 1980, fewer than 600,000 people were arrested for drug abuse violations. By 2019, that number had climbed to more than 1.5 million. Even when people are incarcerated, dangerous drug use continues, with drug and alcohol overdose deaths in prisons increasing by more than 600 percent between 2001 and 2018. Trying to force abstinence on a population through prohibition *will not work*. It did not work for alcohol in the United States and Canada, and it has not worked for drugs.

People will use drugs. Some people will use drugs because the altered state helps with physical or emotional pain. Some lack the insurance or means to access legal drugs to treat their ailments. Some have become physically dependent on prescription medication that they can no longer access. Some people use drugs because they enjoy it. Whatever the reason, people continue to use drugs regardless of the criminal consequences. Fifty years of increasingly punitive drug laws have proven that.

Harsh drug laws have caused significant economic, social, safety, and public and personal health issues for drug users and non–drug users alike. Prohibition doesn't eliminate the sale of illegal substances. It merely ensures that forbidden drugs are available only through underground markets. Just as alcohol prohibition led to the creation of illicit trade operations, which provided access to alcohol when people could not get it legally, drug prohibition encourages the creation of organizations that will service a drug market when the legitimate economy refuses to do so. Those organizations cannot call on regulators, the courts, or police to protect their earnings or assist in dispute resolution like regular businesses. Instead, they engage in their own methods of enforcement outside the legitimate legal system, which fuels violent crime. Multiple studies have shown that increasing prohibitive drug enforcement is positively associated with increases in violent crime (which tells us a little bit about what we need to do if we want to prevent violent crime, but more on that in the following chapter).

Punitive drug laws also prevent street drugs from being screened or controlled for safety. There is no regulator making sure the drugs are not tampered with in ways that make them more dangerous. There is no one to ensure the drugs are at a manageable level of potency. And when the police arrest a street-level supplier, it leaves dependent people who use with no choice but to find another supplier, whose stock may be contaminated or toxic—less safe for the user. The laws that focus on punishing users and suppliers make it so that the majority of resources are going to policing, surveillance, and incarceration, and very few resources are being allocated to treatment that can support health care for people who have a drug dependency.

The U.S. government has spent more than $1 trillion enforcing prohibitive drug policy for nearly half a century. And the only things the war on drugs has been successful at are criminalizing large numbers of Black and Latinx people, fueling the incarceration industry, expanding policing, making drug use far more dangerous than it needs to be, and increasing violent crime.

Then again, perhaps that was always the real purpose of the war on drugs. John Ehrlichman, the domestic affairs adviser to President Richard Nixon and a coconspirator in the Watergate scandal, said as much in an interview with the journalist Dan Baum in 1994:

> You want to know what this was really all about? The Nixon campaign in 1968, and the Nixon White House after that, had two enemies: The antiwar left and Black people. You

understand what I'm saying? We knew we couldn't make it illegal to be either against the war or Black, but by getting the public to associate the hippies with marijuana and Blacks with heroin, and criminalizing both heavily, we could disrupt those communities. We could arrest their leaders, raid their homes, break up their meetings, and vilify them night after night on the evening news. Did we know we were lying about the drugs? Of course we did.

Talk about saying the quiet part out loud.

This is an absolutely stunning admission of what activists had suspected for years. The entire war on drugs was a smoke screen. A convenient scapegoat that could be used to justify state repression of people who opposed the politics and anti-Blackness of the government of the day. It's incredibly rare to get this frank an admission from anyone in power about the real motivations behind laws that end up criminalizing scores of marginalized people. If controlling and vilifying Black people and antiwar activists were the real motivations in this case, we should ask ourselves, How often are policy makers using the police to enact life-destroying strategies like the war on drugs on marginalized communities for motivations entirely different from what they claim?

Nixon's approach has served as a blueprint for how to further marginalize and dehumanize people devalued by society. It's a blueprint that is still followed today, as the war on drugs persists and has stayed true to its original motivations.

The consequences society has instituted for people who are convicted of drug crimes are tantamount to throwing people away. A drug conviction can follow you around for life, even when a prison sentence is complete, making it difficult to obtain housing, social assistance, employment, or admission to college. To eliminate opportunity and social supports for some of the most vulnerable, for people who truly need it, is a cruelty that reveals just how much our society reviles people who use drugs.

So, what would a society that valued people who use drugs look like? How could we set up our institutions to care for the people struggling with the social and health effects of drug use, and to protect people who choose to engage in drug use from becoming harmed by drugs? A simple replacement for the police wouldn't work. We would need to rethink our entire approach to drug use—much like when we reversed the prohibition of alcohol in the early twentieth century.

An approach that would have an immediate effect is to decriminalize drugs. Take police out of the equation. Take incarceration out of the equation. End the billions of dollars per year we spend on failed enforcement measures. Make it impossible to do background checks that block people from services and resources that they need. Eliminate the impetus behind so much violent crime. By doing this, we would increase the level of safety and security among folks who use drugs.

Advocates in some jurisdictions in recent years have been successful in forcing policy makers to take a nonpunitive approach to drug use in programs experimenting with various levels of decriminalization. Despite early success, these programs are already in danger of being defunded and walked back in favor of recriminalization. Take Oregon, for example. In 2020, a ballot measure passed changing the state's approach to engaging with drug users, focusing on partial decriminalization. Police were no longer to arrest drug users, but the program still used police resources. Instead, police issued a $100 citation that could be waived if the recipient entered a drug treatment program. Since being implemented, the program has been discussed as a failure in the press, and police officers have advocated to recriminalize drug users. So, in April 2024, Oregon reversed the policy. Proponents of recriminalization were upset that overdose deaths increased rapidly post-2020; they saw this as a failure of the program. Some even cited the program as its cause, though several researchers have said this isn't the case and instead point to the fentanyl crisis, a health-care system reeling after the pandemic, and a homelessness crisis as exacerbating factors. Less than four years is what this program was given to try to address a drug problem in a crisis situation. Compare that with the decades that policing drug users through the war on drugs has been permitted to fail us and destroy countless Black lives in the process.

Advocates say one of the major issues with the program was its incongruous rollout. The policy was meant to decriminalize drugs *and* increase access to treatment and counseling for drug users. But while partial decriminalization began in 2021, funding for increased treatment only started to be disbursed in May 2022. It would take some time to disburse the funds and set up the new treatment initiatives the program was meant to provide. The timeline between considering a caring approach and falling back on policing was incredible. Oregon did not even allow the approach of pairing treatment with decriminalization to settle in before giving up after little more than a year.

Some activists are stepping in to provide effective services for drug users, at the risk of becoming targets for police action. Take the compassion clubs and safe supply activists in Canada. These programs are led by people who use drugs and take a harm reduction approach to preventing fatalities among drug users. Compassion clubs test drugs to make sure they are safe. Safe supply locations provide access to a safe supply of drugs to remove the risk of toxicity or contamination that the street drug supply may have. Both ideas take police and punishment out of the equation, prioritizing the lives and safety of those using drugs. The programs build on the success of supervised injection sites like Insite, a community-led service in Vancouver born out of the HIV/AIDS epidemic, which today provides drug users immediate access to medical care in the case of an overdose, testing services to ensure substances are not laced, sterile injection equipment to prevent the risk of transmission of infections, and access to mental health, substance use, and primary care health services. The first supervised injection sites in Canada were illegal. Community members and health-care providers risked arrest to ensure the community had access to a service that would keep them safe and wouldn't arrest them. Eventually, through this activism, Canada was pressured to decriminalize this approach, and in 2003 supported Vancouver's Insite, the first legal supervised injection site in North America. Since then, more than six thousand overdoses have been attended to and millions of injections supervised at Insite. No fatalities have occurred there. They don't encourage drug use, nor do they pass judgment on their clients. And they save lives. Similar activism resulted in Canada's first legal safe supply program in 2020, allowing safe supply programs to operate legally in cities across the country.

Given the success of these programs at providing treatment options that keep people safe and alive, how do we then reckon with the actions of police that aim to interrupt them? In Vancouver, access to a compassion club, the Drug User Liberation Front (DULF), that was providing rigorously tested access to heroin, cocaine, and meth for drug users was interrupted when police raided its two founders in October 2023. The compassion club was not legal; much like the activists who advocated for supervised injection sites and safe supply programs, the community-led program operates as a form of civil disobedience, filling a gap where policy makers have failed. The raid caused DULF to cease operations; a condition of the release of the two founders after their arrest was that they not communicate with each other or physically visit the compassion club. Because of the police actions, the compassion club members who relied on the services DULF provided no longer have access to a non-toxic drug supply. In a report by the British Columbia online news source *The Tyee*, one affected user said they first used fentanyl after the police raid forced the closure of DULF. The former compassion club user described how no longer having access to DULF's safe supply of heroin forced them to turn to street fentanyl to avoid withdrawal. In this case, the police made dozens of people who relied on DULF's services more unsafe. In May 2024, the two founders of DULF were charged with possession for the purpose of trafficking. In October 2024, they filed a constitutional challenge, stating their criminalization is a violation of the Canadian Charter of Rights and Freedoms. Their criminal trial has been set for October 2025.

Remember: Criminalization is a *choice*. Drugs were not always criminalized. The United States, Canada, and the U.K. began criminalizing drugs in the early twentieth century, and a major driver for each country was the popularity of opium, a drug associated at the time with Chinese migrants. The first drug prohibition laws were passed in Canada in 1908, in the United States in 1914, and in the U.K. in 1920, each focusing on opium and each driven by xenophobia against Chinese migrants. That our societies are still struggling with ineffective policy born out of racism and more effective at racial discrimination than keeping people safe is shameful. We can and should choose a different path.

Sex Work

We can think of sex work similarly.

Whether you agree with sex work as a legitimate profession or not, a prohibitionist approach has not worked to curb the sale of sex. Instead, all it's done is make sex work riskier for the workers, putting them in more vulnerable circumstances than they would be if their profession was not a crime.

The way sex work is criminalized differs across jurisdictions. In the U.K., sex work is technically legal, but sex workers are criminalized if they advertise sexual services or solicit clients on the street, from their vehicle, or in other public places. It is also illegal to own or manage a brothel, and it is a crime to be a pimp or madam. Clients are criminalized if they seek sexual services in a public place or if they promise to pay for sex with a sex worker who has been forced or threatened into performing this labor. In Canada, sex work is also technically legal, in that it is legal to sell sex, but like in the U.K. it is a crime to run a brothel or be a pimp or madam. It is also a crime to purchase sex, for a business to profit from sex, and to have communications about buying sex. In the United States, state law governs sex work, but it is a crime in virtually all states except Nevada.

Like drugs, sex work was not always criminalized. Today's sex work laws have their root in the mid-nineteenth-century movement to abolish sex work, a crusade which was birthed in Europe and quickly spread to Canada and the United States. The argument then, as it often is now, was moral. Seen as a sin, sex work was something to eliminate, and sexually transmitted infections were the divine punishment. The vigor with which police arrested women who did not meet moral standards, as discussed earlier in this chapter, was related to this movement to abolish sex work. The means for eliminating the presumed evil of sex work included shuttering brothels, "rehabilitating" former sex workers—a euphemism for imprisoning and quarantining them—and punishing men who sought to purchase sex. Opponents of the abolitionist movement advocated for regulation, but England's regulation program in the nineteenth century was oppressive and cruel: women were subjected to forced STI tests, arrested for failing to register as sex workers with government authorities, and incarcerated for having or being suspected of having an STI.

The rhetorical strategy that ultimately won the campaign for sex work abolitionists around the world was the insistence that white women must be saved from slavery. At the time, significant immigration was taking place across Canada and the United States. There was a widespread xenophobic and anti-Semitic belief that Italian, eastern European, Chinese, and Jewish immigrants were kidnapping Anglo-Saxon white women and forcing them into sex work; respectable white women would never have chosen such a sinful profession of their own volition, the reasoning suggested. By the early twentieth century, the successful campaign against so-called white slavery resulted in the League of Nations, precursor to the United Nations, pursuing the abolition of sex work around the globe.

Much like with drugs, abolition was never achieved. Despite the moral discomfort that surrounds it, sex work persists. Countries around the world are rethinking prohibitionist laws that have criminalized sex workers, but the moral discomfort with legalizing sex work that spawned its criminalization just over a century ago also persists.

Proponents of maintaining prohibitionist sex work laws claim that these laws protect vulnerable women from exploitation, protect against human trafficking, and support public health by preventing the spread of sexually transmitted infections. But sex workers themselves disagree with these conclusions, insisting that the enforcement of these laws by police makes them more vulnerable and punishes them for their profession.

In a system in which sex workers are criminalized, clients seeking sex are aware that they may be able to steal from, assault, or force themselves on sex workers and get away with it. Because sex workers are not able to report these crimes without fear of reprisal, malicious clients mistreat them with impunity. Victims and survivors of human trafficking are also negatively affected by criminalization. Not only is it difficult to seek help due to the fear of arrest, trafficking victims and survivors are regularly arrested, with one study suggesting that trafficked people are arrested an average of seven times during their exploitation.

And police are among the most notorious perpetrators of sexual violence against sex workers. An investigative study by *The Buffalo News* found that every five days a police officer in the United States is caught engaging in sexual misconduct. An equally upsetting piece by *Vice* reports that police officers working undercover are sometimes engaging in intimate activities with sex workers just before revealing themselves and making an arrest. The police who engage in these exploitative and abusive behaviors target people disincentivized to report them, both for fear of being arrested and because of an understanding that police are unlikely to face consequences for their misconduct.

Regardless of whether you personally agree with sex work as a profession, people continue to choose it. As with any other job, some sex workers enjoy the work. For some, the money is good. Others choose sex work because of discrimination they face in other jobs, or because alternative choices are not suitable. Regardless of the *why*, we still need to ask the question: What would a world that valued sex workers look like?

Again, eliminating police from the equation would make sex workers safer, ensuring that they can be financially secure, have access to health care, and organize with other sex workers to improve labor conditions.

If we approach these issues from the angle of a service and value the people who engage in behaviors like drug use and sex work, we can look to other services to see how regulation rather than policing and criminalization can more effectively keep our society safe. Services like health care, education, and access to alcohol and tobacco are regulated for the betterment of society. We can look to these services for inspiration as to how regulation can protect both individuals and the broader public.

For both drug use and sex work, a public health and community empowerment approach focused on preventing drug dependency, treating adverse effects when they arise, and keeping people healthy would be markedly better than what we are doing now. A society that values people who use drugs and engage in sex work will provide safe ways for people to engage in these activities—for the workers as well as the community. It will focus on ensuring that the public is well educated on sex, sexual health, drugs, and drug safety, which can help with safe individual decision making. It will ensure every person has access to health care. It will think about how to address the collective emotional and economic difficulties that might lead people who would rather not use drugs or engage in sex work to feel as though they have little choice.

The simple truth is we label social problems and behaviors crimes and leave it to the police to resolve them when the people most affected are not priorities. This is a matter of framing. Our society engages with marginalized communities as if we don't matter. An abolitionist approach requires that we refuse to discard and devalue whole communities. We have to deal with the entire system of rules, values, and institutions that require policing to operate. We don't need to designate so many behaviors as criminal. We can instead take an approach that recognizes the value in building real solutions, rather than lazily leaving it to a militarized force that was never intended to provide solutions in the first place. If we're serious about creating a safer society, we must understand that this is about more than just the police. We have a lot of work ahead of us.

"I CAN HEAR HER BREATHING"

Another world is not only possible, she is on her way. On a quiet day, I can hear her breathing.

—Arundhati Roy

After the unprecedented deluge of protests in 2020, police and their supporters began constructing their dams. The backlash to the progress protesters and activists made has been swift, heartbreaking, and in some cases unfathomable. Just as it took decades to confirm that law enforcement, individuals, and even governmental institutions conspired to crush Black civil rights and liberation movements, we may have to wait to know the complete picture of how those with power conspired to crush an idea that caught hold in the summer of 2020: that we might be collectively safer without police.

Despite attempts to paint it as a fringe movement, defunding the police is a powerful and popular idea. It has caught hold of the imagination of many who are curious about the deep and necessary work of reorganizing our societies. But because the idea of abolishing police threatens the way our society is set up—which may be just what we need—those who rely on maintaining the status quo to hold on to power have fiercely opposed it. This hopeful idea has been met with brutal repression by the police themselves, including the cruel silencing of activists. (The irony being, of course, that the outsized response makes the virtue of the idea all the more plain.) But perhaps the most outrageous example of how the idea of defunding the police has rattled police officers and their supporters is evident in the plans for Atlanta's Cop City.

In 2021, with the approval of the Atlanta City Council, the city's mayor, Keisha Lance Bottoms, and the Atlanta Police Foundation, a private, nonprofit organization dedicated to supporting the city's police department, announced an initiative to build a massive police training compound in the three-hundred-acre Weelaunee Forest (colonized as the South River Forest following the dispossession of the land of the Muscogee Creek Nation). The residents around the area where the site is planned are primarily Black. The plans would destroy critical ecological sites, including wetlands and parts of the Weelaunee Forest, a watershed. The training plans include an intensification of militarized tactics police would then use against civilians. The land has a violent history, once housing a massive plantation and later continuing the tradition of enslaved labor when it housed the Old Atlanta Prison Farm from 1920 to 1990, which used unwaged inmate labor and where inmates were subjected to rape, whippings, malnutrition, and slave-like conditions. The Atlanta Public Safety Training Center, dubbed Cop City by opponents, is intended to be the largest police training facility in the United States at a cost of $90 million—$31 million of which would be provided by public dollars from the City of Atlanta. Under the plan, Atlanta would then lease the facility back from the Atlanta Police Foundation at a cost of $1.2 million per year.

The Atlanta City Council approved the Cop City initiative in September 2021, the same month in which a wrongful death lawsuit was filed against the city by the family of Rayshard Brooks, may he rest in peace. Mr. Brooks was a Black man killed by Garrett Rolfe, an officer of the Atlanta Police Department. The police were responding to a 911 call that was placed when Mr. Brooks fell asleep in the drive-through lane of a fast-food restaurant.

When the police arrived, Mr. Brooks moved his car out of

the line, apparently resolving the initial complaint. Suspecting that Mr. Brooks was intoxicated, the police then engaged him in a lengthy questioning, in which he admitted to having had drinks that night and offered to leave his car where it was and walk to where he was residing on his own. During the conversation, the police appeared most interested in catching Mr. Brooks contradicting himself, seeming to take pleasure when he appeared confused about the street he was on and when he first insisted he drank nothing but a margarita and later insisted he drank nothing but a daiquiri.

If the officers who encountered Mr. Brooks had been more concerned with his safety than his punishment, perhaps they could have offered him a safe ride home or allowed him to walk to where he was staying on his own. Instead, the police strategy led them to kill Mr. Brooks and put all the people at the fast-food restaurant in danger. Mr. Brooks was patted down, interrogated, and underwent a field sobriety test and then a Breathalyzer test. When Officer Rolfe asked Mr. Brooks to put his hands behind his back, he panicked and struggled to get away. In the ensuing struggle, Mr. Brooks grabbed the Taser of another police officer, who had unholstered it. Mr. Brooks managed to break free from the officers and tried to run away, turning once to fire the Taser. Despite police rhetoric that Tasers are safe, "less lethal" weapons, and despite recently being trained in de-escalation techniques, Officer Rolfe responded to Mr. Brooks's firing of his colleague's Taser by firing his gun at Mr. Brooks as he ran, hitting him in the back twice and killing him. The City of Atlanta and Mr. Brooks's family settled the wrongful death lawsuit in 2022.

From the very beginning, this situation could have been handled differently. Is an emergency response necessary for someone asleep in a stationary car, obstructing a fast-food drive-through line? It was an unnecessary escalation with a fatal result, and the incident underscores how interactions with police officers evoke fear in those caught in their purview. Senator Raphael Warnock, the senior pastor at Ebenezer Baptist Church, remarked at Mr. Brooks's funeral that he "wasn't just running from the police. He was running from a system that makes slaves out of people. This is much bigger than the police. This is about a whole system that cries out for renewal and reform."

———

I don't have all the answers. I am comfortable admitting that.

What lies ahead to rectify the curse of policing is monumental. We cannot simply repeal and replace policing and expect whatever it is replaced with to somehow be different when our entire political apparatus, the way our institutions are set up, and the way our economy works are bolstered and supported by the way policing operates. In order to make any headway on all the problems policing presents for so many communities, it will require a reorganization of several institutions, a shake-up in how we value different kinds of people, a shift in how we culturally understand the concepts of safety and security, and political will.

The task is perhaps daunting, seemingly too big or impossible. The monumental lift it would take to shift all these things will require a veritable mass movement of people committed to the idea that we can and must do better. Despite the difficulty of the task, when I look around at my family and my loved ones and think of all the lives that have been interrupted because of policing, I am resolute: We are worth the effort. Every Black life, and our communities that are made to suffer under the most urgent repercussions of policing. For all communities routinely harmed by policing—we are worth it. For the majority of people for whom policing does not work to provide safety or conflict resolution—we are all worth it. The journey to safer societies may be arduous, but it is possible. In fact, I believe this task is not only possible but inevitable. The question that faces us now is how we want to relate to the transformation that is already occurring.

In the aftermath of the 2020 uprisings, my friend Nora Loreto and I had a conversation about policing on our podcast, *Sandy & Nora Talk Politics*, in which we declared victory—that abolitionists had already won the campaign to eliminate policing. Both of us had been doing abolitionist work for years, sometimes together, sometimes apart. What we meant when we said we had won was that 2020 had fundamentally shifted the way scores of people understood the dangers of policing and its anti-Black, racist consequences. That knowledge cannot be reversed. We cannot go back to a world that allows most people to live in blissful ignorance of the often-fatal anti-Black racism our tax contributions fund. That knowledge can transform into political will if communities are presented with options they can support. Finding those strategies is now our task.

There are two principles that I suggest we keep in mind as we think through ideas. First, those of us who suffer under our current system—ourselves, our families, our friends, and our communities as a whole—deserve a courageous commitment to eliminate the dangers of policing. All the stories I have mentioned in this book in which people are victims of a violent and often fatal system of policing represent countless more, and none of them were inevitable. All of them were the result of a system in which the victims at the center of each case were devalued—not important enough to force the political will of those in power. The abuses they endured have far-reaching consequences, with the trauma forever changing their families, friends, witnesses, and communities. Black people and others who are the systematic targets of police violence deserve our attention.

The second principle is that we do not need all the answers to build something new. Oftentimes, when I do workshops or interviews, I am asked to describe what I would replace policing with and how the new society would work. I've come to understand that this question is most often rhetorical; the people asking me this in the final twenty seconds of a five-minute interview or even the final fifteen minutes of a two-hour keynote don't necessarily expect me to describe the intricacies of a new society. They expect me to admit defeat, and to perhaps be vindicated in their own feeling of powerlessness in the face of such a massive obstacle.

But this is an unreasonable request. Not a single institution in our current societal formation was envisioned to perfection prior to its implementation. Think about some of the crucial issues of the present day. We have not yet figured out a perfect way out of the climate crisis, and yet we are implementing policies in an attempt to move in the right direction. We have not figured out how to protect against the ways artificial intelligence could be used as a tool of deception or could result in a radical shifting of our economy, and yet jurisdictions around the world are attempting to implement safeguards to protect people, and unions are struggling to implement collective agreements that protect their workers. During the early days of the COVID-19 pandemic, before we understood the virus, jurisdictions took immediate action to implement policies to protect society.

Our political systems are predicated on having regular reviews of policy, leadership, and bureaucracy so that year after year we can try to make our society better based on the failings and successes we have experienced during the previous period. Policing as it looks today has evolved from how it looked at the end of the eighteenth century and has been up for amendment since its very first year. Why would we expect that we have all the answers now? As with everything else we build in our society, change begins with commitment and curiosity. We must *want* to eliminate what does not work and try to build something that does. It is dangerous to continue to put off the rigorous thought, debate, and hard work necessary to build the institutions of tomorrow and leave in place an institution as utterly devoid of humanity as policing. The idea that we cannot reimagine safety structures through our existing processes is one of several ways policing obstructs our democracies.

The repression police and prosecutors are imparting on the people demonstrating their opposition to Atlanta's Cop City is a tragic example of the ways police respond to democratic activities using authoritarian measures. Since the Cop City compound has been announced, opponents to it have participated in and organized a variety of strategies to have their voices heard. Prior to the Atlanta City Council approving the project, more than eleven hundred residents made public comments, about 70 percent of which opposed the project. The Atlanta City Council approved the project anyway. Environmental activists concerned about the destruction of forestland united with activists concerned about the expansion of policing to hold weeks of action throughout 2021. When the city council failed to respond to the overwhelming opposition to the project, Muscogee Indigenous people led activists to set up camp in the forest to prevent the project's construction, bestowing the name the Weelaunee People's Park on the camp. While the encampment was ongoing, protesters engaged in other peaceful protests, petitions, and sit-ins in an attempt to have the decision reversed. Police responded by raiding the park, destroying community gardens, and using chemical weapons and rubber bullets against peaceful protesters. By the end of 2022, police began arresting protesters, slapping the activists with felony charges of domestic terrorism.

In January 2023, police shot and killed beloved twenty-six-year-old Indigenous activist Tortuguita, may they rest in peace. Tortuguita's autopsy report, uncovered by ABC News, revealed at least fifty-seven gunshot wounds. Police allege they were returning fire, and that Tortuguita shot at them first, but according to the autopsy report there was no gunshot residue on Tortuguita's hands. On audio released three weeks after Tortuguita was killed by the Atlanta Police Department, a police officer is heard suggesting that the initial shot officials had attributed to Tortuguita might have come from the police themselves. Another autopsy commissioned by Tortuguita's family revealed they had their hands up while they were being shot and were likely seated cross-legged when police decided to unleash a barrage of bullets. It's hard to deny that Tortuguita's death was anything less than an extrajudicial political assassination. None of this would have happened if the democratic will of the people of Atlanta was respected over the will of those in power to continue the unfettered and unending expansion of policing. How can the Atlanta City Council justify deciding to enrich the Atlanta Police Foundation and to spend the tens of millions of dollars it has allocated to this project in the face of clear opposition from its constituents? Following Tortuguita's assassination, protests intensified, at times becoming violent. Court documents suggest the City of Atlanta and the Atlanta Police Foundation are spending $41,500 per day to police the site.

As of September 2023, more than sixty people have had criminal charges filed against them under the Georgia Racketeer Influenced and Corrupt Organizations Act—RICO charges. Usually reserved for criminal enterprises conspiring for profit, the harsh charges appear to be aimed at deterring opponents of Cop City from continuing their democratic engagement in opposition of the project.

In a world where political representatives can flippantly ignore the will of their constituents, send in police to crush First Amendment rights, charge people engaging in peaceful protest with domestic terrorism, and protect police who execute peaceful demonstrators voicing their opposition to an undemocratic process, can we say we live in a democracy?

Those who know me well will know that while I tend to be an optimist about many things, I am hopelessly pessimistic about democracy. I don't know that we have an example of democracy that actually works, and much of what we call democracy seems to me to be lip service rather than a real attempt to have people determine their own fates. That said, I don't think our attempts at participatory democracy should be discarded. The brave people interrupting their own lives as a sacrifice to support the Stop Cop City movement are not only struggling against the scourge of policing but also facing policing's attempt to silence them; a force of a so-called democratic society's own creation would rather the process go forward without considering their voices.

Countless people across the world faced the same ugliness from policing when we collectively mobilized against police brutality and anti-Black racism. When we encountered the police, they attacked and brutalized us in an attempt to quash our ideas. Police are deployed in this way whenever there is a mass movement seeking to make a fundamental change in the way our societies function, when those in power would rather not hear us. Policing itself is antidemocratic in its forceful attempt to destroy the ways we can peacefully struggle with one another to build better communities.

Understanding that we do not need all the answers in order to build something better is a principle that is fundamentally democratic; it assumes our human ability to come together and refuse to accept treachery as a consolation prize for lack of perfection. It's a principle that believes in our capacity to chart a new path that insists on being better, even when we haven't figured out where that new path will lead us. And don't we deserve to collectively determine our future? To build communities that support the safety and security of all of us, we need to ask ourselves some big questions.

SAFETY AND SECURITY

What would we do if we were to start from scratch? What is it that we really want? We want our community to be safe, and we want our community to be secure in that safety. If that is our ultimate goal, what would we need to do to support that? Could we focus on prevention of harm rather than on our current focus on catching perpetrators and punishing them? If we were oriented toward prevention, what could we build? What is it that makes wealthier communities safe, if it is not police? What makes people safe? What makes people secure?

Perhaps the best place to start is defining those two concepts. Our common understanding of "safe" is a condition of being that prevents us from experiencing danger or injury. The condition is metaphysical. When I feel most safe, I have the space and comfort to express my true self. Safety permits us to develop a liberated version of ourselves and allows us to express an actualization of our identities and desires. But the condition itself is not entirely knowable. How can one truly know for certain that one is protected from danger or injury? When we invoke the concept of safety, we are signifying a condition through which we can navigate life and its unexpected variables while still being able to express the trueness of our being.

Security, on the other hand, is about the expectation of safety. Can we expect to feel secure in the conditions of safety we've created? The concept of security is about how sustainable the condition of safety is. What makes us secure are the systems and institutions and structures we establish to protect conditions of safety. I feel secure in my home. I feel secure in my parents' home. I feel less secure using public transit. The structures and institutions in which we live are the measure through which we solidify our expectations of safety. Through these institutions, ideally, we enhance our individual and communal ability to anticipate being safe. In our current society, these institutions include policing, law enforcement, and the entire criminal justice apparatus.

Notice that the concepts of both safety and security require proactivity. Both concepts are about creating spaces and communities within which we have a level of comfort and regularity through which we can simply *be*. For wealthier, whiter communities, the conditions of safety are very often proactively taken care of through resources. Of course, financial resources are the most obvious part of that, but what is it that those resources purchase that makes those communities safe? The list is endless: reliable shelter, food security, access to preventative and curative health care, education, economic security, access to safe leisure, access to child care, access to elder care. Each of these things creates safer communities for the people who live in them. In these communities, policing serves as a reactive, seldom used tool to remove, resolve, or otherwise address a threat should one of the resources fail. But for poorer communities lacking resources, there are very few—if any—proactive conditions that allow people to live freely. Therefore, any system based on response has already failed; the threats to safety are endemic to poorer communities. And it's not hard to see why.

If we want to remove these endemic threats to safety, we have to start where they begin and focus on prevention. Could we eliminate the incentive for theft by ensuring economic stability rather than the failed option of deterrence through punishment? Can we ensure the safety of urban spaces by guaranteeing everyone access to shelter and enough space to live with dignity? How would communities change if they knew that children would be well cared for and safe? How would they change if they knew that there would always be time and opportunity for safe leisure? What if we eliminated poverty as one of our primary strategies for creating security in society? Just imagine how such an orientation could eliminate a strong incentive to engage in informal economies and take other extraordinary measures that affect the safety of whole communities.

MENTAL HEALTH

For the odd situation that cannot be solved through deep preventative strategies, people should have access to professionals who can actually help. Several communities and other countries have had success implementing police-free mental health emergency services. We should think about expanding these ideas to address other threats to safety people experience that would not open them up to the dangers policing does. What is stopping us from building a victim-centered emergency service that can support victims of domestic, gender-based, and sexualized violence? We have created ambulatory and fire emergency response systems; can we think of what other community-based, supportive responses would be helpful in times of emergencies?

Some places have already been building these services. Portland Street Response, a first-responder program, is a nonpolice response to mental health crises anyone can access between the hours of 8:00 a.m. and 10:00 p.m. through calling 911 and requesting it. It has been operating throughout the City of Portland since March 2022 and provides callers with access to mental health specialists, medics, and community health workers. The service provides unarmed, civilian support to people experiencing or witnessing distress in a public space, including mental health crises, intoxication, or yelling. The service is not currently available to people inside a private residence and requires that there be no weapons, violence, or obstruction of traffic involved.

The program partnered with Portland State University for independent evaluation—something I have never seen with any policing program. Its Year Two Evaluation report showed positive results. The Portland Street Response service responded to more than seven thousand calls, and only one, co-responded to by police, resulted in an arrest. Recipients of the service are provided with immediate support including but not limited to medical services, food, and clothing and are also provided with follow-ups for housing, medical treatment, and financial support. The service has even found ten recipients permanent housing. In a survey conducted by the evaluation team, anonymous recipients of the service described their experience with the service in a way that lays bare the difference between Portland Street Response and the police:

> What I liked about my initial contact with them is they were really very non-judgmental. You know what I mean? They didn't seem to come out with the attitude of, "Oh, well, this guy's got mental health issues," which I do, "and he's throwing a fit out here." They come out with a little bit more compassion and like, "Hey man, what's going on? So this is what we heard. What's really happening and how can we help?" And it was nice that 911 didn't just show up and start barking orders and acting like I was out there doing something illegal.

Clients also described what it was about the service that was particularly meaningful to them:

> They still come by and go bring me food box and see how am I doing. They're still working with me with my mental health trying to find me to provide primary care for my mental and for medical. And they've made life a lot easier through this transition.

She stuck with me . . . brought food and clothes and blankets and all, made sure I had that. And well, she just kept coming every day. And one day, she came and well she got me into the motel over there for a few days.

This program has been a resounding success, with recommendations to expand and entrench the program with each evaluation. Unfortunately, unlike policing, the program is already in danger, facing hiring freezes and budget cuts. Why would we defund a compassionate program that is working rather than expand it?

A similar program launched in Albuquerque has been lauded as a massive success. The Albuquerque Community Safety Department has received nearly fifty thousand calls for service, with more than half diverted from the police. The service is now operational around the clock, having expanded to twenty-four-hour service in August 2023. In addition to the Community Safety program, Albuquerque's strategy includes a violence prevention program, referring recipients to peer support, housing, transportation, counseling, and other services to support their needs.

In my hometown, after years of activism and protests, the City of Toronto, in partnership with the Gerstein Crisis Centre, created the Toronto Community Crisis Service in 2022 as a new emergency response service available to residents in 60 percent of the city. The Gerstein Crisis Centre has provided equity-based crisis services to Torontonians since 1989 and prioritizes hiring people who have experience living with a mental health condition or an addiction. In addition to diverting appropriate calls from 911, the Toronto Community Crisis Service can be reached through an entirely new crisis support line—211—in which people receive twenty-four-hour support for mental health needs and crises. Like the Portland and Albuquerque services, the program provides immediate civilian support in the form of social workers, nurses, and other community support workers, and provides follow-ups within forty-eight hours for additional services to those who need it. The nonpolice service is trauma informed, community based, and committed to wellness, and works specifically with Black and Indigenous community groups to develop responses that avoid anti-Blackness and anti-Indigeneity in its service provision. In 2023, the city council unanimously voted to expand the nonpolice emergency response service to the entire city, a testament to the incredible success of what residents call Toronto's fourth emergency service.

In 2023, London's Metropolitan Police announced an expansion of a similar program implemented by Humberside police, in which emergency calls are triaged and diverted to nonpolice services in cases of mental health crises. As of November 2023, Met Police will no longer be the primary service provided for people experiencing mental health crises.

These programs are proliferating slowly, but while implementing these responsive programs, we cannot forget to put energy into preventing mental health crises in the first place. While completing my studies, I remember being incredibly frustrated at the way mental health issues were discussed and addressed by college and university administrators. Strategies often included providing students with inadequate services, such as a limited number of hours of counseling, and services that bordered on the insultingly absurd, such as a day when puppies or ponies would be brought to campus for students' enjoyment. What I found most baffling was that administrators were unwilling to discuss some of the roots of student stress and mental health concerns—a lack of access to the funds to afford education, mounting student debt, and the impossibility of maintaining competitive grades while working. I wondered why these administrators didn't want to face the obvious truth: Students will continue to face mental health crises if the affordability of education continues to worsen unaddressed.

We cannot make the same mistake in society at large. Lack of attention to preventative strategies is partly responsible for the way our societies have lazily passed off the responsibility for safety to police. To make sure these new police-free mental health strategies thrive, they should be paired with preventative strategies aimed at addressing the societal origins of mental health problems.

ROAD USE, TRAFFIC, AND BYLAWS ENFORCEMENT

In April 2021, a mere ten miles from where convicted murderer and former police officer Derek Chauvin was on trial for the murder of George Floyd in Minnesota, a young Black father, twenty-year-old Daunte Wright, may he rest in peace, was killed by Brooklyn Center Police Department officer Kimberly Potter. She and another officer pulled Mr. Wright over for minor traffic violations—expired tags and an air freshener hanging from his rearview mirror. Yes, in Minnesota, it is illegal to hang items from a rearview mirror, an outrageous law that provides police with the cover to make pretextual stops. Upon stopping Mr. Wright, the police realized he had a warrant out for his arrest for failing to appear in court for a nonviolent misdemeanor weapons charge. They decided to arrest him. Regardless of what you think of these facts, none of them are punishable via death sentence, the exact consequence Daunte Wright suffered. While the police were engaged with him, Mr. Wright stepped back into his car, and Potter pulled out her handgun, shouting, "I'll tase you! I'll tase you! Taser! Taser! Taser!" just before fatally shooting him. Kimberly Potter was convicted of first- and second-degree manslaughter, and Mr. Wright's family and the City of Brooklyn Center settled a civil wrongful death lawsuit in connection with the homicide for $3.25 million.

There are countless cases of traffic stops that end in killing by police—some of which are likely familiar to you. I discussed Philando Castile's case, which occurred in Minnesota, in chapter 3. There's Memphis's Tyre Nichols, whom I briefly discussed in chapter 5. In Brampton, Canada, there's Jermaine Carby, also discussed in chapter 5. And then there's the case of Sandra Bland, found dead in a Texas jail cell after being detained and held for three days for a minor traffic violation. None of these people should have been subject to an execution as a result of traffic enforcement, which raises the question: Why is traffic enforcement an issue dealt with by armed police officers? Because of the broad powers that police have on roadways, motorists are often stopped for very minor traffic issues, which increases danger. The way that police approach traffic services is not only an affront to personal security; their interactions can lead to obstructions, high-speed chases, and firefights that endanger bystander motorists. And yet traffic stops are the most common reason people come in contact with police officers in the United States.

The cost of police continuing this work is far too high.

And we do not require them for traffic enforcement.

Roads are dangerous. According to the Centers for Disease Control and Prevention, in the United States, road traffic injuries are the leading cause of unnatural death, and the third leading cause of unintentional injury deaths in Canada, per Parachute, Canada's national charity dedicated to injury prevention. There are a few approaches we could take to try to make roads safer, and the laziest is handing the responsibility over to a militarized group that has no effect on road safety. Roads would be safer, for instance, if there were simply fewer vehicles on them, decreasing the opportunity for human error or irresponsible actions by drivers. That means enacting policy that would result in fewer people operating motor vehicles overall. This would require an increase in access to cheap, reliable, and frequent public transportation, with numerous convenient access points. It would mean providing infrastructure for the safe use of bikes and nonmotorized single-occupancy vehicles through separate bicycle lanes. It means providing multiple affordable public transportation options, like bike shares, buses, and light-rail transit. It means creating a society where people can afford to live closer to the places where they work. Much of the funding to make sure that these options are available can come from the funding that is currently going toward violent traffic enforcement through policing.

Even with these strategies, our societies still need ways to make sure motor vehicle transportation is as safe as possible.

In addition to reducing the number of people using motorized vehicles, we can employ traffic-calming strategies that are more effective at preventing road accidents than the failed deterrent strategy of having police lie in wait to chase singular vehicles that have already made traffic more dangerous through their actions. Traffic-calming strategies rely on physical infrastructure designs that are proven to support safer driving. Some examples include speed bumps, the use of roundabouts, narrower lanes, separated bicycle lanes, reduced lanes, raised crosswalks for pedestrians, chicanes, and additional trees as visual markers that help tell motorists how fast they are driving. Notice again that these strategies are based on prevention— taking care of the danger of motor vehicles *before* they can lead to injury and death. These are strategies that require multi-year political action to implement and cannot be achieved by police.

Some advocate for automated machines like speed cameras as ways to eliminate police interaction with motorists. I disagree with these measures. They are akin to having automated police, increase punitive surveillance, are based on a punishment rather than prevention model, and engage only once the danger has *already occurred*. We can save automation for things that *support* us, like vehicle registration renewal—eliminating a reason for police stops. But we should avoid punitive measures focused on trapping people who need to drive.

We can address some issues through the elimination of unnecessary laws and regulations as discussed in chapter 6. For example, several jurisdictions in the United States and Canada have eliminated the need for registration stickers on license plates, one of the reasons Mr. Wright was pulled over before being killed. According to the Pennsylvania Department of Transportation, eliminating registration stickers was supported by a study conducted at Penn State University showing that the measure has "no impact on vehicle registration compliance" and saved Pennsylvania taxpayers upward of $3 million per year.

We can address other issues through a reorientation of how

we approach vehicle safety, from compliance and punishment to correction and support. Instead of seeing the roadway as a revenue generator for jurisdictions that make money from the fees and fines levied on drivers who break rules or engage in unsafe practices, could we focus on keeping our roads as safe as possible? When a motorist has a broken taillight, broken mirror, or other violation, an unarmed civilian traffic safety service could support motorists through correcting the issue so that everyone using the roadway is safer. Some jurisdictions issue what are called fix-it tickets, where motorists can commit to solving a vehicle deficiency by a particular date, rather than being levied a fine. We can push these measures even further. If someone is unable to fix their vehicle for financial reasons, perhaps some of the money saved by eliminating police jurisdiction over traffic enforcement can be used to provide financial support to cover these costs. These are measures that support *everyone* using the road, since one unsafe vehicle endangers far more than just its operator. After all, if we are going to, as a society, require people to work to make a living and survive, and people need to transport themselves to work in order to do so, shouldn't we do what we can to support them doing so safely? This is a people-centered approach. Not a "gotcha."

Similar approaches can be taken for other minor enforcement issues currently taken care of by police. For example, civilians could easily take care of the necessary administration of things like parking and minor bylaw infractions without needing to carry weaponry that can kill people several times over. Services like attending to noise complaints can also be taken care of by civilian staff trained for these purposes. Noise complaints are essentially conflicts between neighbors. Police are not good at de-escalation and conflict resolution. Community well-being requires effective conflict resolution, and if this is a service we wish to provide for communities, we should do it without the deployment of a pseudo-military apparatus with the power and discretion to shoot to kill.

CRIMINAL DISPUTES AND VIOLENCE

I will never forget watching footage of the Miramar, Florida, police shoot-out that occurred on December 5, 2019. I was stunned watching the dozens of police vehicles engaging in a chase of a UPS truck that went viral on the internet. The police seemed to have no concern for the rest of the vehicles in the near-standstill rush-hour traffic. It was horrifying to watch police jump out of their vehicles and use *civilian bystander vehicles as cover* as they opened fire on the UPS truck, killing the occupants inside and endangering everyone on the street. What could have led to this extreme and incredibly dangerous escalation of violence?

The answer: stuff.

The incident began with an armed robbery at a jewelry store. Two individuals held up the store at gunpoint in an attempt to steal diamonds. The store set off a silent alarm to alert the police. Notice that using the police as a safety resource in this case has already failed. The people engaging in the robbery are already at the store and have already been violent in their holdup. In situations of violent crime, this is typical. By the time police arrive, it is often too late; the threat has already escaped or already caused harm. That was certainly the case here, as the store owner and the robbers exchanged gunfire before police arrived, injuring an employee in the process. The robbers then carjacked a UPS vehicle, along with the driver, Mr. Frank Ordoñez, may he rest in peace. Law enforcement from six police departments pursued the UPS vehicle for twenty-three miles in what was at times a high-speed chase. The televised chase came to an end when the UPS truck hit significant traffic at an intersection and was forced to stop. In footage, police can be seen jumping out of their vehicles and firing at the truck from all angles, endangering everyone on the roadway, and taking cover from return fire behind civilian vehicles. Although the police dispute this, a witness whose car the police used to take cover said the police were the first to start the deadly firefight on the roadway. When all was said and done, twenty police officers from six police departments fired more than two hundred shots and four people were killed, including the two people who initiated the robbery, the kidnapped UPS driver, and an innocent bystander who was in his vehicle, Mr. Richard Cutshaw, may he rest in peace.

All of this carnage, destruction, and trauma for stuff that was likely covered by insurance.

The police escalate violent situations, creating more violence, because that is the tool available to them. There are so many things that would have been done differently if the police were attuned to victim and bystander safety rather than punishment and apprehension. They could have stopped the chase when it became clear other people would be in danger, taken the information from the license plate of the UPS truck, and figured out another way to support Mr. Ordoñez without endangering other motorists. The chase went on for approximately an hour. During that time, the police could have evacuated roadways to protect people from the danger *they* caused by engaging in a high-speed chase. They could have tried to negotiate with the people who kidnapped Mr. Ordoñez instead of immediately escalating the situation with the use of force. They did not.

An additional individual, Mr. Carlos Lara, was injured in the melee. Mr. Lara and Mr. Ordoñez's estates filed civil suits in September 2020 against the Miami-Dade Police Department, the Doral Police Department, the Broward Sheriff's Office, the Miramar Police Department, the Pembroke Pines Police Department, and the Florida Highway Patrol for negligence and wrongful death. An investigation into the incident completed in September 2021 by the Florida Department of Law Enforcement (FDLE) was finally released in August 2024. The report describes a horrific scene, with witnesses discovering bullet holes in their vehicles—and in one case, in a car seat—when the shoot-out was over. The findings were delivered to the Broward State Attorney's Office, which confirmed on December 6, 2023, that the findings would be presented to a grand jury to determine whether action should be taken against law enforcement officers involved in the shoot-out. Four police officers—Leslie Lee, Jose Mateo, Rodolfo Mirabal, and Richard Santiesteban—were charged with manslaughter in June 2024. More than four years after the incident, the FDLE report confirmed for the families of the slain victims that it was in fact police fire that killed their loved ones including the driver of the carjacked UPS vehicle, Mr. Frank Ordoñez.

The police were not the answer in this and so many other cases of violent crime and other violations like theft, burglary, robbery, and arson. Recall from chapter 1 that very little police time is spent on violent crime whatsoever. Statistics in the United States, using numbers reported by police themselves, show that police lay a charge in less than 16 percent of cases of thefts, burglary, and motor vehicle thefts, and laying a charge does *not* mean solving a case, achieving a conviction, or providing a resolution. Charges can even result in innocent people taking a plea deal to avoid the risk of incarceration. Charges don't tell us much about the effectiveness of police work. Keep in mind, also, that the police have an interest in inflating numbers to make themselves look as effective as possible. And most important, remember that *not all crime is reported to police.*

In an analysis of data from the U.S. Department of Justice's National Crime Victimization Survey, which relies on survey respondents rather than police data to calculate crime, University of Utah criminal law professor Shima Baradaran Baughman found that only 11 percent of all serious crimes result in arrest and *less than 2 percent* result in a conviction. This, from a country that spends more than $100 billion on policing annually. In England and Wales, less than 6 percent of crimes result in a charge or summons.

So, what will we do about violent crime if we abolish police?

Probably stop deluding ourselves into believing that we are doing anything about it now.

There are many reasons why people may engage in violence, but much of it has to do with the social context creating limited personal opportunities. For example, the two individuals who attempted to rob the jewelry store that led to the shoot-out in Miramar were previously convicted. As discussed in chapter 6, being previously convicted makes it incredibly difficult to make ends meet once released. Perhaps these individuals felt they had little choice but to try something risky to make ends meet. If, as a society, we take measures discussed in chapter 6, we will be able to actually *prevent* violent crime, by making alternative supports readily available for those of us experiencing poverty and other difficulties surviving in society. When an incident occurs resulting in the loss of property, we should avoid actions that put other people in danger and result in homicides. Our cultural addiction to punishment is counterproductive and often results in more harm, danger, and trauma. Instead of prioritizing punishment, why don't we let insurance companies do their jobs, and otherwise focus on a victim-centered approach that provides compensation for lost property and attempts to make victims whole?

I know for some people, this is an impossible thing to consider, because it means as a society we would be doing some version of letting the "bad guys" get away with it. To this I say two things. The first is that we let "bad guys" get away with "it" all the time, both because police are ineffective at the jobs we think they are doing and because police focus on criminalizing only certain communities. As discussed in chapter 4, white-collar crime and the harm that large corporations exact on large swaths of our population often go unconsidered, despite the widespread pain and devastation they cause. We must divorce ourselves from the prejudices we hold that drive us toward accepting harm from the wealthy and insisting on punishment for the poor.

The second thing I would say is that more often than not *all* parties to violence are victims. We must move beyond the juvenile thinking that in situational conflict and harm, one party is "good" and innocent, one party is "bad," and no one else matters. That leads us to the fairy tale that such conflicts can be resolved by getting the "bad guy" and then everyone can live happily ever after. But this is not the case. Conflicts resulting in violence typically start far before the situation in question takes place. What leads perpetrators to use violence as their tool? Are they also victims of unresolved traumas? How can we transform the tools available to people who are desperate or feel as if they have no other choice but to engage in violence? Conflicts also include people we often never hear from: family, community members, and bystanders who are left with the brunt of consequences that we rarely consider. Unresolved trauma and conflict for these unconsidered parties can lead to a continued cycle of violence. What can we do to support the entirety of a community affected by violence? A victim-centered approach would consider all possible victims. These questions have to be part of our thinking if we are truly interested in reducing the prevalence of violence in our communities.

I concede that preventative measures likely won't eliminate violence altogether, but a focus on prevention will certainly help to reduce violent incidents in our lives far better than police do.

So, what do we do when violence does occur? And what do we do in the interim as we work to transform society with a focus on long-term preventative solutions, dispensing with our propensity to devalue particular communities and eliminating the unaddressed ways we create unsafe conditions through entrenched poverty?

Again, let's not be afraid to start from scratch. What are our needs when violence occurs? I think they can be summed up like this: (1) removing victims and potential victims from the threat; (2) taking victims and potential victims to a safer place where they can receive support; (3) incapacitating the violent party's ability to harm; (4) taking the violent party to a safer place where they can receive support; (5) evaluating how to hold responsible parties accountable; and (6) trying to prevent further violence from occurring. A safety-centered approach requires care and attention to several needs to effectively intervene in an ongoing incident of violence. Our current model does not do this work. We must be open to trying new ones.

Some communities have been trying different, community-based approaches with success. Nonpolice violence interruption programs have successfully reduced gun victimization between 20 and 60 percent where they have been implemented. These programs interrupt violence through a local, community-based approach, in which outreach workers who are native to the neighborhoods in which they work and can directly relate to the violence community members experience build relationships and mentorship-like rapports with people to encourage them to engage in conflict resolution without violence and to provide access to resources they need. These programs focus on communities at the highest risk for violence and rely on a local model; they work because community members know, respect, and trust the outreach workers. The model relies on a public health approach, treating violence as an epidemic that can be addressed like a disease. By way of example, the Cure Violence approach, adopted by interruption organizations in communities across sixteen states, in London, and in countries around the world, applies evidence-based public health epidemic-reversal strategies to

1. detect and interrupt (i.e., prevent) potentially violent situations,
2. identify and change the thinking and behavior of the highest risk transmitters (i.e., those most likely to engage in violence), and
3. change group norms that support and perpetuate the use of violence.

While the model was first implemented to address gun violence, Cure Violence has adapted its model for intervention to other types of violence, including domestic violence, gender-based violence, and post-conflict violence. The results are impressive, in one case yielding a 48 percent reduction in shootings in the first week of the program's operations in Chicago.

These programs are effective and can be implemented right now as we work on transforming our societies to prioritize implementing structural conditions to prevent violence and the spread of violence.

GUN CONTROL

We absolutely cannot discuss preventing violence without discussing the problem of gun violence, and how gun proliferation in the United States and across the world is driven by the insatiable, unrelenting, and growing gun industry.

A whole other book could be written about the crisis of gun violence in the United States, and indeed others have. I am not one to agree with claims of U.S. exceptionalism for a whole host of issues, but gun violence is an issue for which the United States is absolutely unique. The United States has the highest gun-related homicide rate in the developed world, at 4.1 homicides per 100,000 people, according to reporting by CNN. Compare that with 0.5 homicides per 100,000 people in Canada, and a rate of 0 per 100,000 people in the U.K. The CNN report states that the United States is also "the only nation in the world where civilian guns outnumber people," at a rate of 120.5 firearms per 100 people. Compare that with 34.7 firearms per 100 people in Canada, and 4.9 firearms per 100 people in the U.K. No other country even comes close to the U.S. level of gun ownership, with U.S. residents estimated to own 46 percent of the world's entire civilian gun supply and one-third of all U.S. adults owning a gun. Manufacturing of guns in the United States is also increasing. The National Rifle Association–led gun lobby is unbelievably powerful and has been successful at keeping gun regulation at bay to the benefit of the corporations making ever-increasing profits from the rising gun sales in the United States. The exception that the United States represents with respect to gun violence is not because there is something inherently different about people in the United States or U.S. culture. It is simply because of a lack of political will to meaningfully address the issue of gun violence through measures the rest of the world has taken, including implementing strict regulations surrounding the use and ownership of guns and reducing the ease with which someone can legally acquire a gun.

The consequences for refusing to meaningfully address gun

ownership in the United States are astronomical. The rate of mass shootings in the United States far outstrips any other developed country. In 2023, there were 655 mass shootings—shootings in which there have been four or more homicides excluding the shooter—nearly double as many days as there are in the year. And now the problem of gun proliferation in the United States has become a worldwide issue, as guns from the United States have crossed borders and fueled gun violence in other countries.

As the U.S. gun market saturates, gun manufacturers looking for new markets have found buyers abroad faster than ever due to a shift in export regulations making worldwide sales simpler. From 2017 to 2021, 33.5 percent of firearms from crime scenes in Canada have been traced back to lawful exports from the United States, and more than 37 percent of firearms outside North America are traceable back to the United States, and these are just the guns that could be traced to lawful exports. Smuggled guns are also a growing problem. The Center for American Progress reports that from 2014 to 2019 more than eleven thousand firearms recovered in Canada were trafficked from the United States, and more than seventy thousand guns were trafficked to Mexico. And these are just the guns that were recovered and traced. The issue could be far more expansive.

The toll is monumental. One of Canada's worst mass shootings, the 2020 Portapique, Nova Scotia, attacks, resulting in twenty-two murders, was carried out using guns smuggled into Canada from the United States. Handguns are also being smuggled into the U.K., with *The New York Times* reporting that a sharp increase in violent crime is occurring at the same time as more weapons are making their way across the pond from the United States.

Like everything else that fuels violence—poverty, anti-Black racism, gendered discrimination, and so on—gun deaths will be reduced only with a focus on prevention. Around the world, regulation has proven to be an effective solution. A report by *The New York Times* found that the U.K. has "one of the lowest gun-related death rates in the world" after banning semiautomatic weapons and most handguns in the 1980s and 1990s. Similar success has been achieved in Australia, Germany, New Zealand, and Norway. Gun violence has gotten so bad because of lobbying by corporations who stand to make a buck off the carnage. Ultimately, it does not matter what the founders intended for the Second Amendment to mean; it matters what makes sense for the country and the world as it stands today. And what does not make sense is staying the course with gun laws when so many lives are being ripped apart in ways that are entirely preventable.

DEMOCRACY

A functioning, robust democracy requires a healthy, educated, participatory followership, and an educated, morally grounded leadership.

—Chinua Achebe

In my years engaging in advocacy with Black Lives Matter, I was often faced with policy makers who would listen to our ideas, only to state that, yes, they understood that there were some problems with policing, but until they had an alternative, their hands were tied. I am fed up with that tired response. Policy makers have a duty to their citizenry. It is their job to do the rigorous, multiyear work of building institutions, infrastructure, and systems that make our societies safer. For years, they have reneged on this responsibility as average people consistently decried the dangers of policing, preferring instead to serve the interests of police fraternal organizations and to benefit from the misleading yet popular "tough on crime" message that works so well in electoral periods. And too many of us have paid with our lives for that refusal to do their jobs. In 2025, there is even less credence in this paltry excuse. Activists, academics, and advocates have made the case, over and over, with different options of paths that can be tried. All that is missing is political will. And I have to wonder, How bad must this crisis get for those in power to take action?

There have been countless studies showing additional strategies we can take to prevent violence in addition to the ones I've mentioned in this book. In *No More Police*, abolitionists Mariame Kaba and Andrea Ritchie reference studies showing that increased green space, improved public lighting, access to education, and accessible health care are all strategies that not only reduce violence in a community but create safer conditions in our society. The beautiful thing is that these sorts of rearrangements benefit everyone, not just the communities disadvantaged by systemic discrimination. We know that the safest communities are not those that are the most policed. They are the wealthiest. They are the ones that have the most resources. What we need are resources for our communities. This means prioritizing communities that are typically systemically dispossessed of resources and deprived of opportunities. This means focusing on violence prevention, treating people who have had traumatic experiences, and offering services to make those who have been harmed whole.

It also means refusing to ignore some of the most consistent and dangerous purveyors of violence in our midst: the police. Police are responsible for about 5 percent of all firearm homicides in the United States, according to a report in *The Guardian*. The police do not prevent violence. Nor do they resolve violence. They *wield* violence, and they wield it against civilians—Black people most urgently. *USA Today* found that more than eighty-five thousand police officers have been investigated or disciplined for cases of police misconduct from 2009 to 2019. This is a veritable crisis. If we want to address violence, preventing police violence should be one of our primary concerns. The heartbreaking ways Black people have their lives stolen from them by police officers cannot be overstated. In 2023, another horrifying case of police torture of primarily Black men was uncovered in Mississippi.

The description that follows is graphic.

Police shocked these Black men on their genitals using Tasers, had metal melted onto their skin with a blowtorch, and waterboarded them and forced them to vomit after thrusting items down their throats. They were choked, beaten, assaulted with sex toys, and threatened with rape. These officers were proud of their actions, calling themselves the Goon Squad, even making commemorative coins emblazoned with the nickname. The former law enforcement officers Christian Dedmon, Hunter Elward, Joshua Hartfield, Brett McAlpin, Jeffrey Middleton, and Daniel Opdyke pleaded guilty to criminal charges. One of these officers was honored as "investigator of the year" in 2013, despite having multiple complaints against him. The people who were subject to these brutal tortures are forever changed by the trauma they endured. I wish I could say this was an isolated incident, but examples of heinous police brutality and torture can be found throughout the history of policing's existence. These issues are consistent and persistent. Decades of attempts at reform have been a complete waste of time. Policing is an irredeemable institution. The only way to protect Black people—and all people—from police violence is to take away their power to harm us, permanently.

This book, the problems it diagnoses, and the solutions it prescribes might sound a bit like an all-encompassing shift of our entire culture—and it is. Those who criticize police abolition for being an underdeveloped and immature solution to a complex problem misunderstand what abolitionists are calling for. We are not simply saying "delete" police, as one would eliminate a typographical error in an otherwise perfect fragment of prose. We are calling for a significant and comprehensive shift in the way our society is constructed. It is not abolitionists who are looking at this problem too superficially. It is those who ask "What would we replace policing with?" who make that error. Replacement is not the goal. The goal is transformation.

The way our societies are currently constructed degrades and oppresses Black people, and the police are deployed as tools to maintain that hierarchical system. So, in a democratic sense, Black people's social movements are meant to uproot the way our societies systemically operate and transform them such that we are liberated from the ways we have been persistently dispossessed. Those who find our movements threatening have something to lose from this transformation: They benefit from our oppression. Black forms of resistance have always been met with coercive repression and backlash. But you, reader, have an opportunity to align yourself with liberation. Do you support apologist thinking, finding excuse after excuse as to why now is not yet the right time to deal with one of the most urgent forms of violence leveled upon Black people with the authorization of our governments? Or do you support the call to end one of the most powerful agents of our oppression?

We have organized society such that there are haves and have-nots—whether you agree with the ethics of this or not. The colonizers have the land. The colonized do not. Someone must protect this relationship, lest the colonized rise up and take back the land. The "ownership" class—those with capital, with resources—has the money. The working class does not. Someone must control this relationship, lest the workers rise up and take the value they create for the owners. White people have majority control of power. Racialized people do not. Someone must protect this dynamic. In each of these relations, there are middling classes who help to create an illusion to the have-nots that there is a road to becoming a have, a road they can traverse. But society works in the way that it does precisely because most people will never be a have. And police are mobilized in the maintenance of this relationship between those considered inferior and those bestowed with power and resources.

A society interested in maintaining these oppressive structures will continue to rely on the police and understand that there is a subset that will necessarily be oppositional to the police—because the police are not in their interest. A society interested in eliminating oppressive structures and moving beyond the genocidal vulgarities of colonialism, racism, anti-Blackness, and class divisions cannot expect to achieve that goal while maintaining an institution designed to maintain those structures.

The assumption that underscores our more than century-long rigid commitment to policing is that violence is required to ensure communal safety. But Black movements, and now you, reader, know that the state's intention in harnessing violence has never been to prevent violence at all. It was to perpetuate it. The initial use of police to perpetuate the violent exploitation of the working poor, the violent ethnic cleansing of Indigenous people, the violent enslavement of Black people, the continued degradation of Black people in the violent maintenance of segregationist laws, the violent discarding of drug users and sex workers—the list of ways that the state employs violence against people is unending. Policing is a fundamentally unjust institution, and this is why creating safety through violence has proven itself to be a failed, fatal strategy.

As a society, we should not be constrained by the limits of our imagination. A reorganization of society with an orientation toward justice, security, and the preservation of life can help us build safer, kinder, more liberated communities—if we dare. Humanity has accomplished the impossible on the strength of belief in a dream. We have traveled to space, built the internet, and created incredible new technologies. We even shifted our entire economy from one reliant on the enslavement of Black people. I cannot accept that it is easier to imagine and build artificial intelligence than it is to imagine and build a world without policing. These major shifts became possible when we refused to be hindered by a box insisting that we have already accomplished all that is possible. Aren't you curious about what it would look like if we were focused on caring for the harmed and preventing harm rather than implementing carceral, punitive half measures that only worsen the issues we seek to resolve? I am curious, and I am committed. We have not reached the pinnacle of human innovation on collective safety. We can and must do better. I believe that policing will have its inevitable end; human creativity and resistance won't allow us to be deluded by policing forever. And I intend to be a part of ushering forward that future as swiftly as possible.

I hope you'll join me.

So much has occurred since I completed this manuscript that I find it necessary to write an afterword.

I lack words evoking the appropriate level of disgust and wrath I felt as I read reports of Sonya Massey's killing by Deputy Sean Grayson. Ms. Massey had called the police for help, fearing a prowler outside her home. The thirty-six-year-old Black woman presciently pleaded with the white officers as she opened her door on July 6, 2024, in Springfield, Illinois, saying: "Please don't hurt me."

The man who would soon kill her responded, "Why would I hurt you? You called us."

Sean Grayson has since been fired and is facing multiple charges, including first degree murder, in Ms. Massey's homicide. In widely shared footage captured from his partner's body camera, Ms. Massey appears calm, sitting on her couch searching for identification the police have requested. Grayson then points to a pot of boiling water on the stove, stating, "We don't need a fire while we're in here." As Ms. Massey picks up the pot and pours the water in the sink, the officers move away from her, and she asks, "Where are you going?" One of the officers laughs as he responds, "Away from your hot, steaming water!" to which she replies, "I rebuke you in the name of Jesus," in a tone of voice appearing to mirror the amusement of the police officer. Grayson suddenly and inexplicably escalates the situation, drawing his gun, pointing it at her, yelling expletives, and demanding she drop the pot. Ms. Massey immediately apologizes and ducks below her kitchen counter. He then shoots her three times in her head, killing her.

May she rest in peace.

The body cameras worn by the police did not save Ms. Massey; neither did the Taser Grayson had on his person. Perhaps if Grayson hadn't had a gun, he wouldn't have killed her. Perhaps if Grayson had not been protected from previous infractions—including two DUIs during his time in the military and complaints of misconduct while he worked at another police service—she wouldn't have been killed. Perhaps.

And almost certainly, if there was a useful service she could have called that night, Sonya Massey would be alive.

Sonya Massey is just one of the hundreds of people police have killed in the United States as of the writing of this afterword in November 2024.

This year, police continued their violent repression of democratic participation with brutal crackdowns of student demonstrations on campuses across North America calling for divestment of their tuition dollars from the Israeli genocidal siege of Palestinians in Gaza, a tactic that was successful in mounting pressure against the South African apartheid regime in the 1990s. Despite the customary commitment to free speech emblematic of most postsecondary education institutions, many colleges and university students, faculty, and staff were subject to intense, ruthless repression by police officers.

More than three thousand students were arrested across the United States, and police arrested dozens of students at similar protests in the United Kingdom and in Canada. Police responded to the peaceful protests with flash-bang grenades, rubber bullets, batons, tear gas, and in one case, at Columbia

University, a police officer fired his gun, in what he said was a mistaken attempt to use his flashlight.

In June, a joint investigation by ProPublica and *The New York Times* revealed NYPD commissioner Edward Caban systematically protected officers accused of misconduct from facing public trials.

Some states have expanded police powers, allowing them to arrest undocumented migrants in conflict with federal law and therefore a clear violation of the Constitution.

In August, a federal judge dismissed felony charges for falsifying a warrant against two police officers involved in the killing of Breonna Taylor. In Judge Charles Simpson's decision, he said there was no link between the false warrant and Ms. Taylor's killing, incomprehensibly blaming her death on her boyfriend.

And Mapping Police Violence data shows police in the United States killed more people in 2024 than they have in the previous ten years.

The unrelenting police violence in the United States is worsening, and as I write this, the most popular policy options touted by policy makers will only place us back in a cycle of ineffectual reforms.

First introduced in 2020 and reintroduced in 2024, the George Floyd Justice in Policing Act is an attempt at reform co-written by then Vice President Kamala Harris and supported by most Democrats, including former president Joe Biden and dozens of advocacy organizations. And, unfortunately, it will not move the needle on police violence. With the exception of its provision to prevent the transfer of military-grade equipment to state and local law enforcement, the bill makes the same bald errors as countless reform attempts before it and would ultimately result in an increase in tools and resources to the police, further endangering the people they are meant to serve.

The bill promises to prohibit racial profiling by police—a practice that is already illegal. It promises to ban no-knock warrants, seemingly in response to the killing of Breonna Taylor. But as discussed in chapter 2, police did not have a no-knock warrant, despite initial reports. They reportedly entered Breonna Taylor's home unannounced anyway. It bans choke-hold restraints—like the one used by Daniel Pantaleo, who killed Eric Garner—a type of restraint already banned in New York at the time of Mr. Garner's killing. It increases training and data collection and provides incredible resources to expand the use of body cameras to all state and federal police.

Despite its namesake, none of the provisions in the proposed legislation would have saved George Floyd. Neither would they have saved Breonna Taylor, Eric Garner, Tyre Nichols, Michael Brown, Sandra Bland, or countless other people whose lives were destroyed by police.

There is competing bill that takes a different approach.

The People's Response Act is a bill that builds on the pre-viously introduced BREATHE Act. It approaches safety as a public health issue, creating a Division of Community Safety, within the Department of Health and Human Services, focused on creating safety and preventing harm before it develops. It pro-vides resources to create nonpolice emergency response pro-grams, expanding the success of grassroots, community-led programs empowering civilians to respond to crises. It provides grants to community organizations to expand noncarceral tools to prevent violence.

The People's Response Act is a powerful step in the right direction that will begin to critically shift our societal infrastruc-ture toward the prevention of harm. These types of changes, along with continuing to remove resources from the ineffectual police, are the only changes that will finally focus on creating safety and eliminate the power of the police to harm us.

I am writing this afterword at the end of November 2024; Donald Trump has just been elected to serve as the U.S. presi-dent for the second time, and the Republicans will control both chambers of Congress. During his campaign, he predictably promised to be tough on crime. Despite an avowed commit-ment to make significant cuts in the service of a smaller, more efficient government, one place Trump has consistently promised to spend with wanton abandon is law enforcement. He has promised to increase funding, resources, and protections for police. Most notably, he has promised to significantly expand carceral institutions in his xenophobic hunt for undocumented migrants. The scale of horrors he plans to implement in his mass deportation plan is unimaginable.

The struggle against policing must be fought at more than just the federal level. The measures we need to take to transform our communities and make them safer are just as important at the municipal, county, and state levels. To this end, the Movement for Black Lives (M4BL), Essie Justice Group, the Civil Rights Corps, Color of Change, and Black Lives Matter (BLM) have created tool kits for local lawmakers, advocates, and activists to advance local versions of the provisions of the People's Response Act, available on the M4BL and BLM websites. As we anticipate worsening police repression under a Trump presidency and a Republican-controlled Congress, it is more important than ever to support initiatives like the ones contained in the People's Response Act at the local and state levels.

The provisions in the People's Response Act *could* have saved George Floyd and Sonya Massey. We cannot continue to be placated by meaningless reform measures like the Justice in Policing Act, nor can we accept measures promising to continue policing's ruinous results in our communities. We are long overdue to move away from the century-long falsehood that police keep us safe. Those of us who oppose anti-Black racism have a moral obligation to decouple the idea of safety from police and usher in a new normal where our efforts to build safe communities focus on health, dignity, and the prevention of harm.

And there is no better time than now.

ACKNOWLEDGMENTS

I love writing, I really do, but writing about a topic so mired in death and destruction is incredibly difficult, and it takes a real community of people to put all that knowledge together, to analyze it, to make it legible, and to keep a writer like me, who wants to remain an eternal optimist, well in the soul. Luckily, I am blessed to have several strong communities of people who surround me, support me, and love me through my most ambitious projects.

First and foremost, I need to thank my parents, Juliette and Donovan, who have given me and my siblings everything of themselves, and to whom I credit for my wits and my sense. They have been an eternal source of support for me, and probably have no idea how helpful some of our dinnertime conversations have been for synthesizing my thoughts. I am eternally grateful for you, Mommy and Daddy.

Deep thank-you also to my partner, Lorson Metelus, for loving me through it, for being a sounding board, and for pushing me forward whenever I felt stuck. While writing this, I experienced a very difficult health challenge requiring major surgery, and I don't know how I would have made it through without you, Lorson. I love you.

To my closest collaborators, I apologize for always having too much going on! Just kidding. I believe all the projects I say yes to complement one another, and I am so lucky to work with so many multitalented people who understand. Rodney Diverlus, my work spouse, thanks for being you, being honest with me, giving me space to breathe and create, and never letting me take the easy way out. Alice Wu, thank you for being one of the best people I know. Your generosity is truly an inspiration for me. To have someone in my corner just making sure that I am good, fed, comfortable, and taking time out for me? I owe you so much. Nora Loreto, thanks for the weekly conversations helping me to work through my own approach to the world's biggest issues, and for taking on the lion's share of the administrative work so I could make this happen. You're one of a kind. Leah Stokes, thank you for being a consistent rock as one of my oldest friends, providing me with such support through my surgery, introducing me to my agent, and being my family out here in California. Who would've thought, back in grade four? The writing retreats, the long phone calls working through our projects—this book literally would not have happened without you. I can't wait to read your next book. It's going to be beautiful. Thank you. Jade Nixon, I cherish our friendship and I am so grateful to have had you working with me as an accountability partner, especially in the moments where the writing got hard. You've been such a great friend and source of support, and I am truly grateful. To Professor David Austin, thank you for being my first reader, and for your kindness, generosity, prodding questions, and support. I am so grateful and humbled by your offering of time, assistance, and wisdom.

To the people I struggle with, the countless activists, disrupters, and agitators from the U.K. to Brazil, to the United States to Canada, there are far too many of you to thank individually. This work draws on your brilliance, your courage, and your tenacity. So many of you give so much of yourselves in ways for which you will never receive the appropriate gratitude, but rest assured—the gratitude is there. While writing this book, the team at Black Lives Matter Canada purchased, renovated, and opened the Wildseed Centre for Art & Activism, a Black-owned community center located in downtown Toronto focused on supporting the most marginalized Black people in our community, supporting the BLM Canada chapters, and nurturing the proliferation of artivist abolitionist work. Any community organizer knows how important it is to have access to unencumbered space to imagine how to bring forth the new world of which we all dream. To have built a queer-led, trans-led, disability-justice-focused space for Black community members to gather, work, and play feels like a miracle. To the best squad I have ever worked with—Pascale Diverlus, Paige Galette, Udokam Iroegbu, Jessica Kirk, Syrus Marcus Ware, and Ravyn Wngz, along with Rodney Diverlus—this book is also for you. You are the most principled, wonderfully caring, consistently brilliant, and remarkably wise people I have ever met. I am so fortunate to be able to create with you. To our OGs, and especially to Angela Robertson, d'bi.young anitafrika, and Mme Michaëlle Jean, thank you all so much for your sage wisdom, picking me up when I was down, and believing in our collective work.

To my oldest friends, Amy Gordon and Bernice Chau, along with Leah Stokes, our check-ins, encouraging one another to keep up our healthy practices, nerdy games, and of course the group chat have all been a lifeline. Thanks for believing in me and being the hilarious people we've all been since our childhoods at Denlow Public School.

Gilary Massa, Adam Awad, Shaun Shepherd, Yasmeen Emadi, Igor Samardzic, Ziyan Hossain—thank you all so much for being such wonderful friends, for believing in me, and for offering me the chance to escape when I've needed it. From Toronto to Panama to Ottawa to San Francisco to Jamaica to Los Angeles—what a blessing I've had to be offered a chance to be reinvigorated on the world's wonderful big playground with you.

To my cousins Amie Archibald-Varley, Jordan Archibald-Varley, and Brent Shepherd, thank you so much for your love, support, and frequent check-ins.

Krisna Saravanamuttu, Brie Berry-Crossfield, Hadia Akhtar Khan, I'm so proud to struggle with you and to call you friends. Thanks for being my sounding boards and being trusted confidants whom I can always count on to help me work through a concept.

To the academic and activist communities who've helped to synthesize my thoughts, I am forever in your debt. My time at the UCLA School of Law in the critical race theory specialization and at the University of Toronto Ontario Institute for Studies in Education was such a critical and potent experience for me. I am grateful for my teachers and guides who have allowed me to study while giving me the space to practice my politics. To Professors Noah Zatz and Devon Carbado at UCLA, thank you for gifting me with the most incredible academic experiences of my very long academic career (during a pandemic, no less!), for encouraging me to develop this book, and for your indispensable feedback. Professor Cheryl Harris, it was an absolute dream to take classes with you and benefit from your brilliance. Professors Joanna Schwartz, Tendayi Achiume, Tony Tolbert, Brenda Suttonwills, Jasleen Kohli, Bryonn Bain, Claudia Peña, Robin D. G. Kelley, Andrew Verstein, Cary Franklin, Julie Cramer, Ingrid Ealy, LaToya Baldwin Clark, Jennifer Chacón, Maximo Langer, Eileen Scallen, Afua Cooper, George Dei, Alisa Trotz, Deb Cowan, and John Portelli, thank you for your tutelage. Alanna Kane and Lila Kalaf Reiner, thank you so much for your support and grounding me when the mess of COVID, the uprisings, and *everything else* would not stop.

I am, of course, also indebted to the writings of thinkers whom I have not had as formal teachers but whom I count as critical to shaping my ideas: Angela Davis, Ruth Wilson Gilmore, Olúfẹ́mi O. Táíwò, Mariame Kaba, Alex Vitale, Simone Browne, Katherine McKittrick, Kimberlé Crenshaw, Michelle Alexander, Andrea Ritchie, Mari Matsuda, and countless others. I have the utmost gratitude for the work you have gifted the world.

Mestre Boneco and Capoeira Brasil Los Angeles. Where

would I be without the capoeira community? I am so grateful to have found a capoeira home in Los Angeles, and to have a space for my body, mind, and soul to work out some of the most emotional parts of creating a work like this. Thanks for the Sunday *rodas* on the beach, and music lessons when my body was healing.

And finally, and crucially, thank you to the team of folks who take care of the logistics of my life and this work. To Morgan Blades and Gab Free—thank you for making sure I don't miss anything and always show up as my best. I appreciate you both so much. To my agent, Will Lippincott from Aevitas Creative Management, what a journey this has been! Thank you so much for pushing me to deepen my thought and to plan for a focused and comprehensive work and for finding some great editors and houses that support my work. Thank you also to my editors Concepción de León at Pantheon Books and Jennifer Lambert at HarperCollins Canada. Concepción, I couldn't have asked for a more thoughtful editor who really understood what I was trying to do with this. Thank you for your gentle nudges and for encouraging me to put more of myself down on the page. And Jennifer, thanks for believing in me, and for your excitement with this project.

A luta continua.

NOTES

INTRODUCTION

4   **She was stunned**: U.S. Department of Justice, "Clearances," Uniform Crime Report.

5   **In August 2016, Black Lives Matter Toronto:** Britneff, "Heart Condition, 'Aggravating' Factors Contributed to Abdi's Death"; Osman, " 'Homicide by Heart Attack.' "

5   **when Mr. Abdi stopped moving:** Helmer, "A Full Picture of Abdirahman Abdi's Final Moments Has Finally Been Painted"; Osman, "The Montsion Trial Resumes."

6   **Months later, Constable Daniel Montsion**: Britneff, "Heart Condition, 'Aggravating' Factors Contributed to Abdi's Death"; Osman, " 'Homicide by Heart Attack' "; Helmer, " 'When Will Our Lives Matter?' "; Weir, "Const. Daniel Montsion Not Guilty in Death."

6   **On October 25, 2024, the Province of Ontario**: Ontario Solicitor General, "Date Announced for the Inquest into the Death of Abdirahman Abdi."

9   **Despite nearly four hundred**: Serrano, " 'Somber Day' in Uvalde."

10   **failed to stop the shooter**: Knowles, Swaine, and Lee, "Updated Timeline: How Police Responded."

10   **Just as in the Parkland mass shooting**: Martínez-Beltrán, "Uvalde Parents Demand Investigation"; Reilly, "Schools Are Putting More Cops on Campus."

10   **policy makers' response**: Bleiberg and Weber, "Uvalde Report."

11   **Could the shooter**: Asher, "Salvador Ramos"; Kesslen, "Uvalde Killer Was Mocked."

13   **In news reports, Ms. Korchinski-Paquet's family**: Nasser, "Release evidence in Regis Korchinski-Paquet death. . . ."

14   **Peter Hamby's famous 2020 interview**: Hamby, "Barack Obama."

15   **But the data shows**: Phillips, "Centrist Dems Are Wrong."

15   **The simple phrase is supported**: Movement 4 Black Lives, Breathe Act.

17   **This was a man**: Riess, Almasy, and Levenson, "Justin Trudeau Says."

17 **In fact, in a year**: Tunney, "Systemic Racism Exists in RCMP"; Government of Canada, *Budget 2021*.

CHAPTER ONE: WE'VE BEEN DISINFORMED

19 **The police procedural is the lifeblood**: Color of Change, *Normalizing Injustice*, 9.

19 **On any random date**: TV Guide, tvguide.com.

20 **In the United States and Canada**: National Center for Education Statistics, "Private School Enrollment"; Statistics Canada, "Key Trends in Elementary to Postsecondary Student Enrolments"; National Statistics, *Schools, Pupils, and Their Characteristics*.

21 **In 2018, less than 25 percent**: Harrell and Davis, "Contacts Between Police and the Public, 2018—Statistical Tables."

21 **A 2003 study**: Reiner, "Policing and the Media."

21 **Similar data**: Statistics Canada, "Decrease in the Rate of Police Strength"; U.S. Department of Justice, "Police Employees."

23 **Popular culture has**: Rosenberg, "In Pop Culture."

24 **One of the most famous**: Allen, *Tiger*, 184.

24 **On January 18**: "Lexow Committee Report," *New York Times*, 1.

24 **Keep in mind**: NYPD, "About NYPD."

24 **In 1910, the International Association of Chiefs of Police**: International Association of Chiefs of Police, "Membership"; Reiner, "Policing and the Media."

25 **In 1916**: Reiner, "Policing and the Media."

25 **"law, natural or divine"**: Doherty, *Pre-Code Hollywood*, 351.

25 **By then, the infamous Federal Bureau**: Rosenberg, "How Police Censorship."

25 **Hollywood producers**: Grady, "How 70 Years of Cop Shows."

25 **The combination of the Hays Code**: Reiner, "Policing and the Media."

25 **The show often**: Grady, "How 70 Years of Cop Shows."

25 **In return for**: Rosenberg, "How Police Censorship."

26 **The organization was known**: Rasmussen, "Police Scandal Is Worst Since 1930s."

26 **The force was even**: Domanick, "Public Corruption, L.A.-Style."

26 **On Christmas Day 1951**: Rasmussen, " 'Bloody Christmas' of 1951."

27 **"routine, harmless, necessary"**: Color of Change, *Normalizing Injustice*, 12.

27 **murder being the most common**: Ibid., 118.

28 **According to the Uniform Crime Reporting**: U.S. Department of Justice, "Violent Crime."

28 **An investigation by**: Asher and Horwitz, "How Do the Police Actually Spend Their Time?"

28 **In the U.K., for instance**: Office for National Statistics, "Nature of Violent Crime," 2.

28 **And though the U.K. Office for National Statistics**: Ibid., 4.

28 **much like *Law & Order***: Frazer-Carroll, "Copaganda."

29 **According to the Innocence Project**: Innocence Project, "Why Do Innocent People Plead Guilty?"

30   **Mr. Browder refused**: Furst, *Time: The Kalief Browder Story.*

30   **In 2019, Mr. Browder's**: Romo, "New York City Reaches $3.3 Million Settlement."

30   **Racial profiling barely**: Color of Change, *Normalizing Injustice*, 81.

31   **While some television shows**: Frazer-Carroll, "Copaganda."

31   **Though people of color**: Quandt and Jones, "Research Roundup: Violent Crimes."

31   **network executives and producers**: Color of Change, *Normalizing Injustice*, 6.

31   **Color of Change reported that on police procedurals**: Ibid., 117.

31   **As a result**: Ibid., 121.

31   **Color of Change found**: Ibid., 31.

32   **What makes the system**: Ibid., 32.

33   **Research consistently demonstrates**: Ibid., xx.

33   **Citing a Kaiser Family**: Ibid., 121.

34   **On December 13, 2022**: Hudson and Loreto, "Theft Is Only Good When the Rich Do It."

34   **The mainstream and widely read**: Carlson, "Not Just Inflation."

34   **Curiously, we came across**: Allen, "Top Retailers Say."

34   **Aside from the publications**: Hartmans, "Target Said It's Lost $400 Million"; Lee, "Shoplifting Fuels a $94.5 Billion Problem"; Wertz, "Shoplifting Has Become a $100 Billion Problem"; Zilber, "Shoplifting Has Reportedly Become a $94.5B Problem."

35   ***not* responsible for 50 percent**: Medina, "Retail Group Retracts Startling Claim."

35   **In a Twitter thread**: Karakatsanis, Twitter.

35   **In 2021, these articles**: Channick, "Rising Crime Scaring Some Visitors"; Thompson, "DAs, Retailers Say California Needs Tougher Retail Theft Law"; Corkery and Maheshwari, "Thefts, Always an Issue for Retailers."

35   **According to Karakatsanis**: Karakatsanis, "The Three Functions of Copaganda."

35   **Blaming the inflationary**: Medina, "Retail Group Retracts Startling Claim."

37   **Police procedurals**: Color of Change, *Normalizing Injustice.*

37   **In Los Angeles alone**: Lau, "Police PR Machine Under Scrutiny."

37   **At some point**: Heath-Rawlings, Twitter.

39   **in 2023**: Parker and McDaniel, "From Freddie Gray to Tyre Nichols."

40   **Instead, for decades**: Cooke and Sturges, "Police and Media Relations in an Era of Freedom of Information," 412.

40   **As we've learned**: Chermak, "Image Control," 22.

40   **When victims are affluent**: Cooke and Sturges, "Police and Media Relations in an Era of Freedom of Information," 412.

40   **Police are the number one source**: Chermak, "Image Control," 22.

41   **professional media departments**: Freckelton, "Police Statistics and the Media," 247.

41   **They essentially act**: Chermak, "Image Control," 27–35.

41   **Yet this mutual interest**: Chibnall, *Law-and-Order News*, 155.

41   **Reporters and news outlets**: Chermak, "Image Control," 36.

42   **Critical reporting**: Ibid., 23.

42   **Researchers in the U.K.**: Freckelton, "Police Statistics and the Media," 247.

42   **"Man Dies After"**: Elder, "Investigative Update."

42   **There is no mention**: Chappell, "Derek Chauvin Is Sentenced."

43   **But crimes that are**: Chermak, "Image Control," 35.

44   **in the U.K., researchers**: Cooke and Sturges, "Police and Media Relations in an Era of Freedom of Information," 411.

45   **In the 1980s**: Beale, "News Media's Influence," 425.

45   **As news conglomerates**: Chermak, "Image Control," 39.

45   **News media began**: Beale, "News Media's Influence," 426.

45   **In a paper**: Ibid., 398, 422.

46   **When reports from the first**: Ibid., 423.

46   **Research on crime reporting**: Ibid., 418.

47   **In Canada, alternative media sources**: Denis, "Copaganda."

47   **The police managed**: Shaw, "Leaked VPD Report an Inflated Work of Fiction."

47   **The police clearly**: Johal and Magusiak, "Police Across Canada."

47   **According to government records**: Alberta Lobbyist Registry, OL-11699-03, 4.

47   **In response to**: Moule, "Under Siege?," 1.

48   **There is no evidence**: Ibid.

48   **In the fall of 2015**: Ibid., 2.

48   **Some police officers**: Ibid.

49   **In some states**: Ibid., 7.

49   **There's a communications theory**: Van der Meer, Kroon, and Vliegenthart, "Do News Media Kill?," 508.

50   **Researchers studying cultivation theory**: Beale, "News Media's Influence," 398.

CHAPTER TWO: ORIGIN STORIES

54   **The first modern**: Rahman, Clarke, and Byrne, "Art of Breaking People Down," 16.

55   **Prior to implementing**: Boyle, "Police in Ireland Before the Union: I," 121.

55   **Prior to creating**: Ibid., 125.

56   **England first tried**: Boyle, "Police in Ireland Before the Union: II," 101–6; Boyle, "Police in Ireland Before the Union: III," 330.

56   **A petition submitted**: Boyle, "Police in Ireland Before the Union: III," 331–32.

56   **The British government**: Ibid., 332.

57   **Through successive advancements**: Sinclair, "'Irish' Policeman and the Empire," 178.

57   **In Canada, the North West Mounted Police**: Ibid., 185.

57   **They brutally attacked**: Gouldhawke, "Condensed History of Canada's Colonial Cops."

58   **They kidnapped Indigenous children**: Rahman, Clarke, and Byrne, "Art of Breaking People Down," 25.

58   **Canada's last residential school**: "Your Questions Answered About Canada's Residential School System," CBC News.

58   **The NWMP was not**: Ennab, "Rupturing the Myth of the Peaceful Western Canadian Frontier," 88–161.

58   **The RCMP's colonial legacy**: Royal Canadian Mounted Police, "Current Operations"; Gouldhawke, "Condensed History of Canada's Colonial Cops."

59   **Consider the story**: Martinez, "Recuperating Histories of Violence," 661.

59   **Mr. Bazán and Mr. Longoria**: Ibid., 665.

60   **The Rangers regularly**: Ibid., 678.

61   **Imagine learning that**: Hersher, "Key Moments in the Dakota Access Pipeline Fight."

61   **According to Greenpeace**: Reid, "Oil and Water."

62   **In fact, the safety**: Brown and Sadasivam, "Pipeline Company Spent Big on Police."

62   **They interrupted and dispersed**: Brown, Parrish, and Speri, "Battle of Treaty Camp."

63   **An investigation by *The Guardian***: Dhillon and Parrish, "Exclusive: Canada Police Prepared to Shoot."

64   **These examples I have**: Little, "3 Arrested as B.C. RCMP Resume Enforcement."

64   **Among the profitable**: Rugemer, "Development of Mastery and Race," 434.

64   **Enslaved people across**: Stevens-Acevedo, "Santo Domingo Slave Revolt of 1521," v.

65   **But the revolt**: Ibid., 12.

65   **In Barbados, the colonizers**: Rugemer, "Development of Mastery and Race," 429.

65   **The South Carolina slave code**: Ibid., 430.

66   **The South Carolina slave code called**: Brucato, "Policing Race and Racing Police," 127.

66   **The slave code in South Carolina**: Ibid., 130.

66   **Similar to the initial**: Ibid., 128.

66   **The slave patrols had broad**: Turner, Giacopassi, and Vandiver, "Ignoring the Past," 185.

66   **By the end of the eighteenth**: Hassett-Walker, "How You Start Is How You Finish?"

67   **"Neither slavery nor"**: U.S. Const. amend. XIII, §1.

67   **The Black codes dictated**: Hassett-Walker, "How You Start Is How You Finish?"

67   **Among these new laws**: Robinson, "Black Bodies on the Ground," 556.

68   **During this time**: Roberts, "Abolition Constitutionalism," 29–32.

68   **These Black codes**: Bell, *Race, Racism, and American Law*, chap. 2.

69   **The enslavement of Black**: Colley, "Nova Scotia's First Black Superintendent."

70   **You can draw that line**: Bogel-Burroughs and Kovaleski, "Breonna Taylor Raid."

70   **The warrant was later**: Oppel Jr., Taylor, and Bogel-Burroughs, "What to Know About Breonna Taylor's Death."

70   **As a former professor**: Carbado, "From Stopping Black People to Killing Black People," 129–30.

71   **The police executed**: Lovan, "Q&A: What Were the Results of Breonna Taylor Investigation?"

71   **On November 1, 2024, a federal jury**: U.S. Department of Justice, Office of Public Affairs, "Former Louisville, Kentucky, Metro Police Officer Found Guilty."

71   **The city of Louisville, Kentucky**: Morales, Levenson, Joseph, and Carrega, "Louisville Agrees to Pay Breonna Taylor's Family."

72   **Black drivers in the United States**: Weitzer and Brunson, "Policing Different Racial Groups," 131.

72   **Black people in my hometown**: Ontario Human Rights Commission, *Collective Impact*, 3.

72   **Black people in the United States**: Schwartz and Jahn, "Mapping Fatal Police Violence," 5.

72   **Or the fact that Greater**: "Greater Manchester Police," BBC.

73   **Prior to the police**: Boyle, "Police in Ireland Before the Union: II," 121; Monkkonen, "History of Urban Police," 549–50; Waxman, "How the U.S. Got Its Police Force."

74   **Take the first**: Linebaugh, *London Hanged*, 425.

74   **At the time**: Ibid., 404–6.

75   **Patrick Colquhoun, one of the founders**: Ibid., 428.

75   **In the northern United States**: Potter, *History of Policing*, 2; Waxman, "How the U.S. Got Its Police Force."

76   **These business owners were**: Nalla and Newman, "Is White-Collar Policing, Policing?," 306, 313; Potter, *History of Policing*, 4–7; Waxman, "How the U.S. Got Its Police Force."

77   **From 1880 to 1900**: Lipold and Isaac, "Repressing Worker Dissent," 3; Potter, *History of Policing*, 6.

78   **The investigation revealed**: U.S. Department of Justice, *Investigation of the Ferguson Police Department*, 9.

79   **A class-action lawsuit**: Fines & Fees Justice Center, "Fant et al. v. City of Ferguson"; ArchCity Defenders, "Court Preliminarily Approves Class Action Settlement."

79   **Imagine that you**: Vandell, "Man Had $39,500 Seized by Arizona Police."

80   **The police can confiscate**: Miller, "Civil Asset Forfeiture," 2.

80   **According to a class-action lawsuit**: *Christos Sourovelis et al. v. City of Philadelphia et al.*; Institute for Justice, "Philadelphia's Civil Forfeiture Machine."

81   **In Philadelphia, the asset**: *Christos Sourovelis et al. v. City of Philadelphia et al.*; Mock, "'Policing for Profit' in Philadelphia."

81 **From 281 to 2019**: Knepper et al., *Policing for Profit*, 15.

81 **An investigation by**: O'Harrow, Rich, and Tan, "Asset Seizures Fuel Police Spending."

82 **A study by Lucy Parsons Labs**: Ciaramella, "Poor Neighborhoods Hit Hardest."

82 **John Yoder and Brad Cates**: Yoder and Cates, "Government Self-Interest Corrupted."

83 **The Supreme Court**: *Halima Tariffa Culley, et al. v. Steven T. Marshall.*

83 **Police also maintain**: Goodwin, Shepard, and Sloan, *Police Brutality Bonds.*

CHAPTER THREE: WHAT WE'VE WROUGHT

88 **Writing in *The Washington Post***: Vitale, "Five Myths About Policing."

88 **Abolitionist organizer**: Kaba, "Yes, We Mean Literally Abolish the Police."

88 **The same is true**: Heath, "80% of Police Officers Time."

88 **The British Crime Survey**: Reiner, "Who Governs?," 171.

89 **Controlling space is one**: Boddie, "Racially Territorial Policing," 480.

89 **While official apartheid laws**: Capers, "Policing, Race, and Place," 69–72.

90 **Though the decision discusses**: Carbado, "From Stopping Black People to Killing Black People," 31.

90 **Like the *Brignoni-Ponce***: Government of Ontario Reg. 58/16, Police Services Act, §5.

91 **One 2002 study**: Capers, "Policing, Race, and Place," 67; Meehan and Ponder, "Race and Place," 415.

93 **The heavier police presence**: Boddie, "Racially Territorial Policing," 481.

93 **"High-crime area"**: Ibid., 497.

94 **Larnie Thomas and Mathias Ometu**: CBS Minnesota, "Man from Viral Video Sues"; Eaton, "City Lands Big Win."

94 **Neli Latson, who was eighteen**: Vargas, "Black Disabled Teen."

94 **He was later re-incarcerated**: Autistic Self Advocacy Network.

95 **His family also filed**: *Reinald Latson v. Harold Clarke.*

96 **The truth is**: Capers, "Policing, Race, and Place," 63.

96 **Selling cigarettes in violation**: Siff, "4 EMS Workers Suspended"; Baker, Goodman, and Mueller, "Beyond the Chokehold."

97 **More than *five years later***: Southall, "Daniel Pantaleo."

97 **No one was made safer**: Wang, "Erica Garner."

97 **The theory behind**: Hinkle and Weisburd, "Irony of Broken Windows Policing," 503.

99 **An analysis by the New York**: Gregorian, Bult, and Ryley, "Exclusive: Daily News Analysis Finds Racial Disparities."

100 **In support of this**: Balko, *Rise of the Warrior Cop*, 11.

100 **A paper commissioned**: Rahr and Rice, "From Warriors to Guardians," 6.

100 **Philando Castile, a thirty-two-year-old**: Warnke, "Opinion: Sandra Bland, Philando Castile, and Now Charleena Lyles."

100 **When Yanez asked**: Peterson, "Why the Philando Castile Police-Shooting."

101 **We can't know**: Hauptman, "'Warrior Mindset' Police Training."

101 **He has trained**: Grossman Academy, "About the Colonel."

102 **Our experience was**: Daugherty, "Story of Mother Sentenced to Jail"; Edwards, "This Mom Went to Prison."

103 **Despite the increased**: Nelson, Leung, and Cobb, *Right to Remain a Student*, 9–14.

104 **students at Northern Secondary School**: MajorKraze, "Student Arrested at Northern Secondary School for No Reason."

104 **Reports from the time**: Rushowy, "Arrested Student Suspended."

105 **This mirrors the safer**: Thomas and Mohdin, "Nearly 1,000 Police Officers Operating in UK Schools."

105 **The same is true in the United States**: Kupchik et al., "Police Ambassadors," 392; DePaoli and McCombs, *Safe Schools, Thriving Students*, 6.

106 **The stories contained in the map**: #PoliceFreeSchools Advancement Project, "#AssaultAt Map."

107 **Between the United States**: Kupchik et al., "Police Ambassadors," 392.

107 **In the U.K., nearly one thousand**: Thomas and Mohdin, "Nearly 1,000 Police Officers Operating in UK Schools."

107 **These police officers performed**: Badshah, "Met Police Urged to Admit Racism."

107 **A disproportionate number**: Nagesh, "Child Q: Schoolgirl Strip-Search Not Isolated."

107 **In one case**: Badshah, "Met Police Urged to Admit Racism."

107 **Child Q and her parents**: "Hackney Schoolgirl Strip-Searched," BBC News.

108 **In fact, one of the metrics**: Thomas and Mohdin, "Nearly 1,000 Police Officers Operating in UK Schools."

108 **In a study of crimes**: Baughman, "How Effective Are Police?," 95.

CHAPTER FOUR: BETRAYAL OF TRUST

110 **While social control for the behavior**: Nalla and Newman, "Is White-Collar Policing, Policing?," 307.

111 **In a release**: U.S. Attorney's Office, "Monsanto Agrees to Plead Guilty."

111 **One study suggests**: Holtz, "UW Study: Exposure to Chemical in Roundup."

111 **Monsanto has been sued**: Gaines, "Roundup Lawsuit Update."

111 **Although he was initially awarded**: Egelko, "Award to Vallejo Groundskeeper."

111 **Bayer, the company**: Agence France Presse, "Higher Prices for Herbicides."

111 **Large numbers of people**: Cliff and Wall-Parker, "Statistical Analysis of White-Collar Crime," 6.

112 **During the COVID-19 pandemic**: Jayanetti, "At Least 130,000 Households in England Made Homeless"; Ronayne, Casey, and Mulvihill, "Homelessness Surging"; Sweet, "Vulnerability to Homelessness Much Higher."

113 **These were the words**: KC Defender Staff, "KCPD Said Missing Black Women Reports in KC Were 'Completely Unfounded.'"

113 **The twenty-two-year-old**: Ibid.; Lowe, "Jaynie Crosdale."

114 **In the United States, Black women**: Alexander and Willie, "Epidemic of Missing Black Women."

114 **In Canada, Indigenous women**: Native Women's Association of Canada, "Fact Sheet: Missing and Murdered," 3.

114 **And in the U.K.**: Norton Cultural Centre, "Frequently Asked Questions."

116 **A minority of sexual**: Bureau of Justice Statistics, *Criminal Victimization*, 6; Department of Justice Canada, "Sexual Assault," 1; Rape Crisis England & Wales, "Rape and Sexual Assault Statistics."

116 **Daniel Holtzclaw is a former**: Redden, "Daniel Holtzclaw."

116 **According to the U.S. Department**: Bureau of Justice Statistics, *Criminal Victimization*, 6; Department of Justice Canada, "Sexual Assault," 1; Rape Crisis England & Wales, "Rape and Sexual Assault Statistics."

116 **In the United States**: Domestic Shelters, "Domestic Abuse Topline Facts."

117 **In Canada, nearly**: Canadian Women's Foundation, "Facts About Sexual Assault."

117 **One-quarter of all women**: USAFacts, "Data Says Domestic Violence Incidents Are Down."

117 **intimate partner violence is**: Hafemeister, "If All You Have Is a Hammer," 920.

117 **Intimate partner violence suffers**: Ibid., 922.

119 **Police officers often disbelieve**: Gruber, "How Police Became the Go-to Response."

120 **Since the widespread**: Ibid.

120 **Nearly two-thirds**: Hafemeister, "If All You Have Is a Hammer," 963.

120 **Since the adoption**: Rajan and McCloskey, "Victims of Intimate Partner Violence."

120 **In cases of dual arrest**: Leisenring, "Victims' Perceptions of Police Response," 157.

121 **One study showed**: Gruber, "How Police Became the Go-to Response."

121 **And yet the majority**: Ibid.

CHAPTER FIVE: HOW WE'VE FAILED

127 *Even when* **a police officer**: *Pearson v. Callahan*; Schwartz, "Case Against Qualified Immunity," 1802.

127 **The fatal case**: *Gladis Callwood v. Jay Jones*, writ; *Gladis Callwood v. Jay Jones*, respondents' brief.

129 **Gladis Callwood, Mr. Illidge's mother**: *Gladis Callwood v. Jay Jones*.

129 **In the matter of**: *Gladis Callwood v. Jay Jones*. 11th Cir.

130 **Mr. Reinhold was a forty-two-year-old**: McGreevy and Spitzer, "OCDA Report: Officer-Involved Shooting."

130 **According to the Orange**: Orange County Sheriff-Coroner Department, "Homeless Outreach and Liaison," 1.

131 **The following day**: Orange County DA, "OCDA Report Officer-Involved Shooting—Kurt Reinhold."

133 **"In order for Deputy Duran"**: McGreevy and Spitzer, "OCDA Report: Officer-Involved Shooting."

134 **Association of Orange**: Ray and Spitzer, "Recipient Committee Campaign Statement," 6, January 19, 2020.

134 **the Santa Ana**: Ray and Spitzer, "Recipient Committee Campaign Statement," 10, July 24, 2020.

134 **the Huntington Beach**: Ray and Spitzer, "Recipient Committee Campaign Statement," 11, January 19, 2020; Ray and Spitzer, "Recipient Committee Campaign Statement," 33, January 19, 2022.

134 **the Westminster Police**: Ray and Spitzer, "Recipient Committee Campaign Statement," 24, January 19, 2020.

134 **the Pasadena Police**: Ibid., 17.

134 **the Anaheim Police**: Ray and Spitzer, "Recipient Committee Campaign Statement," 4, July 24, 2020.

134 **the City of Orange**: Ibid.

134 **the California Statewide**: Fleming, "Who Is Bankrolling Orange County DA's Re-election?"

134 **the Orange County**: Ray and Spitzer, "Recipient Committee Campaign Statement," 7, July 24, 2020.

134 **the PAC of the Irvine**: Ibid., 8.

134 **the Tustin Police**: Ibid., 11.

134 **and the Garden Grove**: Ray and Spitzer, "Recipient Committee Campaign Statement," 27, January 19, 2022; Ray and Spitzer, "Recipient Committee Campaign Statement," 10, January 19, 2020.

135 **In December 2020**: Smith, "County Awards $7.5 Million."

136 **The Federal Rules**: U.S. Judiciary, Federal Rules of Criminal Procedure, 10.

136 **In a world**: Levine, "Who Shouldn't Prosecute the Police," 1471.

137 **According to Mapping**: Mapping Police Violence, "2022 Police Violence Report."

137 **The Police Integrity Research Group**: Stinson and Wentzlof, "On-Duty Shootings: Police Officers Charged," 1.

139 **Andrew Loku, may he rest**: Gillis, "Andrew Loku Was Traumatized."

139 **According to the SIU report**: Special Investigations Unit, "SIU Report on Andrew Loku's Shooting."

140 **Days after the shooting**: Gillis, "Andrew Loku Was Traumatized."

140 **In one officer's account**: Gillis, "Rookie Cop Says Shooting Andrew Loku."

140 **Witnesses say Mr. Loku**: Khandaker, "Black Lives Matter Blasts Censored Details"; Gillis, "One Death, Two Versions."

140 **The vast majority**: DiMatteo, "Police Watchdog SIU Clears 95 Per Cent of Cops."

141 **The report reveals**: Special Investigations Unit, "SIU Report on Andrew Loku's Shooting."

141 **Consider the case of Jermaine Carby**: Gallant, "Officer Defends Taking Knife from Scene."

141 **The SIU report**: Ontario Special Investigations Unit, "SIU Concludes Shooting Death Investigation in Brampton."

142 **Mr. Carby's family**: Khandaker, "Family of Man Killed by Ontario Cops."

142 **Mr. Loparco raised**: Ontario Special Investigations Unit, "SIU Concludes Shooting Death Investigation in Brampton."

142 **According to the Cato**: Olson, "Police Misconduct and 'Law Enforcement Officers' Bill of Rights' Laws."

143 **The former Ontario ombudsman**: Marin, *Oversight Unseen*, 10, 92, 109; Marin, *Oversight Undermined*, 5, 20, 35, 44, 48.

143 **In the United States**: Council on Criminal Justice, "Civilian Oversight," 2.

143 **In the case of**: Ontario Ombudsman, "Oversight Unseen—Facts and Highlights."

144 **Studies suggest they**: Ariel et al., "Wearing Body Cameras Increases Assaults," 750.

145 **The scientific research**: Yokum, Ravishankar, and Coppock, "Evaluating the Effects of Police Body-Worn Cameras," 3, 21.

145 **Even though body cameras**: Zansberg, "Public Access to Police Body-Worn Camera Recordings."

145 **In fact, the global market**: Lacy, "Two Companies Fight to Corner."

146 **Police see body cameras**: Dodd, "Ministers Looking at Body-Worn Facial Recognition"; Lee and Chin-Rothmann, "Police Surveillance and Facial Recognition."

146 *Wired* **reported on**: Newman, "Police Bodycams Can Be Hacked."

148 **In footage taken**: Black Lives Matter London, "In April 2023, Zodoq Obatolah."

148 **Police shot the unarmed**: Russell, "Vigil and March Held."

148 **But let's be perfectly clear**: Zipes, "Sudden Cardiac Arrest and Death," 2418.

149 **A Reuters investigation**: Smith et al., "Shock Tactics: The Vulnerable."

149 **Being from one**: Minhas et al., "Family Income and Cardiovascular Disease," 1.

149 **Even though children**: Wald and Thurau, *Catch & Stun*, 17.

149 **An American Public Media**: Gilbert, Caputo, and Hing, "When Tasers Fail."

150 **In the 2016 case**: Feith, "Black Man Was Hit in the Head."

150 **Officer Gilbert was**: "Police Officer Acquitted in Fatal Shooting," CBC News.

151 **And yet companies**: Wrap Technologies, "BolaWrap."

152 **And throughout the time**: Meadow, "Police Brutality Statistics."

153 **"Do you see"**: *Woodruff v. City of Detroit*.

154 **In fact, a study**: Romine, "Facial Recognition Technology."

154 **As reported by** *The Verge*: Stroud, "Heat Listed."

155 **Chicago stopped using**: Gorner and Sweeny, "For Years Chicago Police Rated the Risk."

156 **On October 3**: *Steen v. City of Pensacola*.

157 **As a result**: Suarez-Balcazar et al., "Race, Poverty, and Disability," 355.

157 **The commission identified**: National Advisory Commission on Civil Disorders, *Report*.

158 **As the Knapp Commission**: Krauss, "Bad Apple Shake-Ups," 30.

CHAPTER SIX: MANUFACTURING CRIME

163 **On New Year's Eve**: Fernandez, "BART Police Bloodied Woman."

163 **On body camera**: "Warning: Graphic: BART Officers Accused," KTVU Fox 2 San Francisco.

163 **According to a suit**: *Devereaux v. Lucas*, August 2021.

163 **Ms. Devereaux's case**: *Devereaux v. Lucas*, April 2023.

165 **If you are living**: Melore, "Cost-of-Living Crisis in UK"; Dickler, "60% of Americans Are Still Living Paycheck to Paycheck"; Ritchie, "Almost Half of Canadians Living Paycheque to Paycheque"; WTW, "40% of UK Employees Live Payday-to-Payday"; Leonhardt, "Living Paycheck to Paycheck Is Common."

166 **In fact, research**: Gibbs, "Myth That Tough Sanctions Deter Crime"; Paternoster, "How Much Do We Really Know About Criminal Deterrence," 765.

167 **"Good Morning All"**: Childs and Zahniser, "LAPD Condemns Officer's Email."

170 **Take the story**: Zed, "Toronto Tiny Shelters."

171 **And then the City**: Draaisma, "Toronto Carpenter Who Builds Tiny Shelters."

171 **Some reports suggest**: Fraieli, "Taxes Are Being Used to Fight Rather Than Solve Homelessness."

173 **It's why we occasionally**: Nichols, "It's Not Illegal to Live Together as an Unmarried Couple."

173 **In July 2015**: ACLU, Iowa Civil Rights Commission Complaint on Behalf of Meagan Taylor.

173 **In an audio recording**: Strangio, "No, Seeing a Transgender Person Is Not a Reason to Call 911."

175 **One day in 1919**: Stern, *Trials of Nina McCall*, 73, 5, 133; "Arrests Halted After Women Taken," *Sacramento Bee*, 1, 5; Stern, "America's Forgotten Mass Imprisonment."

176 **Enacted in 1974**: U.S. Department of Housing and Urban Development, "Housing Choice Vouchers Fact Sheet."

176 **Landlords often refuse**: Cunningham et al., *Pilot Study of Landlord Acceptance*.

176 **Writing for the American**: Rhoades, "Freedom of Choice for Low-Income Renters."

177 **The city's Black**: Ocen, "New Racially Restrictive Covenant," 1572.

177 **In January 2007**: Swain, "Renting While Black," 1.

178 **They also sent**: *Williams v. City of Antioch*, May 2008.

178 **A report issued**: Hayat, "Section 8 Is the New N-Word," 64.

178 **Police would place**: Ocen, "New Racially Restrictive Covenant," 1576.

179 **Mary Scott was**: *Williams v. City of Antioch*, April 2012.

180 **In 2016, after**: McGillivray, "Group of Lawyers Step Up to Defend Men."

180 **For six weeks**: Reason, "Toronto Police Cracking Down on Public Sex."

180 **Constable Ward later pleaded**: Davis, "Toronto Police Officer Admits to Inappropriate."

184 **Currently, more people**: New York Times Editorial Board, "America Has Lost the War on Drugs"; Revolving Doors, "Rethinking Drugs."

184 **The war on drugs**: Coyne and Hall, *Four Decades and Counting.*

184 **By 2019, that number**: U.S. Department of Justice, "Arrests."

184 **Even when people**: Schwartzapfel and Jenkins, "Inside the Nation's Overdose Crisis."

185 **Multiple studies have shown**: Coyne and Hall, *Four Decades and Counting.*

185 **Punitive drug laws**: Victor and del Pozo, "Here's Why Police Drug Busts Don't Work."

185 **The U.S. government has spent**: Coyne and Hall, *Four Decades and Counting.*

185 **"You want to know"**: Baum, "Legalize It All."

187 **Take Oregon, for example**: Wilson, "Oregon Pioneered a Radical Drug Policy"; Szalavitz, "Portugal Has Succeeded Where We've Failed"; Botkin, "Law Enforcement Officials Seek Means"; Hayden, "Measure 110 Shows Early Successes"; Gebelhoff, "No, Oregon's Drug Decriminalization Law Was Not a Failure"; Hinch, "What Happened When Oregon Decriminalized Hard Drugs"; Mathis, "Why Did Oregon Recriminalize Drug Possession."

187 **Some even cited**: Wilson, "Oregon Pioneered a Radical Drug Policy."

188 **But while partial**: Hayden, "Measure 110 Shows Early Successes."

188 **The programs build**: PHS Community Services Society, "Insite"; Allingham, "Fight for Safe Supply of Drugs."

188 **Eventually, through this activism**: Mickleburgh, "B.C. Safe-Injection Site Wins."

188 **Since then, more than**: Gordon, "What's the Evidence That Supervised Drug Injection Sites."

189 **In Vancouver, access**: Dellplain, "Future of DULF Compassion Club."

189 **In a report by the British**: Gamage, "'DULF, as We Knew It, Is Dead.'"

189 **In May 2024, the two founders of DULF**: File Number 270084, Vancouver, B.C. British Columbia Court Services Online. justice.gov .bc.ca/cso/criminal/file/charges.do?fileID=7264113.0009.

189 **In October 2024, they filed a constitutional challenge**: Greer, "Founders of B.C. Drug 'Compassion Club' File Charter Challenge."

190 **The first drug**: Rosenfeld, "Overdose Awareness Day"; Transform Drug Policy Foundation, "Short History of the Misuse of Drugs Act"; Davison, "Brief History of Drug Criminalization."

190 **In the U.K., sex work**: City of London Police, "Sex Worker Safety."

190 **In Canada, sex work**: Department of Justice Canada, Prostitution Criminal Law Reform.

190 **In the United States**: Decriminalize Sex Work, "Prostitution Laws by State."

190 **Today's sex work laws**: Stern, *Trials of Nina McCall*, 11.

191 **The rhetorical strategy**: García, "Beware of Pity," 99; University of Toronto Libraries, *Legislating the "White Slave Panic"*; Stern, *Trials of Nina McCall*, 24.

192 **Not only is it difficult**: Decriminalize Sex Work, "Human Trafficking and Sex Work."

192 **An investigative study**: Spina, "When a Protector Becomes a Predator."

192 **An equally upsetting**: Kale, "Police Are Allegedly Sleeping with Sex Workers."

CHAPTER SEVEN: "I CAN HEAR HER BREATHING"

194 **Another world is not only**: Roy, *War Talk*, 75.

195 **In 2021, with the approval**: Pratt, "'Birds Stopped Singing'"; Stop Cop City, "No Police Military Base in Weelaunee Forest."

195 **The plans would destroy**: Defend the Atlanta Forest, "Frequently Asked Questions."

195 **The land has**: Public Safety Training Center, "Atlanta Public Safety Training Center"; Atlanta Community Press Collective, "Brief History of the Atlanta City Prison Farm."

195 **Under the plan**: Public Safety Training Center, "Atlanta Public Safety Training Center"; Dixon and Wheatley, "Where 'Cop City' Leaders Stumbled"; Atlanta Community Press Collective, "Backroom Deals and Elasticity Clause"; Gardner, "Stopping Cop City."

195 **Mr. Brooks was**: Associated Press, "Atlanta to Pay $1 Million Settlement."

196 **Mr. Brooks was patted**: Atlanta News First, "APD Bodycam Footage," YouTube, youtube.com; Zennie62, "Brosnan Body Cam," YouTube, youtube.com; Georgia Bureau of Investigation, "Wendy's Surveillance Video."

196 **In the ensuing struggle**: Ortiz, "What to Know About the Death of Rayshard Brooks."

196 **Senator Raphael Warnock**: Ibid.

197 **In the aftermath**: Hudson and Loreto, "Episode 108—We Have Already Won."

199 **Prior to the Atlanta City Council**: Atlanta Community Press Collective, "Backroom Deals and Elasticity Clause"; Dixon and Wheatley, "Where 'Cop City' Leaders Stumbled"; Pratt, "'Birds Stopped Singing.'"

200 **Environmental activists concerned**: Block Cop City, "Brief Timeline of the Movement to Stop Cop City."

200 **In January 2023**: Alfonseca, "DeKalb County Releases Autopsy."

200 **Another autopsy commissioned**: Goldberg, "Remembering Tortuguita"; Binder, "Manuel 'Tortuguita' Terán's Independent Autopsy."

201 **Court documents suggest**: Ruch, "Training Center Security Costs $41,500 a Day."

201 **As of September 2023**: Young, Conlon, and Yan, "61 'Cop City' Protesters Indicted on RICO Charges."

204 **The service is not currently**: City of Portland, Oregon, "Portland Street Response Frequently Asked Questions."

205 **The program partnered**: Townley and Leickly, *Portland Street Response*, 22, 32.

205 **"What I liked"**: Ibid., 52.

205 **"They still come"**: Ibid., 51.

206 **"She stuck with me"**: Ibid.

206 **Unfortunately, unlike policing**: Hayden and Kavanaugh, "Portland Street Response's Future"; Zielinski, "Portland Street Response, Despite Successes."

206 **The Albuquerque Community**: One Albuquerque, "Two Years of Service from Community Safety."

206 **In addition to the Community**: Ruiz-Angel and Erhard, *City of Albuquerque Community Safety Department FY24 Q1 Report*, 8.

206 **In my hometown**: Centre for Addiction and Mental Health, *Toronto Community Crisis Service*.

207 **In 2023, the city**: "City Council Votes Unanimously to Expand Community Crisis Service," CBC News.

207 **In 2023, London's**: Pidd, "How Humberside Police's Pioneering Policy."

208 **She and another officer**: Lavoie, "Explainer: Can Officers Stop Drivers for Air Fresheners?"

208 **While the police were**: "New Video of Ex-cop Fatally Shooting Daunte Wright," *Good Morning America*.

208 **Kimberly Potter was convicted**: Timsit, "Minn. City to Pay $3.25M in Police Killing."

208 **And then there's**: Lemieux, "What Happened to Sandra Bland?"

209 **And yet traffic stops**: Bureau of Justice Statistics, "Traffic Stops."

209 **road traffic injuries**: Centers for Disease Control and Prevention, "Global Road Safety"; Parachute, "Road Safety."

210 **For example, several jurisdictions**: Pennsylvania Department of Transportation, "Elimination of Stickers."

212 **That was certainly the case**: Rabin, "After 3 Years, Families Still Don't Know Who Killed Loved Ones."

213 **An additional individual**: *Nguyen v. Miami Dade Police Department*.

213 **An investigation into the incident**: Olmeda, "Grand Jury Will Review Fatal 2019 Shooting"; Gothner, "All Bullets Killing UPS Driver, Bystander in Miramar Shootout Came from Officers"; Ojo and Torres, "Police Officers Surrender to Face Charges"; Florida Department of Law Enforcement, Case Number: MI-27-0120.

214 **In an analysis**: Baughman, "How Effective Are Police?," 95.

214 **In England and Wales**: Home Office, *Official Statistics: Crime Outcomes in England and Wales*.

215 **The second thing**: Roman et al., *Victim-Offender Overlap*.

216 **Nonpolice violence interruption**: St. Julien, "Community-Based Violence Interruption Programs."

217 **By way of example**: Cure Violence Global, "Our Impact."

218 **The United States has the highest**: Fox et al., "How US Gun Culture Stacks Up with the World."

219 **The rate of mass shootings**: Gun Violence Archive, "Mass Shootings in 2023."

219 **As the U.S. gun market**: Riley, Kocieniewski, and Fan, "How the US Drives Gun Exports."

219 **One of Canada's worst**: Center for American Progress, "Frequently Asked Questions About Gun Trafficking."

219 **Handguns are also**: Bradley, "How American Guns Are Fueling U.K. Crime."

219 **A report by *The New York Times***: Fisher, "Other Countries Had Mass Shootings."

220 **Similar success has been achieved**: "Gun Control, Explained," *New York Times.*

220 **"A functioning, robust democracy"**: Achebe, "Chinua Achebe on Corruption and Hope in Nigeria."

221 **In *No More Police***: Kaba and Ritchie, *No More Police*, 69.

221 **Police are responsible**: Beckett, "One in 20 US Homicides Are Committed by Police."

221 ***USA Today* found**: Kelly and Nichols, "We Found 85,000 Cops Who've Been Investigated for Misconduct."

221 **In 2023, another horrifying case**: Che, "6 Ex-officers Plead Guilty to State Charges"; Howey and Rosenfield, "How a 'Goon Squad' of Deputies Got Away with Years of Brutality."

AFTERWORD

225 **Ms. Massey had called**: Negussie and Ghebremedhin, "Sonya Massey Case."

225 **In widely shared footage**: Illinois State Police, "Sangamon County Sheriff's Office July 6, 2024 OIS Incident."

226 **Perhaps if Grayson**: Negussie and Ghebremedhin, "Sonya Massey Case."

226 **Sonya Massey is just one**: Mapping Police Violence, "Mapping Police Violence."

226 **More than three thousand students**: *New York Times*, "Where Protesters on U.S. Campuses Have Been Arrested or Detained."

226 **at Columbia University**: Watson, Keller, Thompson, and Dazio, "More Than 2,100 People Have Been Arrested."

227 **In June, a joint investigation**: Umansky, "New Yorkers Were Choked, Beaten and Tased."

227 **Some states have expanded**: Cline, "Louisiana Proposes Bill"; Valerie Gonzalez, "What We Know About Texas' New Law."

227 **In August, a federal judge**: CBS News, "Judge Rules Breonna Taylor's Boyfriend Caused Her Death."

227 **And Mapping Police Violence**: Mapping Police Violence, "Mapping Police Violence."

227 **The bill promises**: House Committee on the Judiciary, "Justice in Policing Act."

228 **a type of restraint**: Peischel, "Activists Say Democrats' Proposed Chokehold Ban Won't Work."

228 **The People's Response Act**: Community Safety Agenda, "People's Response Act."

BIBLIOGRAPHY

Achebe, Chinua, interviewed by Scott Baldauf. "Chinua Achebe on Corruption and Hope in Nigeria." *Christian Science Monitor*, March 22, 2013. www.csmonitor.com/World/Africa/2013/0322/Chinua-Achebe-on-corruption-and-hope-in-Nigeria.

ACLU. Iowa Civil Rights Commission Complaint on Behalf of Meagan Taylor. June 28, 2016. aclu.org.

Agence France-Presse. "Higher Prices for Herbicides Boost Bayer Profits in 2022." *Barron's*, Feb. 28, 2023.

Alberta Lobbyist Registry. "Organization Lobbyist Registration—Semi-annual Renewal." Calgary: Alberta Office of the Ethics Commissioner, 2021.

Alexander, K. A., and T. C. Willie. "An Epidemic of Missing Black Women Has Been Ignored for Too Long." *Hill*, Oct. 10, 2023. thehill.com.

Alfonseca, K. "DeKalb County Releases Autopsy in 'Cop City' Protester Manuel Teran's Death." ABC News, April 19, 2023. abcnews.go.com.

Allen, A. "Top Retailers Say Theft Has Reached Historic Highs." *Washington Free Beacon*, Dec. 7, 2022.

Allen, O. E. *The Tiger.* New York: Addison-Wesley, 1993.

Allingham, J. "Fight for Safe Supply of Drugs Is 'This Generation's Insite,' Advocates Say." CBC News, Sept. 14, 2019. www.cbc.ca.

ArchCity Defenders. "Court Preliminarily Approves Class Action Settlement on Behalf of Thousands of People Jailed by the City of Ferguson for Money Damages." Feb. 27, 2024.

Ariel, B., A. Sutherland, D. Henstock, J. Young, P. Drover, J. Sykes, . . . R. Henderson. "Wearing Body Cameras Increases Assaults Against Officers and Does Not Reduce Police Use of Force: Results from a Global Multi-site Experiment." *European Journal of Criminology* 13, no. 6 (2016): 744–55.

Asher, A. "Salvador Ramos Shot Grandmother in Face After 'Fighting over Graduation' Before School Attack." *Independent*, May 25, 2022.

Asher, J., and B. Horwitz. "How Do the Police Actually Spend Their Time?" *New York Times*, June 19, 2020.

Associated Press. "Atlanta to Pay $1 Million Settlement to Family of Rayshard Brooks." PBS, Nov. 21, 2022. pbs.org.

Atlanta Community Press Collective. "Backroom Deals and Elasticity Clause Increase Public Cost of Cop City." May 24, 2023. atlpresscollective.com.

———. "A Brief History of the Atlanta City Prison Farm." Aug. 14, 2021. atlpresscollective.com.

Atlanta News First. "APD Bodycam Footage of Shooting of Rayshard Brooks." YouTube, June 13, 2020.

Autistic Self Advocacy Network. "ASAN Calls for Neli Latson's Release." Nov. 24, 2014. autisticadvocacy.org.

Badshah, N. "Met Police Urged to Admit Racism After Strip-Search of Black Girl in Hackney." *Guardian*, April 1, 2022.

Baker, A., J. D. Goodman, and B. Mueller. "Beyond the Chokehold: The Path to Eric Garner's Death." *New York Times*, June 13, 2015.

Balko, R. *Rise of the Warrior Cop: The Militarization of America's Police Forces.* New York: PublicAffairs, 2013.

Baughman, S. "How Effective Are Police? The Problem of Clearance Rates and Criminal Accountability." *Alabama Law Review* 72, no. 1 (2020): 47–130.

Baum, D. "Legalize It All." *Harper's Magazine*, April 2016. harpers.org.

BBC. "Greater Manchester Police Branded 'Institutionally Racist.'" July 27, 2021. www.bbc.com.

BBC News. "Hackney Schoolgirl Strip-Searched by Met Police Was Taken out of Exam." March 16, 2022. bbc.com.

Beale, S. S. "The News Media's Influence on Criminal Justice Policy: How Market-Driven News Promotes Punitiveness." *William & Mary Law Review* 48, no. 2 (Nov. 2006): 397–481.

Bearden v. Georgia, 461 U.S. 660 (1983).

Beckett, L. "One in 20 US Homicides Are Committed by Police—and the Numbers Aren't Falling." *Guardian*, Feb. 15, 2023.

Bell, D. *Race, Racism, and American Law: Leading Cases and Materials*, 2023 ed. Frederick, MD: Aspen Publishing, 2023.

Binder, A. "Manuel 'Tortuguita' Terán's Independent Autopsy Report Released at Press Conference." Unicorn Riot, March 13, 2023. unicornriot .ninja.

Black Lives Matter London. Facebook, Sept. 14, 2023. facebook.com.

Bleiberg, J., and P. J. Weber. "Uvalde Report: 376 Officers but 'Egregiously Poor' Decisions." Associated Press, July 17, 2022.

Block Cop City. "Brief Timeline of the Movement to Stop Cop City." Nov. 2023. blockcopcity.org/timeline.

Boddie, E. C. "Racially Territorial Policing in Black Neighborhoods." *University of Chicago Law Review* 89, no. 2 (2022): 477–98.

Bogel-Burroughs, N., and S. F. Kovaleski. "Breonna Taylor Raid Puts Focus on Officers Who Lie for Search Warrants." *New York Times*, Aug. 6, 2022.

Botkin, B. "Law Enforcement Officials Seek Means Beyond Jail to Address Drug Epidemic." *Oregon Capital Chronicle*, Nov. 6, 2023.

Boyle, K. "Police in Ireland Before the Union: I." *Irish Jurist* 7, no. 1 (1972): 115–37.

———. "Police in Ireland Before the Union: II." *Irish Jurist* 8, no. 1 (1973): 90–116.

———. "Police in Ireland Before the Union: III." *Irish Jurist* 8, no. 2 (1973): 323–48.

Bradley, J. "How American Guns Are Fueling U.K. Crime." *New York Times*, Aug. 12, 2020.

Britneff, Beatrice. "Heart Condition, 'Aggravating' Factors Contributed to Abdi's Death, Pathologist Testifies in Ottawa Constable's Trial." *Global News*, June 4, 2019. globalnews.ca/news/5350408/pathologist-testifies-abdi-cause -of-death-police-officer-trial.

Brown, A., W. Parrish, and A. Speri. "The Battle of Treaty Camp." *Intercept*, Oct. 27, 2017. theintercept.com.

Brown, A., and N. Sadasivam. "Pipeline Company Spent Big on Police Gear to Use Against Standing Rock Protesters." *Intercept*, May 22, 2023. theintercept.com.

Brucato, B. "Policing Race and Racing Police: The Origin of US Police in Slave Patrols." *Social Justice* 47, no. 3 (2020): 115–36.

Bureau of Justice Statistics. *Criminal Victimization, 2022.* U.S. Department of Justice, 2023.

Canadian Women's Foundation. "The Facts About Sexual Assault and Harassment." Nov. 22, 2022. canadianwomen.org/the-facts/sexual-assault -harassment/.

Capers, B. "Policing, Place, and Race." *Harvard Civil Rights–Civil Liberties Law Review* 44, no. 1 (2009): 43–78.

Carbado, D. W. "From Stopping Black People to Killing Black People: The Fourth Amendment Pathways to Police Violence." *California Law Review* 105, no. 1 (2017): 125–64.

Carlson, G. "Not Just Inflation: Shoplifting and Soft-on-Crime Policies in the U.S. Push Prices Up, Too." *Globe and Mail*, Dec. 10, 2022.

CBC News. "City Council Votes Unanimously to Expand Community Crisis Service Across Toronto." Nov. 9, 2023. cbc.ca/news.

———. "Const. Daniel Montsion Not Guilty in Death of Abdirahman Abdi." Oct. 20, 2020. cbc.ca/news.

———. "Police Officer Acquitted in Fatal Shooting of Bony Jean-Pierre in Montréal-Nord." Feb. 4, 2021. cbc.ca/news.

———. "Your Questions Answered About Canada's Residential School System." June 4, 2021. cbc.ca/news.

CBS Minnesota. "Man from Viral Video Sues City of Edina, Police Officer." CBS News, Oct. 16, 2016. cbsnews.com.

CBS News. "Judge Rules Breonna Taylor's Boyfriend Caused Her Death." Aug. 26, 2024. cbsnews.com.

Center for American Progress. "Frequently Asked Questions About Gun Trafficking." Aug. 21, 2021. www.americanprogress.org.

Centers for Disease Control and Prevention. "Global Road Safety." Jan. 10, 2023. www.cdc.gov.

Centre for Addiction and Mental Health. *Toronto Community Crisis Service: One-*

Year Outcome Evaluation Report. Toronto: Centre for Addiction and Mental Health, 2023.

Channick, R. "Rising Crime Scaring Some Visitors Away from Michigan Avenue and Other Chicago Destinations During Crucial Holiday Shopping Season." *Chicago Tribune*, Dec. 11, 2021.

Chappell, B. "Derek Chauvin Is Sentenced to 22½ Years for George Floyd's Murder." National Public Radio, June 25, 2021. npr.org.

Che, C. "6 Ex-officers Plead Guilty to State Charges in Torture of Two Black Men." *New York Times*, Aug. 14, 2023.

Chermak, S. "Image Control: How Police Affect the Presentation of Crime News." *American Journal of Police* 14, no. 2 (1995): 21–44.

Chibnall, S. *Law-and-Order News.* London: Routledge, 2001.

Childs, J., and D. Zahniser. "LAPD Condemns Officer's Email on 'Hush Hush' Plan for Mass Arrests at Encampment Cleanup." *Los Angeles Times*, June 28, 2023.

Christos Sourovelis et al. v. City of Philadephia et al., 2:13-cv-04687-ER (U.S. District Court for the Eastern District of Pennsylvania, Feb. 23, 2017).

Ciaramella, C. "Poor Neighborhoods Hit Hardest by Asset Forfeiture in Chicago, Data Shows." *Reason*, June 13, 2017. reason.com.

City of London Police. "Sex Worker Safety." 2023. www.cityoflondon.police.uk.

City of Portland, Oregon. "Portland Street Response Frequently Asked Questions." July 11, 2023. portland.gov.

Cliff, G., and A. Wall-Parker. "Statistical Analysis of White-Collar Crime." In *Oxford Research Encyclopedia of Criminology and Criminal Justice*, April 26, 2017.

Cline, Sara. "Louisiana Proposes Bill." Associated Press, April 8, 2024.

Colley, S. B. "Nova Scotia's First Black Superintendent Appointed to Tri-county School Board." CBC News, March 24, 2017. cbcnews.ca.

Color of Change. *Normalizing Injustice: The Dangerous Misrepresentations That Define Television's Scripted Crime Genre.* USC Annenberg Norman Lear Center, 2020.

Community Safety Agenda. "People's Response Act." communitysafety.us.

Consent Decree on Plaintiff's Claims for Injunctive Relief in *Christos Sourovelis et al. v. City of Philadelphia*, 2:14-cv-04687-ER (United States, Sept. 18, 2018).

Cooke, L., and P. Sturges. "Police and Media Relations in an Era of Freedom of Information." *Policing and Society: An International Journal of Research and Policy* 19, no. 4 (2009): 406–24.

Corkery, M., and S. Maheshwari. "Thefts, Always an Issue for Retailers, Become More Brazen." *New York Times*, Dec. 3, 2021.

Council on Criminal Justice. "Civilian Oversight." Policy Assessment, Task Force on Policing, April 2021.

Court of British Columbia. File Number 270084. Vancouver, B.C. British Columbia Court Services Online. justice.gov.bc.ca/cso/criminal/file/charges .do?fileID=7264113.0009.

Coyne, C. J., and A. R. Hall. *Four Decades and Counting: The Continued Failure of the War on Drugs.* Cato Institute, April 12, 2017. cato.org.

Cunningham, M. K., M. M. Galvez, C. Aranda, R. Santos, D. Wissoker, A. D. Oneto, . . . J. Crawford. *A Pilot Study of Landlord Acceptance of Housing Choice Vouchers.* Urban Institute, Aug. 20, 2018. www.urban.org.

Cure Violence Global. "Our Impact." 2021. cvg.org/impact.

Daugherty, O. "Story of Mother Sentenced to Jail for Enrolling Child in Different District Resurfaced amid College Scandal." *Hill*, March 14, 2019. thehill.com.

Davis, Angela Y. *Freedom Is a Constant Struggle: Ferguson, Palestine, and the Foundations of a Movement*. Ed. Frank Barat. Chicago: Haymarket Books, 2016.

Davis, S. S. "Toronto Police Officer Admits to Inappropriate Sexual Relationship with Youth Group Member." *Toronto Star*, Dec. 9, 2017.

Davison, C. "A Brief History of Drug Criminalization in Canada." Law Now, Aug. 19, 2022. www.lawnow.org.

Decriminalize Sex Work. "Human Trafficking and Sex Work." 2023. decriminalize sex.work.

———. "Prostitution Laws by State." Sept. 3, 2023. decriminalizesex.work.

Defend the Atlanta Forest. "Frequently Asked Questions." 2023. defendthe atlantaforest.org/faq.

Dellplain, M. "Future of DULF Compassion Club Will Hinge on Judicial Review." Healthy Debate, March 4, 2024. healthydebate.ca.

Denis, J. S. "'Copaganda': Critics Challenge Police Report on Social Spending." *Tyee*, Nov. 9, 2022. thetyee.ca.

DePaoli, J., and J. McCombs. *Safe Schools, Thriving Students*. Palo Alto, Calif.: Learning Policy Institute, 2023.

Department of Justice Canada. Prostitution Criminal Law Reform: Bill C-36, the Protection of Communities and Exploited Persons Act. Government of Canada, Dec. 6, 2014. www.justice.gc.ca.

———. "Sexual Assault." JustFacts, 2019.

Devereaux v. Lucas, 4:21-cv-06169 (U.S. District Court for the Northern District of California, Aug. 11, 2021).

Devereaux v. Lucas, 3:21-cv-06169 (U.S. District Court for the Northern District of California, April 20, 2023).

Dhillon, J., and W. Parrish. "Canada Police Prepared to Shoot Indigenous Activists, Documents Show." *Guardian*, Dec. 19, 2019.

Dickler, J. "60% of Americans Are Still Living Paycheck to Paycheck as Inflation Hits Workers' Wages." CNBC News, Sept. 27, 2023. cnbc.com.

DiMatteo, E. "Police Watchdog SIU Clears 95 Per Cent of Cops Investigated in 2019." *NOW Magazine*, July 13, 2020. nowtoronto.com.

Dixon, K., and T. Wheatley. "Where 'Cop City' Leaders Stumbled When Seeking Public Support." *Axios Atlanta*, June 6, 2023. axios.com.

Dodd, V. "Ministers Looking at Body-Worn Facial Recognition Technology for Police." *Guardian*, May 16, 2023.

Doherty, T. *Pre-Code Hollywood: Sex, Immorality, and Insurrection in American Cinema, 1930–1934*. New York: Columbia University Press, 1999.

Domanick, J. "Public Corruption, L.A.-Style: Where Have the Notorious Gone?" *Los Angeles Times*, Jan. 25, 1998.

Domestic Shelters. "Domestic Abuse Topline Facts and Statistics." Jan. 7, 2015. www.domesticshelters.org.

Draaisma, M. "Toronto Carpenter Who Builds Tiny Shelters for Unhoused People Calls on City to Drop Legal Fight." CBC News, Feb. 22, 2021. cbc .ca/news.

Eaton, E. "City Lands Big Win in Lawsuit Filed by Black Jogger Wrongfully Arrested by San Antonio Police." *San Antonio Express-News*, Nov. 22, 2023.

Edwards, A. A. "This Mom Went to Prison for Enrolling Her Son in a School Outside Her District." Refinery29, March 15, 2019. refinery29.com.

Egelko, B. "Award to Vallejo Groundskeeper in Monsanto Cancer Case Slashed Again—Verdict Upheld." *San Francisco Chronicle*, July 20, 2020.

Elder, J. "Investigative Update on Critical Incident." *Inside MPD*, May 26, 2020. Wayback Machine. web.archive.org/web/20210331182901/https://www.insidempd.com/2020/05/26/man-dies-after-medical-incident-during-police-interaction.

Ennab, F. S. "Rupturing the Myth of the Peaceful Western Canadian Frontier: A Socio-historical Study of Colonization, Violence, and the North West Mounted Police, 1873–1905." Master's thesis, University of Manitoba, 2010.

Feith, J. "Black Man Was Hit in the Head by a Rubber Bullet, Trial of Montreal Cop Hears." *Gazette* (Montreal), Nov. 10, 2020. montrealgazette.com.

Fernandez, L. "BART Police Bloodied Woman Who Skipped $3.60 Fare, Video Shows." FOX KTVU 2, Aug. 11, 2021. ktvu.com.

Fines & Fees Justice Center. "Fant et al. v. City of Ferguson." March 19, 2020. finesandfeesjusticecenter.org.

Fisher, M. "Other Countries Had Mass Shootings. Then They Changed Their Gun Laws." *New York Times*, May 25, 2022.

Fleming, R. "Who Is Bankrolling Orange County DA's Re-election Campaign?" Davis Vanguard, Sept. 15, 2021. www.davisvanguard.org.

Florida Department of Law Enforcement (Case Number: MI-27-0120). Seventeenth Judicial Circuit of Florida. Investigative Summary Use of Force Investigation. Incident Date: Dec. 5, 2019. scribd.com/document/763900670/FDLE-UPS-MI-27-0120-Investigative-Summary-Redacted#download&from_embed.

Fox, K., K. Shveda, N. Croker, and M. Chacon. "How US Gun Culture Stacks Up with the World." CNN, Oct. 26, 2023. cnn.com.

Fraieli, A. "Taxes Are Being Used to Fight Rather Than Solve Homelessness Across the Country; It's Making Life More Difficult for Those Who Are Unhoused, and Isn't Cheap on the Taxpayer Either." *Homeless Voice*, May 10, 2021. homelessvoice.org.

Frazer-Carroll, M. "Copaganda: Why Film and TV Portrayals of the Police Are Under Fire." *Independent*, July 9, 2020.

Freckelton, I. "Police Statistics and the Media." *Legal Service Bulletin* 12 (1987): 247.

French-Marcelin, M., and S. Hinger. *Bullies in Blue: The Origins and Consequences of School Policing*. American Civil Liberties Union, April 12, 2017.

Furst, J., dir. *Time: The Kalief Browder Story*. 2017.

Gaines, M. "Roundup Lawsuit Update December 2023." *Forbes*, Nov. 3, 2023. forbes.com.

Gallant, J. "Officer Defends Taking Knife from Scene of Jermaine Carby's Killing by Police." *Toronto Star*, May 16, 2016.

Gamage, M. "'DULF, as We Knew It, Is Dead.'" *Tyee*, Nov. 10, 2023. thetyee.ca.

García, M. R. "Beware of Pity: The League of Nations' Treatment of Prostitution." *Monde(s)* 1, no. 19 (2021): 97–117.

Gardner, L. "Stopping Cop City: A Timeline of Suppression and Resistance." *Georgia Voice*, Nov. 23, 2023.

Gebelhoff, R. "No, Oregon's Drug Decriminalization Law Was Not a Failure." *Washington Post*, March 5, 2024.

Georgia Bureau of Investigation. "Wendy's Surveillance Video—OIS Atlanta—6.12.20." YouTube, June 12, 2020.

Gibbs, P. "The Myth That Tough Sanctions Deter Crime—Revealed by the Sentencing Council." Transform Justice, Oct. 7, 2022. transformjustice.org.uk.

Gilbert, C., A. Caputo, and G. Hing. "When Tasers Fail." APM Reports, May 9, 2019. apmreports.org.

Gillis, W. "Andrew Loku Was Traumatized from Kidnapping, Torture in South Sudan." *Toronto Star*, June 5, 2017.

———. "One Death, Two Versions: Finding the Facts in the Killing of Andrew Loku." *Toronto Star*, April 22, 2016.

———. "Rookie Cop Says Shooting Andrew Loku Was the Only Option." *Toronto Star*, June 15, 2017.

Gladis Callwood v. Jay Jones, Brief of Respondents on Petition for a Writ of Certiorari (U.S. Supreme Court, June 18, 2018).

Gladis Callwood v. Jay Jones, Petition for Writ of Certiorari (U.S. Supreme Court, May 18, 2018).

Gladis Callwood v. Jay Jones, 16-1754 (U.S. Court of Appeals for the Eleventh Circuit, Feb. 18, 2018).

Goldberg, S. K. "Remembering Tortuguita, Indigenous Queer and Non-binary Environmental Activist and Forest Defender." Human Rights Campaign, March 21, 2023. www.hrc.org/news.

Gonzalez, Valerie. "What We Know About Texas' New Law." Associated Press, Dec. 20, 2024.

Good Morning America. "New Video of Ex-cop Fatally Shooting Daunte Wright Shown in Court l GMA." YouTube, Dec. 9, 2021.

Goodwin, A., W. Shepard, and C. Sloan. *Police Brutality Bonds: How Wall Street Profits from Police Violence*. Acre Campaigns, June 2020. acrecampaigns.org.

Gordon, E. "What's the Evidence That Supervised Drug Injection Sites Save Lives?" National Public Radio, Sept. 7, 2018. www.npr.org.

Gorner, J., and A. Sweeny. "For Years Chicago Police Rated the Risk of Tens of Thousands Being Caught Up in Violence. That Controversial Effort Has Quietly Been Ended." *Chicago Tribune*, June 24, 2020.

Gothner, Chris. "All Bullets Killing UPS Driver, Bystander in Miramar Shootout Came from Officers, FDLE Report Says." Local10.com, Aug. 29, 2024.

Gouldhawke, M. "A Condensed History of Canada's Colonial Cops." *New Inquiry*, March 10, 2020. thenewinquiry.com.

Government of Canada. *Budget 2021: A Recovery Plan for Jobs, Growth, and Resilience*. Ottawa: Her Majesty the Queen in Right of Canada, 2021.

Government of Ontario. Ontario Reg. 58/16: Collection of Identifying Information in Certain Circumstances—Prohibition and Duties. Police Services Act, R.S.O. 1990. Toronto, Ontario, Canada: Government of Ontario, March 21, 2016.

Grady, C. "How 70 Years of Cop Shows Taught Us to Valorize the Police." *Vox*, April 12, 2021. www.vox.com.

Graziano, L. M., and J. F. Gauthier. "Media Consumption and Perceptions of Police Legitimacy." *Policing: An International Journal* 41, no. 5 (2018): 593–607.

Greer, Darryl. "Founders of B.C. Drug 'Compassion Club' File Charter Challenge." CBC, Oct. 15, 2024. cbc.ca/news/canada/british-columbia/dulf-drug-compassion-club-charter-challenge-1.7352605.

Gregorian, D., L. Bult, and S. Ryley. "Exclusive: Daily News Analysis Finds Racial Disparities in Summonses for Minor Violations in 'Broken Windows' Policing." New York *Daily News*, Aug. 4, 2014.

Grossman Academy. "About the Colonel." Accessed March 2023. www.grossmanacademy.com/about-the-colonel.

Gruber, A. "How Police Became the Go-to Response to Domestic Violence." *Slate*, July 7, 2020. slate.com.

Gun Violence Archive. "Mass Shootings in 2023." Dec. 2023. gunviolencarchive.org.

Hafemeister, T. L. "If All You Have Is a Hammer: Society's Ineffective Response to Intimate Partner Violence." *Catholic University Law Review* 60, no. 1 (2011): 919–1002.

Halima Tariffa Culley et al., Petitioners v. Steven T. Marshall, Attorney General of Alabama, et al., 21-13805, 21-13484 (U.S. Supreme Court, 2023).

Hamby, P. "Peter Hamby Interviews President Obama—Part 1." *Good Luck America*, Snap Originals. YouTube, Dec. 2, 2020.

Harrell, E., and E. Davis. "Contacts Between Police and the Public, 2018—Statistical Tables." Bureau of Justice Statistics, 2020.

Hartmans, A. "Target Said It's Lost $400 Million This Year due to 'Inventory Shrink'—and Organized Retail Crime Is Mostly to Blame." *Business Insider*, Nov. 18, 2022. www.businessinsider.com.

Hassett-Walker, C. "How You Start Is How You Finish? The Slave Patrol and Jim Crow Origins of Policing." American Bar Association, Jan. 11, 2021. americanbar.org.

Hauptman, M. "'Warrior Mindset' Police Training Proliferated. Then, High-Profile Deaths Put It Under Scrutiny." *Washington Post*, Aug. 21, 2021.

Hayat, N. B. "Section 8 Is the New N-Word: Policing Integration in the Age of Black Mobility." *Washington University Journal of Law & Policy* 51, no. 1 (2016): 61–93.

Hayden, J. "Measure 110 Shows Early Successes Despite Backlash." Street Roots, Oct. 25, 2023. www.streetroots.org.

Hayden, N., and S. D. Kavanaugh. "Portland Street Response's Future Hangs in Balance: 'I Feel Like It's About to Implode.'" Oregon Live, June 26, 2023. oregonlive.com.

Heath, W. "80% of Police Officers Time Spent Dealing with Non-crime." Justice Gap, March 3, 2020. www.thejusticegap.com.

Heath-Rawlings, J. Twitter, July 5, 2022. twitter.com/TheGameSheet/status/1544355813891923969.

Helmer, A. "A Full Picture of Abdirahman Abdi's Final Moments Has Finally Been Painted." *Ottawa Citzen*, May 2, 2019.

———. "'When Will Our Lives Matter?' Pain and Heartbreak Follow Ottawa Officer's Full Acquittal in Abdirahman Abdi Manslaughter Trial." *Ottawa Citizen*, October 21, 2020.

Hersher, R. "Key Moments in the Dakota Access Pipeline Fight." National Public Radio, Feb. 22, 2017. npr.org.

Hinch, J. "What Happened When Oregon Decriminalized Hard Drugs." *Atlantic*, July 19, 2023. www.theatlantic.com.

Hinkle, J. C., and D. Weisburd. "The Irony of Broken Windows Policing: A Micro-place Study of the Relationship Between Disorder, Focused Police Crackdowns, and Fear of Crime." *Journal of Criminal Justice* 36, no. 6 (Nov. 2008): 503–12.

Holtz, J. "UW Study: Exposure to Chemical in Roundup Increases Risk for Cancer." University of Washington, Feb. 13, 2019. washington.edu.

Home Office. *Official Statistics: Crime Outcomes in England and Wales 2022 to 2023.* July 20, 2023. www.gov.uk.

House Committee on the Judiciary. "Justice in Policing Act." democrats-judiciary .house.gov.

Howey, B., and N. Rosenfield. "How a 'Goon Squad' of Deputies Got Away with Years of Brutality." *New York Times*, Nov. 30, 2023.

Hudson, S., and N. Loreto. "Episode 108—We Have Already Won." *Sandy & Nora Talk Politics*, July 7, 2020. sandyandnora.com.

———. "Episode 220—Theft Is Only Good When the Rich Do It." *Sandy & Nora Talk Politics*, Dec. 13, 2022. sandyandnora.com.

Illinois State Police. "Sangamon County Sheriff's Office July 6, 2024 OIS Incident."

Illinois v. Wardlow, 528 U.S. 119 (2000).

Innocence Project. "Why Do Innocent People Plead Guilty?" 2018. guiltyplea problem.org.

Institute for Justice. "Philadelphia's Civil Forfeiture Machine Facts and Figures." Accessed April 11, 2024. ij.org/philadelphia-facts-and-figures/.

International Association of Chiefs of Police. "Membership." Oct. 2022. www .theiacp.org/membership.

Jayanetti, C. "At Least 130,000 Households in England Made Homeless in Pandemic." *Guardian*, June 13, 2021.

Johal, R., and S. Magusiak. "Police Across Canada Are Hiring a Tech Company to Justify Bigger Budgets and Belittle Social Services." Press Progress, Nov. 12, 2022. pressprogress.ca.

Kaba, M. "Yes, We Mean Literally Abolish the Police." *New York Times*, June 12, 2020.

Kaba, M., and A. J. Ritchie. *No More Police: A Case for Abolition.* New York: New Press, 2022.

Kale, S. "Police Are Allegedly Sleeping with Sex Workers Before Arresting Them." *Vice News*, May 3, 2017. vice.com.

Karakatsanis, A. "The Three Functions of Copaganda." *Alec's Copaganda Newsletter*, July 21, 2022. equalityalec.substack.com.

———. Twitter. Dec. 12, 2021. twitter.com.

KC Defender Staff. "KCPD Said Missing Black Women Reports in KC Were 'Completely Unfounded.' Less Than a Month Later, One Escaped After Being Kidnapped from Prospect & Tortured in a Basement for over a Month." *Kansas City Defender*, Oct. 14, 2022. kansascitydefender.com.

Kelly, J., and M. Nichols. "We Found 85,000 Cops Who've Been Investigated for Misconduct. Now You Can Read Their Records." *USA Today*, April 24, 2019.

Kesslen, B. "Uvalde Killer Was Mocked as a 'School Shooter,' Griped About Bullying at School Before Deadly Rampage." *New York Post*, July 18, 2022.

Khandaker, T. "Black Lives Matter Blasts Censored Details in Report on Fatal Shooting by Toronto Police." *Vice News*, April 30, 2016. vice.com.

———. "Family of Man Killed by Ontario Cops Sues for $12 Million." *Vice News*, Sept. 28, 2016. vice.com.

Knepper, L., J. McDonald, K. Sanchez, and E. S. Pohl. *Policing for Profit: The Abuse of Civil Asset Forfeiture: 3rd Edition*. Institute for Justice, 2020.

Knowles, H., J. Swaine, and J. S. Lee. "Updated Timeline: How Police Responded to the Texas School Shooter." *Washington Post*, June 21, 2022.

Krauss, C. "Bad Apple Shake-Ups: A 20-Year Police Cycle." *New York Times*, July 8, 1994.

KTVU FOX 2 San Francisco. "Warning: Graphic: BART Officers Accused of Excessive Force on Woman Who Didn't Pay Fare." YouTube, Aug. 11, 2021. youtube.com.

Kupchik, A., F. C. Curran, B. W. Fisher, and S. L. Viano. "Police Ambassadors: Student-Police Interactions in School and Legal Socialization." *Law & Society Review* 54, no. 2 (2020): 391–422.

Lacy, A. "Two Companies Fight to Corner the Police Body Camera Market." *Intercept*, Dec. 8, 2021. theintercept.com.

Lau, M. "Police PR Machine Under Scrutiny for Inaccurate Reporting, Alleged Pro-cop Bias." *Los Angeles Times*, Aug. 30, 2020.

Lavoie, D. "Explainer: Can Officers Stop Drivers for Air Fresheners?" Associated Press, April 15, 2021.

Lee, J. "Shoplifting Fuels a $94.5 Billion Problem at American Stores." *Wall Street Journal*, Dec. 23, 2022.

Lee, N. T., and C. Chin-Rothmann. "Police Surveillance and Facial Recognition: Why Data Privacy Is Imperative for Communities of Color." Brookings, April 12, 2022. brookings.edu.

Leisenring, A. "Victims' Perceptions of Police Response to Intimate Partner Violence." *Journal of Police Crisis Negotiations* 12, no. 2 (Nov. 2012): 146–64.

Lemieux, J. "What Happened to Sandra Bland?" *Ebony*, July 13, 2019. ebony.com.

Leonhardt, M. "Living Paycheck to Paycheck Is Common, Even Among Those Who Make More Than $100,000." *Barron's*, Oct. 14, 2023.

Levine, K. "Who Shouldn't Prosecute the Police." *Iowa Law Review* 101, no. 4 (2016): 1447–96.

Linebaugh, P. *The London Hanged*. London: Verso, 2006.

Lipold, P. F., and L. W. Isaac. "Repressing Worker Dissent: Lethal Violence Against Strikers in the Early American Labor Movement." *Labor History* 63, no. 1 (2022): 1–23.

Liptak, A., and S. Dewan. "Supreme Court Limits Police Powers to Seize Private Property." *New York Times*, Feb. 20, 2019.

Little, S. "3 Arrested as B.C. RCMP Resume Enforcement Against Fairy Creek Old-Growth Logging Blockade." *Global News*, Aug. 15, 2023. globalnews.ca.

Lovan, D. "Q&A: What Were the Results of Breonna Taylor Investigation?" Associated Press, Sept. 23, 2020.

Lowe, P. "Jaynie Crosdale, Slain Woman Connected to Timothy Haslett Case, Was 'Full of Energy and Life.'" KCUR, Aug. 28, 2023. kcur.org.

MajorKraze. "Student Arrested at Northern Secondary School for No Reason." YouTube, 2009.

Mapping Police Violence. "2022 Police Violence Report." 2022. policeviolence report.org.

Marin, A. *Oversight Undermined: Investigation into the Ministry of the Attorney General's Implementation of Recommendations Concerning Reform of the Special Investigations Unit.* Ombudsman Report, Ontario Ombudsman, 2011.

———. *Oversight Unseen: Investigation into the Special Investigations Unit's Operational Effectiveness and Credibility.* Ombudsman Report, Ontario Ombudsman, 2008.

Martinez, M. M. "Recuperating Histories of Violence in the Americas: Vernacular History-Making on the US-Mexico Border." *American Quarterly* 66, no. 3 (Sept. 2014): 661–89.

Martínez-Beltrán, S. "Uvalde Parents Demand Investigation into Resource Officers Who Responded to Shooting." KUT News, Sept. 28, 2022. www.kut.org.

Mathis, J. "Why Did Oregon Recriminalize Drug Possession?" *Week*, April 4, 2024.

McGillivray, K. "Group of Lawyers Step Up to Defend Men Charged in Etobicoke Park Sting." CBC News, Nov. 16, 2016. cbc.ca/news.

McGreevy, S. J., and T. Spitzer. "OCDA Report: Officer-Involved Shooting—Kurt Andreas Reinhold." Office of the District Attorney Orange County, 2022.

Meadow, R. "Police Brutality Statistics: What the Data Says About Police Violence in America." Police Brutality Center, June 27, 2022. policebrutalitycenter .org.

Medina, E. "Retail Group Retracts Startling Claim About 'Organized' Shoplifting." *New York Times*, Dec. 9, 2023.

Meehan, A. J., and M. C. Ponder. "Race and Place: The Ecology of Racial Profiling African American Motorists." *Justice Quarterly* 19, no. 3 (2002): 399–430.

Melore, C. "Cost-of-Living Crisis in UK Leaves Third of British Living Paycheck to Paycheck." Study Finds, March 31, 2023. studyfinds.org.

Mickleburgh, R. "B.C. Safe-Injection Site Wins Police Immunity." *Globe and Mail*, June 25, 2003.

Miller, C. "Civil Asset Forfeiture: Unfair, Undemocratic, and Un-American." Southern Poverty Law Center, Oct. 30, 2017.

Minhas, A. M., V. Jain, M. Li, R. W. Ariss, M. Fudim, E. D. Michos, . . . A. Mehta. "Family Income and Cardiovascular Disease Risk in American Adults." *Scientific Reports* 13 (2023).

Mock, B. "'Policing for Profit' in Philadelphia Comes to an End." *Bloomberg*, Sept. 18, 2018.

Monkkonen, E. H. "History of Urban Police." *Crime and Justice: A Review of Research* 15 (1992): 547–80.

Morales, M., E. Levenson, E. Joseph, and C. Carrega. "Louisville Agrees to Pay

Breonna Taylor's Family $12 Million and Enact Police Reforms in Historic Settlement." CNN, Sept. 15, 2020. cnn.com/2020/09/15/us/breonna-taylor -louisville-settlement/index.html.

Moule, R. K., Jr. "Under Siege? Assessing Public Perceptions of the 'War on Police.'" *Journal of Criminal Justice* 66 (Jan.—Feb. 2020).

Movement 4 Black Lives. The Breathe Act. 2021. breatheact.org.

Nagesh, A. "Child Q: Schoolgirl Strip-Search Not Isolated Issue, Police Data Suggests." BBC, Aug. 8, 2022. www.bbc.com.

Nalla, M. K., and G. R. Newman. "Is White-Collar Policing, Policing?" *Policing and Society: An International Journal of Research and Policy* 3, no. 4 (1994): 303–18.

Nasser, Shanifa. "Release Evidence in Regis Korchinski-Paquet Death or Turn It Over to Outside Agency, Family Lawyer Says." CBC, June 10, 2020. cbc.ca/news/canada/toronto/regis-korchinski-paquet-toronto-1.5606704.

National Advisory Commission on Civil Disorders. *Report of the National Advisory Commission on Civil Disorders.* U.S. Department of Justice Office of Justice Programs, 1967. ojp.gov.

National Center for Education Statistics, U.S. Department of Education. "Private School Enrollment." May 2022. nces.ed.gov/programs/coe/indicator/cgc.

National Statistics, Government of the United Kingdsom. *Schools, Pupils, and Their Characteristics: Academic Year 2022/23.* Nov. 23, 2023. explore-education -statistics.service.gov.uk.

Native Women's Association of Canada. "Fact Sheet: Missing and Murdered Aboriginal Women and Girls." Ottawa: Native Women's Association of Canada, 2010.

Negussie, Tesfaye, and Sabina Ghebremedhin. "Sonya Massey Case: Ex-Deputy Charged in Woman's IL Shooting Death." ABC News. abc7chicago.com.

Nelson, L., V. Leung, and J. Cobb. *The Right to Remain a Student: How California School Policies Fail to Protect and Serve.* American Civil Liberties Union of California, Oct. 2016.

Newman, L. H. "Police Bodycams Can Be Hacked to Doctor Footage." *Wired,* Aug. 11, 2018. wired.com.

New York Times. "Gun Control, Explained." Jan. 26, 2023.

———. "Lexow Committee Report: New-York's Police Described as Allies of Criminals. The Entire Department Corrupt: Evidence of a Systematic Protection of Crime, with Blackmail for Its Only Object." Jan. 18, 1895, 1–2.

———. "Where Protesters on U.S. Campuses Have Been Arrested or Detained," July 22, 2024.

New York Times Editorial Board. "America Has Lost the War on Drugs. Here's What Needs to Happen Next." *New York Times,* Feb. 22, 2023.

Nguyen v. Miami Dade Police Department (Circuit Court of the 17th Judicial Circuit in and for Broward County, Florida, Sept. 14, 2020).

Nichols, A. L. "It's Not Illegal to Live Together as an Unmarried Couple Anymore in Michigan." *Michigan Advance,* July 13, 2023. michiganadvance.com.

Norton Cultural Centre. "Frequently Asked Questions." Missing Black People, 2021. missingblackpeople.com/faq.

NYPD. "About NYPD." Oct. 2022. www.nyc.gov.

Ocen, P. "The New Racially Restrictive Covenant: Race, Welfare, and the Policing of Black Women in Subsidized Housing." *UCLA Law Review* 59, no. 6 (2012): 1540–82.

Office for National Statistics. "The Nature of Violent Crime in England and Wales: Year Ending March 2022." Office for National Statistics, Nov. 9, 2022. www.ons.gov.uk.

O'Harrow, R., Jr., S. Rich, and S. Tan. "Asset Seizures Fuel Police Spending." *Washington Post*, Oct. 11, 2014.

Ojo, Joseph, and Andrea Torres. "Police Officers Surrender to Face Charges over Shooting That Killed 4 in Miramar After Pursuit Started in Coral Gables." Local10.com, June 21, 2024.

Olmeda, R. "Grand Jury Will Review Fatal 2019 Shooting of UPS Driver and His Kidnappers." *South Florida Sun Sentinel*, Dec. 6, 2023.

Olson, W. "Police Misconduct and 'Law Enforcement Officers' Bill of Rights' Laws." Cato Institute, April 24, 2015. cato.org.

One Albuquerque. "Two Years of Service from Community Safety First Responders." Albuquerque Community Safety, Sept. 2023. cabq.gov/acs.

Ontario Human Rights Commission. *A Collective Impact: Interim Report on the Inquiry into Racial Profiling and Racial Discrimination of Black Persons by the Toronto Police Service.* Toronto: Government of Ontario, 2018.

Ontario Ombudsman. "Oversight Unseen—Facts and Highlights." Ombudsman Ontario, 2008.

Ontario Solicitor General. "Date Announced for the Inquest into the Death of Abdirahman Abdi." Press release, Oct. 25, 2024. news.ontario.ca/en/release/1005219/date-announced-for-the-inquest-into-the-death-of-abdi rahman-abdi.

Ontario Special Investigations Unit. "SIU Concludes Shooting Death Investigation in Brampton." Press release, July 21, 2015.

Oppel, R.A. Jr., D. B. Taylor, and N. Bogel-Burroughs. "What to Know About Breonna Taylor's Death." *New York Times*, Aug. 23, 2024.

Orange County DA. "OCDA Report Officer-Involved Shooting—Kurt Reinhold." YouTube, Feb. 11, 2022. youtube.com.

Orange County Sheriff-Coroner Department. "Policy 408—Homeless Outreach and Liaison." Orange County SD Policy Manual, Feb. 4, 2021. ocsheriff.gov.

Ortiz, A. "What to Know About the Death of Rayshard Brooks." *New York Times*, Nov. 21, 2022.

Osman, Laura. "'Homicide by Heart Attack': Pathologist Examines How Abdirahman Abdi Died." CBC, June 4, 2019. cbc.ca/news/canada/ottawa/abdirahman-abdi-heart-attack-montsion-trial-1.5161383.

———. "The Montsion Trial Resumes: What the Crown Says Happened to Abdirahman Abdi." CBC, May 29, 2019. cbc.ca/news/canada/ottawa/montsion-abdi-timeline-1.5152894.

Parachute. "Road Safety." 2023. parachute.ca/en/injury-topic/road-safety.

Parker, A., and J. McDaniel. "From Freddie Gray to Tyre Nichols, Early Police Claims Often Misleading." *Washington Post*, Feb. 17, 2023.

Paternoster, R. "How Much Do We Really Know About Criminal Deterrence." *Journal of Criminal Law and Criminology* 100, no. 3 (2010).

Pearson v. Callahan, 555 U.S. 233 (2009).

Peischel, Will. "Activists Say Democrats' Proposed Chokehold Ban Won't Work." *Mother Jones*, June 10, 2020. motherjones.com.

Pennsylvania Department of Transportation. "Elimination of Stickers: Frequently Asked Questions." 2023. www.dmv.pa.gov.

Peterson, A. "Why the Philando Castile Police-Shooting Video Disappeared from Facebook—Then Came Back." *Washington Post*, July 7, 2016.

Phillips, S. "Centrist Dems Are Wrong About November's Losses." *Nation*, Dec. 21, 2020. www.thenation.com.

PHS Community Services. "Insite." 2024. www.phs.ca/program/insite/.

Pidd, H. "How Humberside Police's Pioneering Policy on Mental Health Calls Paid Off." *Guardian*, May 30, 2023.

#PoliceFreeSchools Advancement Project. "#AssaultAt Map." 2003. policefree schools.org/map.

Potter, G. *The History of Policing in the United States*. Eastern Kentucky University, June 25–July 30, 2013.

Pratt, T. "'The Birds Stopped Singing': Inside the Battle for Atlanta's South River Forest." *Atlanta*, Jan. 20, 2023. atlantamagazine.com.

Public Safety Training Center. "Atlanta Public Safety Training Center." 2023. atltrainingcenter.com.

Quandt, K. R., and A. Jones. "Research Roundup: Violent Crimes Against Black and Latinx People Receive Less Coverage and Less Justice." Prison Policy Initiative, March 18, 2021. prisonpolicy.org.

Rabin, C. "After 3 Years, Families Still Don't Know Who Killed Loved Ones During UPS Hijack Shootout." *Miami Herald*, Dec. 2, 2022.

Rahman, A., M. A. Clarke, and S. Byrne. "The Art of Breaking People Down: The British Colonial Model in Ireland and Canada." *Canadian Journal of Peace and Conflict Studies* 49, no. 2 (2017): 15–38.

Rahr, S., and S. K. Rice. "From Warriors to Guardians: Recommitting American Police Culture to Democratic Ideals." *New Perspectives in Policing*, April 2015.

Rajan, M., and K. A. McCloskey, "Victims of Intimate Partner Violence: Arrest Rates Across Recent Studies." *Journal of Aggression, Maltreatment & Trauma* 15, no. 3–4 (2007): 27–52.

Rape Crisis England & Wales. "Rape and Sexual Assault Statistics." Accessed March 2023. rapecrisis.org.uk/get-informed/statistics-sexual-violence/.

Rasmussen, C. "The 'Bloody Christmas' of 1951." *Los Angeles Times*, Dec. 21, 1997.

———. "Police Scandal Is Worst Since 1930s." *Los Angeles Times*, Sept. 17, 1999.

Ray, L., and T. Spitzer. "Recipient Committee Campaign Statement." State of California, California Fair Political Practices Commission. Netfile Public Portal for Campaign Finance Disclosure, 2020.

———. "Recipient Committee Campaign Statement." State of California, California Fair Political Practices Commission. Netfile Public Portal for Campaign Finance Disclosure, 2022.

Reason, C. "Toronto Police Cracking Down on Public Sex in Etobicoke Park." *Toronto Star*, Nov. 13, 2016. thestar.com.

Redden, M. "Daniel Holtzclaw: Former Oklahoma City Police Officer Guilty of Rape." *Guardian*, Dec. 10, 2015. theguardian.com.

Reginald Latson v. Harold Clarke, 18-2457 (U.S. Court of Appeals for the Fourth Circuit, Dec. 18, 2019).

Reid, L. "Oil and Water: ETP and Sunoco's History of Pipeline Spills." Greenpeace, April 17, 2018. greenpeace.org.

Reilly, K. "Schools Are Putting More Cops on Campus—Despite the 'Abject Failure' in Uvalde." *Time*, June 22, 2022. time.com.

Reiner, R. "Policing and the Media." In *Handbook of Policing*. Vol. 2, edited by T. Newburn. London: Routledge, 2008.

———. "Who Governs? Democracy, Plutocracy, Science, and Prophecy in Policing." *Criminology & Criminal Justice* 13, no. 2 (April 2013): 161–80.

Revolving Doors. "Rethinking Drugs: Criminalisation Is Causing Harm." March 15, 2023. revolving-doors.org.uk.

Rhoades, G. "Freedom of Choice for Low-Income Renters Still Elusive as States and Cities Scramble to Confront Housing Voucher Discrimination." American Bar Association, Jan. 6, 2023. www.americanbar.org.

Riess, R., S. Almasy, and E. Levenson. "Justin Trudeau Says He Does Not Know How Many Times He's Worn Blackface in His Life." CNN, Sept. 20, 2019. cnn.com.

Riley, M., D. Kocieniewski, and E. Fan. "How the US Drives Gun Exports and Fuels Violence Around the World." *Bloomberg*, July 24, 2023.

Ritchie, S. "Almost Half of Canadians Living Paycheque to Paycheque as Conservative Support Grows: Poll." *Globe and Mail*, Sept. 2, 2023.

Roberts, D. E. "Abolition Constitutionalism." *Harvard Law Review* 133, no. 1 (Nov. 2019): 1–122.

Robinson, M. A. "Black Bodies on the Ground: Policing Disparities in the African American Community—an Analysis of Newsprint from January 1, 2015, Through December 31, 2015." *Journal of Black Studies* 48, no. 6 (Sept. 2017): 551–71.

Roman, C. G., C. S. Harding, H. J. Klein, L. Hamilton, and J. Koehnlein. *The Victim-Offender Overlap: Examining Police and Service System Networks of Response Among Violent Street Conflicts*. Office of Justice Programs, April 2020. www.ojp.gov/pdffiles1/nij/grants/254626.pdf.

Romine, C. H. "Facial Recognition Technology." National Institute of Standards and Technology. U.S. House of Representatives Committee on Homeland Security, 2020.

Romo, V. "New York City Reaches $3.3 Million Settlement with Kalief Browder's Family." National Public Radio, Jan. 25, 2019. npr.org.

Ronayne, K., M. Casey, and G. Mulvihill. "Homelessness Surging in Many US Cities amid End of Pandemic Relief Measures." NBC Bay Area, Oct. 6, 2022. nbcbayarea.com.

Rosenberg, A. "How Police Censorship Shaped Hollywood." *Washington Post*, Oct. 24, 2016.

———. "In Pop Culture, There Are No Bad Police Shootings." *Washington Post*, Oct. 26, 2016.

Rosenfeld, J. "Overdose Awareness Day: How Drug Overdoses and White

Supremacy Are Linked in the U.S." *Teen Vogue*, Aug. 31, 2020. www.teen
    vogue.com.
Roy, Arundhati. *War Talk*. Boston: South End Press, 2003.
Royal Canadian Mounted Police. "Current Operations." June 21, 2022. rcmp
    -grc.gc.ca/en/current-operations.
Ruch, J. "Training Center Security Costs $41,500 a Day, Planner Claims."
    SaportaReport, Feb. 16, 2023. saportareport.com.
Rugemer, E. B. "The Development of Mastery and Race in the Comprehensive
    Slave Codes of the Greater Caribbean During the Seventeenth Century."
    William and Mary Quarterly 70, no. 3 (July 2013): 429–58.
Ruiz-Angel, M., and A. Erhard. *City of Albuquerque Community Safety Department
    FY24 Q1 Report*. Albuquerque: City of Albuquerque, 2023.
Rushowy, K. "Arrested Student Suspended from Northern Secondary." *Toronto
    Star*, Oct. 7, 2009.
Russell, H. "Vigil and March Held for Man Who Fell to His Death
    'Shortly After Being Tasered' by Police in Peckham." *Southwark News*,
    Oct. 2023.
Sacramento Bee. "Arrests Halted After Women Taken." Feb. 26, 1919.
Schwartz, G. L., and J. L. Jahn. "Mapping Fatal Police Violence Across U.S.
    Metropolitan Areas: Overall Rates and Racial/Ethnic Inequities, 2013–
    2017." *PLoS ONE* 15, no. 6 (2020): 5.
Schwartz, J. C. "The Case Against Qualified Immunity." *Notre Dame Law Review*
    93, no. 5 (2018): 1797–852.
Schwartzapfel, B., and J. Jenkins. "Inside the Nation's Overdose Crisis in Prisons
    and Jails." Marshall Project, July 15, 2021. themarshallproject.org.
Serrano, A. "'Somber Day' in Uvalde as Community Commemorates One
    Year Since Robb Elementary Shooting." *Texas Tribune*, May 24, 2023. texas
    tribune.org.
Shaw, Rob. "Rob Shaw: Leaked VPD Report an Inflated Work of Fiction."
    Business in Vancouver, Nov. 8, 2022. biv.com/vnews/commentary/rob-shaw
    -leaked-pd-report-inflated-work-fiction-8269528.
Shine, J. "'Dragnet' Was Straight Up LAPD Propaganda, on National TV for
    Years." *Timeline*, June 20, 2017. timeline.com.
Siff, A. "4 EMS Workers Suspended Without Pay in Chokehold Arrest." NBC
    New York, July 21, 2014. nbcnewyork.com.
Sinclair, G. "The 'Irish' Policeman and the Empire: Influencing the Policing
    of the British Empire—Commonwealth." *Irish Historical Studies* 36, no. 142
    (Nov. 2008): 173–87.
Smith, C. J. "County Awards $7.5 Million to Family of Slain Homeless Man
    Kurt Reinhold." *San Clemente Times*, May 10, 2023.
Smith, G., J. Szep, P. Eisler, L. So, and L. Girion. "Shock Tactics | Part 7: The
    Vulnerable." Reuters, Feb. 7, 2018.
Southall, A. "Daniel Pantaleo, Officer Who Held Eric Garner in Chokehold, Is
    Fired." *New York Times*, Aug. 19, 2019.
Special Investigations Unit. "SIU Report on Andrew Loku's Shooting Death."
    Scribd, April 29, 2016. scribd.com.
Spina, M. "When a Protector Becomes a Predator." *Buffalo News*, Nov. 22, 2015.

Statistics Canada. "Decrease in the Rate of Police Strength in Canada in 2022." Government of Canada, 2023.

———. "Key Trends in Elementary to Postsecondary Student Enrolments, Graduations, and Tuition Fees." Nov. 28, 2023. www150.statcan.gc.ca.

Steen v. City of Pensacola, 809 F. Supp. 2d 1342 (U.S. District Court for the Northern District of Florida, Pensacola Division, Aug. 22, 2011).

Stern, S. W. "America's Forgotten Mass Imprisonment of Women Believed to Be Sexually Immoral." History, July 21, 2019. history.com.

———. *The Trials of Nina McCall: Sex, Surveillance, and the Decades-Long Government Plan to Imprison "Promiscuous" Women*. Boston: Beacon Press, 2018.

Stevens-Acevedo, A. "The Santo Domingo Slave Revolt of 1521 and the Slave Laws of 1522: Black Slavery and Black Resistance in the Early Colonial Americas." CUNY Dominican Studies Institute, 2019.

Stinson, P. M., and C. Wentzlof. "On-Duty Shootings: Police Officers Charged with Murder or Manslaughter, 2005–2019." Research Brief One-Sheet, Bowling Green State University, Police Integrity Research Group, 2019.

St. Julien, J. "Community-Based Violence Interruption Programs Can Reduce Gun Violence." Center for American Progress, July 14, 2022. www.americanprogress.org.

Stop Cop City. "No Police Military Base in Weelaunee Forest." 2023. stopcop.city.

Strangio, C. "No, Seeing a Transgender Person Is Not a Reason to Call 911." ACLU, Dec. 8, 2015. aclu.org.

Stroud, M. "Heat Listed." *Verge*, May 24, 2021. theverge.com.

Suarez-Balcazar, Y., F. Balcazar, T. Taylor-Ritzler, A. Ali, and R. Hasnain. "Race, Poverty, and Disability: A Social Justice Dilemma." In *Reinventing Race, Reinventing Racism*, ed. J. J. Betancur and C. Herring, 351–70. Boston: Brill, 2013.

Swain, R. "Renting While Black: Antioch Tenants Charge Police with Campaign of Intimidation." *ACLU News* 71, no. 4 (2008): 1–4.

Sweet, J. "Vulnerability to Homelessness Much Higher Than Before Pandemic, Researcher Says." CBC News, Feb. 28, 2023. cbc.ca/news.

Szalavitz, M. "Portugal Has Succeeded Where We've Failed with Addiction." *New York Times*, Aug. 29, 2023.

Thomas, T., and A. Mohdin. "Nearly 1,000 Police Officers Operating in UK Schools, Figures Show." *Guardian*, Jan. 16, 2023.

Thompson, D. "DAs, Retailers Say California Needs Tougher Retail Theft Law." Associated Press, Dec. 3, 2021.

Timbs v. Indiana, 17-1091 (U.S. Supreme Court, Feb. 20, 2019).

Timsit, A. "Minn. City to Pay $3.25M in Police Killing of Daunte Wright." *Washington Post*, June 22, 2022.

Torstar Open Data Team. "Break and Enter Reported at One East York Home (July 5)." *Toronto Star*, July 5, 2022.

Townley, G., and E. Leickly. *Portland Street Response: Year Two Program Evaluation*. City of Portland, Bureau of Fire & Rescue. Portland State University, June 2023.

Traffic Stops. Accessed Nov. 2023. bjs.gov.

Transform Drug Policy Foundation. "A Short History of the Misuse of Drugs Act."

TRANSFORM, Nov. 4, 2021. transformdrugs.org/blog/a-short-history-of-the-misuse-of-drugs-act.

Tunney, C. "Systemic Racism Exists in RCMP, Trudeau Argues—After Commissioner Says She's 'Struggling' with the Term." *CBC News*, June 11, 2020. cbc.ca/news.

Turner, K. B., D. Giacopassi, and M. Vandiver. "Ignoring the Past: Coverage of Slavery and Slave Patrols in Criminal Justice Texts." *Journal of Criminal Justice Education* 17, no. 1 (April 2006): 181–95.

TV Guide, a Fandom Company. *TV Guide*. 2022. tvguide.com.

Umansky, Eric. "New Yorkers Were Choked, Beaten and Tased," ProPublica, June 27, 2024. propublica.org.

United States v. Brignoni-Ponce, 422 U.S. 873 (1975).

University of Toronto Libraries. *Legislating the "White Slave Panic," 1885–1914*. 2023. exhibits.library.utoronto.ca.

USAFacts. "Data Says Domestic Violence Incidents Are Down, but Half of All Victims Don't Report to Police." Oct. 21, 2021. usafacts.org.

U.S. Attorney's Office, Central District of California. "Monsanto Agrees to Plead Guilty to Illegally Using Pesticide at Corn Growing Fields in Hawaii and to Pay Additional $12 Million." Press release, Sept. 2021. www.justice.gov/.

U.S. Department of Housing and Urban Development. "Housing Choice Vouchers Fact Sheet." Accessed Oct. 2023. hud.gov.

U.S. Department of Justice. "Arrests." In *Crime in the United States, 2019*. Federal Bureau of Investigation, 2020.

———. "Clearances." In *Crime in the United States, 2019*. Federal Bureau of Investigation, 2020.

———. *Crime in the United States, 2017*. Federal Bureau of Investigation. 2018.

———. *Investigation of the Ferguson Police Department*. U.S. Government, Civil Rights Division, 2015.

———. "Police Employees." In *Crime in the United States, 2018*. Federal Bureau of Investigation, 2018.

———. "Violent Crime." In *Crime in the United States, 2019*. Federal Bureau of Investigation, 2020.

U.S. Department of Justice, Office of Public Affairs. "Former Louisville, Kentucky, Metro Police Officer Found Guilty of Federal Civil Rights Crimes Related to the Breonna Taylor Case." Press release, Nov. 1, 2024. justice.gov/opa/pr/former-louisville-kentucky-metro-police-officer-found-guilty-federal-civil-rights-crimes.

U.S. Judiciary. Federal Rules of Criminal Procedure. Administrative Office of the U.S. Courts, 2022.

Vandell, P. "Man Had $39,500 Seized by Arizona Police for Nearly 3 Years. He Finally Received His Money Back." *USA Today*, March 23, 2023.

van der Meer, T. G., A. C. Kroon, and R. Vliegenthart. "Do News Media Kill? How a Biased News Reality Can Overshadow Real Societal Risks, the Case of Aviation and Road Traffic Accidents." *Social Forces* 101, no. 1 (Sept. 2022): 506–30.

Vargas, T. "A Black Disabled Teen Went Unheard in Prison. People Are Now Listening." *Washington Post*, Feb. 25, 2023.

Victor, G., and B. del Pozo. "Here's Why Police Drug Busts Don't Work." Harvard Public Health, July 25, 2023. harvardpublichealth.org.

Vitale, A. "Five Myths About Policing." *Washington Post*, June 26, 2020.

Wald, J., and L. H. Thurau. *Catch & Stun: The Use and Abuse of Conducted Electrical Weapons (CEWS) on Children and Youth*. Strategies for Youth, Jan. 2022.

Wang, V. "Erica Garner, Activist and Daughter of Eric Garner, Dies at 27." *New York Times*, Dec. 30, 2017.

Warnke, M. B. "Opinion: Sandra Bland, Philando Castile, and Now Charleena Lyles. Scream Their Names for All to Hear." *Los Angeles Times*, June 19, 2017.

Watson, Julie, Christopher L. Keller, Carolyn Thompson, and Stefanie Dazio. "More Than 2,100 People Have Been Arrested." Associated Press, May 1, 2024.

Waxman, O. B. "How the U.S. Got Its Police Force." *Time*, May 18, 2017. time .com.

Weir, David. CBC News, "Const. Daniel Montsion Not Guilty in Death . . . ," cbc.ca/news.

Weitzer, R., and R. Brunson. "Policing Different Racial Groups in the United States." *Cahiers Politiestudies* (2015): 129–45.

Wertz, J. "Shoplifting Has Become a $100 Billion Problem for Retailers." *Forbes*, Nov. 20, 2022. forbes.com.

Williams v. City of Antioch, No. C-08-2301 SBA (U.S. District Court for the Northern District of California, May 2, 2008).

Williams v. City of Antioch, 4:08-cv-02301-SBA (U.S. District Court for the Northern District of California, April 6, 2012).

Wilson, C. "Oregon Pioneered a Radical Drug Policy. Now It's Reconsidering." National Public Radio, Feb. 7, 2024. www.npr.org.

Woodruff v. City of Detroit, 5:23-cv-11886-JEL-APP (U.S. District Court for the Eastern District of Michigan Southern Division, Aug. 3, 2023).

Wrap Technologies. "What Is BolaWrap?" Accessed Sept. 2023. wrap.com.

WTW. "40% of UK Employees Live Payday-to-Payday and Half Overspend Each Month, Straining Family Relationships." Press release, Feb. 12, 2020. wtwco.com.

Yoder, J., and B. Cates. "Government Self-Interest Corrupted a Crime-Fighting Tool into an Evil." *Washington Post*, Sept. 18, 2014.

Yokum, D., A. Ravishankar, and A. Coppock. "Evaluating the Effects of Police Body-Worn Cameras: A Randomized Controlled Trial." Working Paper, The Lab @ DC, Oct. 20, 2017.

Young, R., K. Conlon, and H. Yan. "61 'Cop City' Protesters Indicted on RICO Charges. Opponents Question the Timeline and Motivation." CNN, Sept. 6, 2023. cnn.com.

Zansberg, S. "Public Access to Police Body-Worn Camera Recordings (Status Report 2020)." American Bar Association, Jan. 21, 2021. americanbar.org.

Zed, K. "Toronto Tiny Shelters." GoFundMe, Oct. 22, 2023. www.gofundme .com.

Zennie62. "Brosnan Body Cam: Atlanta Police Fighting, Shooting Unarmed Rayshard Brooks, University Ave Wendy's." YouTube, June 14, 2020.

Zielinski, A. "Portland Street Response, Despite Successes, Faces an Uncertain Future." OPB, June 27, 2023. www.opb.org.

Zilber, A. "Shoplifting Has Reportedly Become a $94.5B Problem for US Retailers." *New York Post*, Dec. 23, 2022.

Zipes, D. "Sudden Cardiac Arrest and Death Following Application of Shocks from a TASER Electronic Control Device." *Circulation* 125, no. 20 (2012): 2417–22.

A NOTE ABOUT THE AUTHOR

SANDY HUDSON is a multidisciplinary creative, writer, and activist. Her work has appeared in *The Washington Post, Toronto Star*, and *HuffPost*, among other publications. Hudson holds a JD from the UCLA School of Law and an MA in social justice education from the University of Toronto. She cohosts the podcast *Sandy & Nora Talk Politics* and is coauthor of the bestselling anthology *Until We Are Free: Reflections on Black Lives Matter in Canada*. Hudson is a cofounder of Black Lives Matter Canada, as well as the Black Legal Action Centre, a specialty legal aid clinic that services Black communities in Ontario. She is currently based in Los Angeles and is co-executive producer of the eight-part CBC documentary series *Black Life: Untold Stories*, an official selection of the 2023 Toronto International Film Festival.

A NOTE ON THE TYPE

This book was set in Janson, a typeface long thought to have been made by the Dutchman Anton Janson, who was a practicing typefounder in Leipzig during the years 1668–1687. However, it has been conclusively demonstrated that these types are actually the work of Nicholas Kis (1650–1702), a Hungarian, who most probably learned his trade from the master Dutch typefounder Dirk Voskens. The type is an excellent example of the influential and sturdy Dutch types that prevailed in England up to the time William Caslon (1692–1766) developed his own incomparable designs from them.

Typeset by Scribe,
Philadelphia, Pennsylvania

Designed by Casey Hampton